The
THIRD MAN
OF THE DOUBLE HELIX

MAURICE WILKINS (1916–2004) was born in Pongoroa, New Zealand. He studied physics at Cambridge, graduating in 1938, and went on to work in J.T. (later Sir John) Randall's research group at Birmingham. In 1944 he moved to Berkeley, California, to work on the Manhattan Project. After the war he joined Randall's new biophysics group at St Andrews. The group moved in 1946 to King's College London and it was here where Wilkins began X-ray diffraction studies of DNA. These X-ray measurements, made with Rosalind Franklin and others, eventually established the correctness of the double helix structure of DNA proposed in 1953 by Watson and Crick at the Cavendish Laboratory, Cambridge. In 1962, Crick, Watson, and Wilkins were jointly awarded the Nobel Prize for Physiology or Medicine for this discovery.

Maurice Wilkins was appointed CBE in 1963, and was elected a Fellow of the Royal Society in 1959. He was appointed Emeritus Professor of Biophysics at King's College London in 1981, where he remained until his death in 2004. He was married, in 1959, to Patricia Chidgey; they had two sons and two daughters.

The
THIRD MAN
OF THE DOUBLE HELIX

THE AUTOBIOGRAPHY OF
MAURICE WILKINS

OXFORD
UNIVERSITY PRESS

OXFORD
UNIVERSITY PRESS

Great Clarendon Street, Oxford OX2 6DP

Oxford University Press is a department of the University of Oxford.
It furthers the University's objective of excellence in research, scholarship,
and education by publishing worldwide in

Oxford New York

Auckland Bangkok Buenos Aires Cape Town Chennai
Dar es Salaam Delhi Hong Kong Istanbul Karachi Kolkata
Kuala Lumpur Madrid Melbourne Mexico City Mumbai Nairobi
São Paulo Shanghai Taipei Tokyo Toronto

Oxford is a registered trade mark of Oxford University Press
in the UK and in certain other countries

Published in the United States by
Oxford University Press Inc., New York

Database right Oxford University Press (maker)

First published 2003

First published in paperback 2005

British Library Cataloguing in Publication Data

Data available

Library of Congress Cataloguing in Publication Data

Data available

ISBN 0-19-280667-X (Pbk.)   978-0-19-280667-3 (Pbk.)

1

Printed in Great Britain by
Clays Ltd, St Ives plc

CONTENTS

Preface *vii*

List of plates *xii*

1
Distant shores *1*

2
Finding my feet *30*

3
In a world at war *59*

4
Randall's circus *87*

5
Crystal genes *114*

6
Go back to your microscopes! *140*

7
How does DNA keep its secrets? *168*

8
The double helix *196*

9
Living with the double helix *222*

10
A broader view *246*

Index *267*

PREFACE

I was remarkably fortunate in the way my career as a physicist developed. It began when a local headmaster called at our house to see my father, the school doctor. My father told his visitor about the flying model aeroplanes I had made in my workshop, and the headmaster replied that I should go to Cambridge and do research in the Cavendish Laboratory. I had never heard of the Cavendish, but I remembered the name; and years later I became a student there, enjoying tutorials with M.L.E. Oliphant, the Deputy Director of Research.

During my student years at Cambridge, Hitler was preparing for war. I became very concerned about science-based warfare, and worked for the Cambridge Scientists Anti-War Group rather than on my degree studies. So I did not qualify for a research grant in Cambridge and could not see a way to pursue the work I had decided to do. I wanted to research luminescence, because quantum mechanics gave a very lively picture of electrons moving in luminescent crystals. But back home in Birmingham I remembered that Oliphant had, after my first year at

Cambridge, moved to Birmingham University as Head of Physics, where he had begun building the biggest atom smasher in Britain. I telephoned Oliphant, who told me that J.T. Randall, who was an expert on luminescence, had joined his lab and was looking for a research assistant. Randall's research was exactly the kind of physics I had chosen to do. I quickly went across Birmingham to the University, found Randall stimulating, and signed on as a member of Oliphant's staff.

Before World War II, many British scientists were getting ready for Hitler. My job was to find ways of improving radar screens, which used luminescence just as televisions screens do today. Oliphant got the most important problem – how to make radar beams strong enough to see through heavy clouds or fog. Randall had begun working on generators for making very strong beams of microwaves, and soon he had the first working resonator magnetron. At first, most scientists could not believe how powerful it was, but when perfected the magnetron gave air supremacy to the Allies. The next important problem was the atom bomb, and Oliphant took us all to California to work on that project.

Working with Randall again back in Britain after the War, I looked for more positive applications of my skills. I chose to study the structure of genes – later recognized as DNA – because the quantum pioneer Erwin Schrödinger described genes as 'aperiodic crystals', and that seemed to me remarkably like the luminescent crystals I had studied before the War. Another great quantum theorist, Niels Bohr, was keen to link physics and biology, and his colleague Max Delbrück took that message to many young biologists, including Jim Watson whose inspired approach to DNA contributed much to the new genetics. Thus the quantum mechanics of crystals that gave us transistors and the information technology revolution is also linked with the revolution in genetics.

In the early post-War years, the molecule DNA was known to be associated in some way with processes of biological inheritance, and in Randall's lab at King's College London we set about elucidating its structure. For a couple of years our group was joined by one colleague with whom I sometimes did not get along: the very talented X-ray scientist Rosalind Franklin. The tension between us made research very difficult. Nevertheless, while our efforts led to some dead ends and some about-turns, the team of researchers at King's laid the foundations for the double helix structure that Jim Watson and Francis Crick demonstrated so persuasively with their model in 1953. After many more years of detailed work to confirm the validity and explore the implications of our DNA structure, Watson, Crick and I were awarded a Nobel Prize in 1962.

Some years afterwards my career took a more difficult turn. In 1968 Jim Watson wrote a book about our discovery which made some of us, Francis and me included, uncomfortable. Rosalind Franklin had died of cancer in 1958 and so she was unable to comment on Jim's book, but in 1974, the writer Anne Sayre published a book about Rosalind disputing Jim's portrayal of her. This book enabled some activists to mount a campaign in Rosalind's name to improve the lot of women in science. This was no doubt well-intentioned and indeed useful, but one side-effect was that Rosalind's male colleagues were to some extent demonised. The most prominent demon seemed to be me. Since then, the Franklin/Wilkins story has often been told as an example of the unjustness of male scientists towards their women colleagues, and questions have been raised over whether credit was distributed fairly when the Nobel Prize was awarded. I have found this situation distressing over the years, and I expect that this book is in some way my attempt to respond to these questions, and to tell my side of that story.

The title of this book, *The Third Man of the Double Helix*, is not the one I would have chosen. I have deferred to the advice of my publishers on that issue! However, this title does resonate with some of the tensions, accusations, confusions and controversies that have attended the telling and retelling of the DNA story.

The later years of my career have been devoted to the exploration of the social issues raised by advances in science. I believe that the tensions in the DNA story may shed some light on how tensions in other spheres might be avoided or addressed. But I hope also that this book will show that scientists are not outside of the social concerns about their work, and that they can and should usefully reflect more broadly on their role in the world. At a time of heightened international tensions and new science-based threats, I believe that these lessons are particularly relevant.

This book has been many years in the making. I am very glad to have this opportunity to thank my family for their support, and especially my wife Patricia for her patience and insight.

I would also like to thank my many friends and colleagues, especially Watson Fuller and Herbert Wilson for their scientific contributions and Jane Gregory for her hard work in the editing of this book.

M.H.F.W.
London, 2003

LIST OF PLATES

1. 'Skerries', 30 Kilburn Parade, Wellington.

2. Maurice, his sister Eithne, and their father Edgar, in 1917.

3. Edgar showing Maurice and Eithne how a watch works, *c.* 1919.

4. Eithne and Maurice, 1919.

5. Maurice, Eithne, and Jasmine Wilkins with their mother Evelyn, 1927.

6. Maurice in 1929 with scale model Hawker Fury aeroplane (which still hangs in his bedroom today).

7. Maurice skipping, 1930s.

8. Maurice in 1934 with home-made 'hot box' solar energy panel and home-made astronomical telescopes.

9. Edgar and Granny Wilkins ,1931.

10. Edgar and Evelyn Wilkins during the Second World War.

11. Maurice: self-portrait, 1930s.

12. Anti-war demonstration in London, 1936 – 'scholarships not battleships'.

13. Maurice during experiments on gas-proof rooms carried out by the Cambridge Scientists Anti-War Group, Trinity College, 1937-8.

14. Maurice during experiments on incendiary bombs carried out by the Cambridge Scientists Anti-War Group in W. A. Wooster's garden in 1938.

15. Birmingham University Luminescence Laboratory: 1939.

16. Laboratory sketch by Maurice.

17. Ruth.

18. Berkeley: the Magnetron team, August 1945.

19. Excavating the quadrangle at King's College for the new Wheatstone Physics Laboratory. (Courtesy of King's College London.)

20. Two bottles containing DNA used in the X-ray work in the early 1950s by Wilkins and Gosling and by Franklin and Gosling. (Courtesy of King's College London.)

21. Phillips micro camera used in the early 1950s for recording X-ray diffraction patterns from fibres of DNA. (Courtesy of King's College London.)

22. Cylindrical camera used in the 1950s for recording an X-ray diffraction pattern from a fibre of DNA. (Courtesy of King's College London.)

23. Maurice adjusting the position of an X-ray camera to maximize the intensity of the X-rays incident on the specimen. (Courtesy of King's College London.)

24. Maurice's X-ray sketch, from a letter to Francis Crick, and Rosalind's X-ray. (Sketch courtesy of King's College London; X-ray: © Science Photo Library)

25. Diagram based on the figure in the original paper by Watson and Crick describing the DNA double helix. (Courtesy of King's College London.)

26. Wire model of the DNA double helix in which the base-pairs are represented by flat metal plates with wires representing the bonds to atoms in the sugar-phosphate chain. (Courtesy of King's College London.)

27. Rosalind Franklin and Maurice, at a Gordon research Conference in the USA, late 1950s. (Courtesy of Achber Studio, Laconia, New Hampshire.)

28. Maurice (late 1950s) identifying features in a model of the DNA double-helix built for lectures to general audiences. (Courtesy of King's College London.)

29. Space-filling model of the B form of DNA from Courtauld atomic components. (Courtesy of King's College London.)

30. Maurice (with Don Marvin) assembling a space filling model of the B form of the DNA double helix, *c.* 1960. (Courtesy of King's College London.)

31. Device used from early 1960s for drawing a fibre of DNA from a gel by controlled separation of two glass rods on which the gel was supported. (Courtesy of King's College London.)

32. Notes by Maurice made in around 1960 during work on the structure of nucleohistone, the major component of chromatin. (Courtesy of King's College London.)

33. Nobel laureates, 1962: Maurice Wilkins, John Steinbeck, John Kendrew, Max Perutz, Francis Crick, Jim Watson. (© The Nobel Foundation, 1962.)

34. Christmas 1962 celebration of the award of the Nobel Prize to Francis Crick, Jim Watson, and Maurice Wilkins, showing Maurice looking out from a model of the double helix and photographs of Maurice and Pat and their children at the Stockholm presentation celebrations. (Courtesy of King's College London.)

35. Maurice and Sir John Randall at a Drury Lane party, 1960s.

36. King's College Biophysics Unit laboratory workers, Drury Lane, 1960s.

37. The Wilkins family on a cross-channel ferry on the way to Corsica, 1967: Patricia, William, Sarah, George, and Emily.

38. Maurice with Pope John Paul II, 1980s.

39. Maurice at King's, 1998. (Picture: Carolyn Djanogly.)

CHAPTER I

DISTANT SHORES

I am glad to have been brought up in the constructive spirit and breadth of vision that has its roots in the seventeenth-century English Revolution, when freedom of thought replaced Authoritarianism. My earliest known ancestor, Philip Henry, a minister, joined the move away from Authoritarianism and became, like his contemporary Isaac Newton, a Nonconformist and a Unitarian, seeing one God, not three. In 1662 the English Church tried to turn the clock back by reinstating authority in its Statute of Conformity, and Henry was one of many to give up his ministry in protest. Unitarians set up their own Chapels and schools, and took a leading part in the growth of science and the Industrial Revolution. Joseph Priestley, the discoverer of oxygen, was a Unitarian, and, in industrial Manchester in the north of England, taught some of my ancestors. He then moved to Birmingham where he set up the Lunar Society, where scientists and industrialists met each month on a night when the moonlight made it easier for them to get to the meeting. Alongside Priestley's laboratory was a library, where he studied the sacred texts of many religions.

Another of my ancestors was apprenticed to the pioneering railway engineer George Stevenson: Frederick Swanwick, who was born in 1810, was the youngest son of a manufacturer in industrial Manchester, and his apprenticeship spared him the classical education in the Public Schools where his brothers were sent. Stevenson set up the first passenger railway, between Liverpool and Manchester, and, as the railways spread over Britain, one of Fred's jobs was to persuade landowners to let railways cross their land. In facing the many problems of industrialization he saw clearly the need for new developments in education, and with influential supporters, including the Archbishop of Canterbury, he campaigned for public schools to teach science, modern history and economics. He was able to establish colleges and libraries for working men.

Anna Swanwick, who was born in 1813 – she was Fred's cousin and my father's great aunt – was a pioneer in education. There were no good schools for girls, so Anna and her mother and sisters set up their own self-education group. Anna gained a high reputation as a translator of Goethe and classical Greek writers, and was awarded an Honorary degree by Aberdeen University. She became a well-known public figure, and organized free reading rooms, libraries and lectures for working people, especially women. In 1848 F.D. Maurice, the Christian Socialist, set up Queen's College in London, the first higher education centre for women in the British Isles, and Anna was chosen to oversee the work of the male staff. She and her mother also helped to establish Bedford College for Women, and Anna became its President.

Progressive educational ideas flourished in Anna's family. Her niece Mary Hutton kept notebooks describing her experiences of the education devised for her and her sisters by their parents, who saw education as a process of exploration and enquiry. The family left their home in Dublin, Ireland, and moved to Edenfield, a country house with a farm. In the house, books were the biggest source of new experience – there were novels, astronomy books, histories and fairy tales – and on the farm, the workers taught the girls about the animals and their care. Mary explored the wildlife around her: one spring, she collected caterpillars from the rosebushes to feed to baby robins. There were gymnastics and dancing and weekly swimming in the sea. Mary's father took her to Hallé Concerts and to hear the best sermons, and, instead of school, private tutors came to Edenfield. That was how William Wilkins, my grandfather, met his future wife Mary.

William Mortimer Wilkins, William Wilkins' father, had been an army surgeon in India and Afghanistan. At the age of 59 he married a girl of 19 in Kent in southern England, and they had six children in the six years before he died. His widow and her children became very poor, but William, the eldest son, saved the family by working in a railway office from the age of 16 to 20. Then he worked as a teacher at a school where he could also study, and at 23 he took entrance exams at Trinity College Dublin with outstanding success. This success continued throughout his university work, and he subsequently secured, at a very young age, the headship of Dublin High School. His younger brother George was also brilliant, and became a Fellow and Professor of Hebrew at Trinity. Their sister Eliza obtained an Honours Degree at the Royal University of Ireland only two years after the first British women graduates at University College London. Charles, the youngest brother, was a brilliant mathematician but died from smallpox just before graduating (the Wilkins Prize in Mathematics for Women was set up at Trinity College in his memory). During his short career he was, however, a lucky find as a tutor at Edenfield for Mary Hutton and her sisters. William seems to have done some tutoring there too, and that was how he and Mary met.

Mary studied at the newly founded Newnham College, Cambridge, and spent some time at Anna Swanwick's home in London. Among the many cultural centres she visited was the Royal Institution, the famous science laboratory and lecture hall, where Anna was one of the first women Members. Mary was related to Professor Adams, the Astronomer Royal, and she wrote to William of an entertaining meeting with him in Cambridge. Though she did well in her studies, Mary was not concerned to obtain a degree: her interest, like William Wilkins', was in teaching children, and a Diploma enabled her to teach at Bath High School for Girls in England. After two successful years there, she married William and soon was creating a home in Dublin where her children learnt in ways similar to those she had experienced at Edenfield. The idea of education as exploration was unusual at the time – most schooling was very rigid, and children were not encouraged to think for themselves. At around this time, Einstein's schoolteachers were offended by the dull boy who resisted their attempts to teach him, and only in his third school, where he had some freedom to learn by exploring for himself, did he gain any benefit from formal education.

William and Mary were brought together in an exciting educational situation. They were both keenly interested in education, and they shared many basic ideas. They were also enthusiastic gymnasts, and strongly agreed about the importance of bodily health; and they spent long holidays at Skerries on the coast just north of Dublin, sharing their passion for natural history. However, the marriage was not to last. It is not clear when the break-up began, but a clash of attitudes seems likely: William had struggled very hard with the aid of education to overcome acute poverty, and saw examinations as very important – he was very glad to see entry to the British Civil Service opened to all classes through exams, rather than depending on upper-class connections. Mary's background was very different, mainly in relation to money. Her parents had employed servants and farm workers; her father paid her fees at Cambridge. Her many relatives had fairly rich homes, which Mary visited at holidays. Her history was one of economic security and comfort. But when her father died, Mary's mother sold Edenfield and moved with her unmarried daughters to Italy where most of her relatives were, and since most of the Swanwick relatives were in England, Mary had little family support in Dublin. The marriage breakdown became notorious: James Joyce wrote in *Ulysses* that Mary 'had her work cut out for her'. The Huttons and Wilkinses had little contact thereafter.

Nevertheless, William and Mary had raised their family of three children: Maurice, Edgar and Una. Maurice, my uncle, seemed happy as a boy at Dublin High School where his father was Headmaster, and he did clerical work there in his very good 'copperplate'. In contrast, Maurice's younger brother Edgar, my father, had almost illegible handwriting, and he was very unhappy at school; William felt ashamed of him. Edgar would have been much happier with the Edenfield 'explore for yourself' way of learning. Mary was a very great help to him, providing him with a real carpenter's bench and tools, and encouraging his enthusiasm for bird-watching at Skerries. William was a keen cyclist and gymnast, and Edgar put much energy into those activities. I think he wished to show his father he could be a success, even if he did not like ordinary school.

Edgar grew up into a very energetic man: cycling in the mountains, high-diving off the rocks, and running naked with his pals around the beaches. He was a committed vegetarian. There were endless escapades: pushing a rich landowner's boat into the centre of his best drawing room; and walking on his hands with his feet in the air around the wall on the top of an ancient tower. Then, as a medical student at Trinity College, Dublin, he won outright the annual cycling trophy: the great silver rose bowl I was to be christened in. But a life of cycle racing, conjuring tricks, gymnastics and Turkish baths did not provide him with a sufficiently challenging vision of his future. At Skerries he had met Eveline Whittacker, a police chief's daughter from Dublin, an affectionate and beautiful woman with long blonde hair and a great deal of common sense. They were married in the autumn of 1913. Medicine, vegetarianism and healthy living pointed the way forward, as did the prospect of helping to educate any children that might arise from his marriage. But it seemed that Ireland could not provide him with the opportunities he needed. Edgar looked much further: he had heard that New Zealand wanted doctors, and in 1913 he and Eveline set sail for the other side of the world.

In New Zealand, Edgar found a practice near Wellington. He cycled on his rounds; some eyebrows were raised when people heard he was vegetarian, and he learned to use an agent to collect his fees. Edgar and Eveline's first child, my sister Eithne, was born in Wellington in 1914. The family then spent a memorable few years in the dramatically beautiful mountain country at Pongoroa, where notices warned that the winds could blow travellers off the roads. They built a typical wooden house there – interrupted only when their timber was blown away. I was born in that house on 15 December 1916, and it still stands.

Eveline enjoyed learning to bake bread, and helping Edgar with anaesthetics. He admired the pioneering farmers and timber men of Pongoroa and was glad to help look after their needs, but he wanted to work with other doctors, find out more about healthcare generally and explore the possibilities of preventive medicine. So we moved to the nearby town of Paihatua, where there was a hospital. This led to contact with school medicine which interested Edgar very much because of its role in child development and its largely preventive nature. Preventive medicine became his primary interest, and he was fortunate to be appointed New Zealand Director of School Hygiene, a post that took us back to Wellington.

My first clear memories are from Wellington. For me, the name evokes much joy. In Wellington, it seemed that there was always sun, blue sky and peaceful white clouds gently moving, symbolizing my joyful life and dreamlike contentment in the loving security of my family. I have many vivid memories of our elegant one-storey house with its verandah and white palings on pretty, respectable Kelburn Parade. On a steep slope above the city, it gave us a view of the grand sweep of Wellington Bay, and 'Skerries' on our front gate reminded my parents of where they first met in the Irish sun and air. Just across the way, the large buildings of Victoria College reassured them by expressing the value of education and learning. We had parties in our big drawing room at the front of the house. We had a piano and a very special hand-made gramophone – what a liberation that gramophone was! With it we could have the best music performed by the best musicians whenever we liked. We enjoyed all the music our father bought as he explored the records in the music shop, especially the *Tancredi Overture*, Mischa Elman playing Schubert's *Ave Maria*, *A la Luz de la Luna* and the *Spinning Quartet* from *Martha*. I remember specially *L'Après Midi d'Une Faune* because Father taught us to hear it with the sound of the sawmills, as he had at Pongoroa, coming over the hills far away, rising and falling with the wind and giving us a sense of wild beauty from beyond this world. We shared with him Italian opera, Gilbert and Sullivan, and John McCormack singing Irish songs. Eithne and I danced and danced, each of us whirling about, and life was like a festival. Memories of dancing with Eithne have haunted me all my life. My mother played the piano so we could sing. My father played only one piece which he called *Moonlight and Roses*, but for us that was very special and quite enough – like the fried porridge which was the only thing he ever cooked.

I enjoyed our food. It gave me a feeling of wholesome security. We ate vegetarian whole food with minimal refining and processing, and cooked it to retain its natural goodness. Our breakfast porridge was made from unrolled grain, heated the previous evening and put in a hay box overnight to conserve energy. To fatten me up, I had cream with my porridge (my mother affectionately called me a skinamalink). We had baked lentils, macaroni cheese, green pea soup, unpolished rice, potatoes steamed in their skins, underdone cabbage (we liked drinking the cabbage water) and lots of fresh vegetables, fruit and nuts. We ate wholemeal bread. We bought stiff white New Zealand honey in a great square tin more than a foot across, and scraped it out into a pot for the table – once we found a little dead moth in it. I was told that I once exclaimed 'toast and honey is nicer than hearing stories', and I used to hold up a piece of toast and move it about in the air making a noise like an aeroplane.

Several of my most intense memories of the Wellington times are about the discovery or emergence of something new. It was an extraordinary revelation when I was able to draw beautiful small shining fish out of the deep dark sea. I very vividly remember searching for hens' eggs in the straw at a neighbour's house, and my great enthusiasm when I found a smooth egg lying in the confusion of the straw. Eithne and I were very impressed when Father and Professor Kirk from Victoria College took us to the Botanical Gardens, and Kirk showed us the trapdoor spiders that lived in little tunnels and clung tightly to their trapdoors to hold them shut when disturbed.

New dimensions were added to our happiness by our summer holidays at Muritai near Wellington, in a bungalow that was almost on the beach. Typically, Father did not try to teach us how to swim, and, while Eithne mastered it, I learnt only to enjoy splashing about. The best time of all at Muritai was when my mother had to go to Wellington and my father took Eithne and me on a long walk along the hills, all the way to Pencarrow lighthouse. I remember walking from one hilltop to the next only to find yet another had come into view — and Father encouraging us by saying the next was the last. Eithne wrote: 'On the way back Daddin sang to the sheep and made us laugh so we couldn't walk, and walked small with his knees bent so that we laughed and couldn't walk and it was a long way back so he made a song about: "We are so hungry and so thirsty and so tired and <u>so</u> glad we are getting <u>so</u> near home."' That was a wonderful day.

We had many small trips into wild places, especially for picnics. After eating we might 'strike up the ridge' with my father — my mother never wishing to join us in such energetic adventure.

Sometimes we would push into the beautiful and almost impene-trable bush in which strange octopus-like plants climbed and twisted around the trees and unusual birds hovered above us. One extraordinary expedition was from a neighbours' holiday cottage. It was on a beach by a very calm stretch of water, and in the quiet evening my father rowed us out gently in a little boat. We came to a strange island just above the level of the sea, and when we stepped out of the boat we were amazed to find that the island consisted of nothing but beautiful little seashells. In the evening light it seemed like fairyland. That was a heavenly memory – our father taking us across the water to another world. We greatly valued his special ability to find and show us what was wonderful, interesting or somehow out-of-this-world. He could sense the magic in things.

My father's ideas about education derived largely from his mother's experience at Edenfield. He believed that children should not go to school at an early age, because there they would only be exposed to second-hand knowledge from books. He wrote that 'The bright child naturally takes to books early enough. It is necessary rather to keep it from this lazier form of gaining knowledge in order to compel it to go out and contact the world with its own hands and feet and eyes and ears.' Father claimed that his attitudes derived from 'modern ideas' as regards the 'psychology and education of the child mind', but I think he was also reacting to his hard school-master father. As a result, Eithne did not begin school until she was 8½, after she had learned to read (and knew all of Peter Rabbit by heart). My father said that in Wellington I picked up from Eithne some of what she had learned at school; and he taught us some maths, science and theology. He claimed that when I was 4½ I argued that God could not be everywhere, only pieces of him could. Eithne and I taught each other geography from a globe and, excited by seeing eclipses of the Sun and the Moon, we studied Sir Robert Ball's big illustrated *Story of the Heavens*. Our telescope, binoculars, microscope and barograph interested us, but the binoculars were best because used the wrong way round they made people look so tiny.

However, the time was fast approaching when we children would need some formal schooling, and Father, with his strong views on education, was concerned that the choice of schools in Wellington might be rather too limited. He was also becoming frustrated with the medical establishment, who were proving resistant to Father's ideas about preventive medicine. He felt that, especially for children, decent living conditions and sound nutrition were the key to good health, whereas his doctor colleagues considered their work to consist only of tending in hospital to children who had become sick. Father eventually tired of battling with the authorities and decided to take his family home to Ireland.

So we packed up and left our cosy home in Wellington. We sailed from Auckland in June 1923, and began our family world cruise – across two enormous oceans, and through Central America via the Panama Canal. It was a big adventure for Eithne and me. We had a little cabin with a porthole facing the rear deck, and there were many other children on board so we played a lot of games. The decks were big, and often Eithne grabbed my hand and we ran up and down and round and round. Or we just leaned on the rail and looked out at the sky and sea – there was so much fresh air and light. The Bible says that God made light and saw 'that it was good': and that was how we felt.

As we travelled North we noticed it slowly but steadily growing warmer. The first time we saw the tropical flying fish, flashing silver as they shot from one wave to another, we were amazed how far they could go. When we came in from the deck and went deep down inside the ship we found extraordinary forces at work there. Several times our father arranged for us to climb with him down steep iron ladders to explore the cavernous engine rooms. In the boiler room we watched the stokers open the furnace and throw coal into its burning mouth. We gazed at the enormous pistons moving up and down and the cranks rotating; and, best of all, we squeezed down by the massive propeller shaft that reached all the way to the stern of the ship, and watched it, all bare bright metal, steadily and incessantly rotating as it worked our way towards England. Day after day, week after week, we shared our experiences, gliding through space and through time and, of course, like moving through life, we barely knew how it would end.

When we reached the Panama Canal we were very excited to get off the boat and spend a day on land. We drove around looking with amazement at the tropical trees and weird birds and monkeys and strange creatures we did not know. In the Canal we were especially interested when the enormous locks filled and emptied so that the ship gradually rose or fell. Then the sailors who lived below looked out of their portholes and shouted and laughed as they threw potatoes at the lizards on the sides of the locks. As we moved north across the Atlantic, the stokers got down to better coal and the ship moved faster. Near the purser's office there was a big map of the ocean and we watched an officer put a line on the map each day to show the distance we had travelled. When we reached the better coal we moved faster and the lines were longer. We looked forward to reaching England, even though, as we moved further and further from the tropics and nearer to life on land and the workaday world ahead, it slowly grew cooler and greyer. But Eithne and I were carried along in a joyful dream, and all the time the stokers went on shovelling coal into the furnaces below.

At last England came in sight, and after passing the enormous *Majestic* and *Mauretania* (which my father said made my eyes pop out of my head), we landed from our own steamer at the great port of Southampton. Standing on the wharf we were excited to see our father's special gramophone being unloaded from our ship. Seeing that arrive safely meant that we could look forward to our good life continuing, and Eithne and I would dance together again. The next leg of the journey took us to the enormous Victoria Station in London where we were bewildered by the immense crowds and bustle. Our real goal, however, was Dublin, about which our parents had talked so much, and all our marvellous relatives. We got our train, caught our ferry boat, and as the boat at last eased itself along the wharf at Dublin the passengers crowded on the deck, and we could feel the great silent anticipation – my parents were not the only ones who had been long out of Ireland.

Our relatives were all very friendly and warm. The one I remember most clearly is Granny Whittacker, my mother's mother, with whom we stayed. Very tall and upright, all in widow's black, she appeared most formidable, but she was very kind and understanding. We had pulled up our roots on the other side of the world, and were deeply disorientated, and Granny Whittacker tried to help us feel at home. One day she organized a very enjoyable visit to the beautiful country lanes outside Dublin. A large party of us went, like Queen Victoria, in open carriages drawn by horses. But our parents were sometimes not at ease in Dublin. The disappearance in the 1916 Rebellion of well-known buildings was not reassuring. Dublin Castle, where my mother had lived with police families, was now guarded with much finesse not by British but by Irish Republican sentries. Standing to attention, their perfect immobility provoked my father to step forward and run his finger along a fixed bayonet, much to the horror of his relatives who were walking him around Dublin. The city seemed empty and ailing, and many people had abandoned it for the countryside as jobs were scarce. Father's older brother Maurice was earning his living as a Headmaster in non-Republican Northern Ireland (later we spent many happy holidays in County Down, with Uncle Maurice and his wife Eva, who had been imprisoned for Suffragist activities). Mother's brother-in-law Bob had taken a job in London. So Father decided that his prospects would be best with the British School Medical Service, although he would need to spend a year studying for a Diploma of Public Health to become a School Doctor. Also if we got back to London soon, Eithne and I could go to school together. That would be a step towards a new happy home.

Life in London began with a furnished house near Uncle Bob's house in Norbury, an unexciting suburb south of London. My father started studying for his DPH at King's College, part of the University of London, and Eithne and I began going to a school close to our home. Eithne had spent a year at school in New Zealand, but I, at age six-and-a-half, had no experience of school at all. My first impression was overwhelming: I remember standing with Eithne, holding her hand in the middle of a very big room with a polished floor, surrounded by an enormous crowd of shrieking children running in all directions. The very next day, Eithne was taken ill and I did not go back to that school. Standing in the noisy schoolroom with Eithne holding my hand was in many ways my last real contact with her. Her whole body was taken over by septicaemia caused by a very dangerous infection; and she was moved through a succession of hospitals to Great Ormond Street Hospital for Children. I visited her many times: I remember climbing big institutional staircases with my parents and passing through many wards and rooms before finding Eithne. But she was not only swallowed up by the great hospitals: she had become physically almost unrecognizable. Her beautiful blond hair had been cut off and her head shaved, and only with an effort could I recognize her face. She was like a victim of some nightmarish scheme, trapped in her bed by a great framework of ropes and pulleys that held her legs up in the air. I had seen pictures of machines for torture like that.

It was difficult for me to know what to do when we stood around the bed. On one occasion, I bumped against it, and Eithne cried out in pain. That was all the communication I had with her, and it felt like a clear rejection. It was an extremely bitter moment, and seemed to mark the end of our close relationship. Possibly if we had been able to talk about her anguish in hospital, and all her sufferings and everlasting disablement, we might have been able to keep alive some of the love and understanding we had enjoyed in New Zealand. Eithne's doctors tried to release her infection by opening up her joints and letting the pus out. There were no antibiotics then. If she lived there was the problem of trying to keep her joints mobile after they had healed. The surgeons would continue operating on Eithne for years. Like William and George Wilkins she did not withstand suffering easily, and she said later that she wished they had let her die because life had been so painful. My father, of course, could not think of letting his wonderful daughter die. Blood transfusion was then only in its early days, but he gave blood when Eithne was in a crisis. Distraught and cast down by sadness, he could do nothing but wander aimlessly about

the streets of London. One day he heard, far away, someone singing opera in Italian, and the uplifting beauty of it moved him
profoundly and he was able to go home. As he told me that story I
realized how much my parents had suffered. Possibly my father
blamed himself for Eithne's illness, because his career had not
sufficient success in New Zealand.

I don't remember feeling especially unhappy or lonely
without Eithne, but my parents were concerned about me and
gave me many very special presents to encourage me, such as tin
soldiers on motorcycles with sidecars containing machine guns, a
very good model Howitzer which fired model shells, and a real
blank cartridge pistol. I went for long walks on Mitcham Common, and had a fox terrier which kept me company until it died of
mange. One clear memory from those walks is of looking at a big
advertisement on a hoarding, and deciding I really should learn to
read. Fairly soon Mary, my Granny Wilkins, arrived and took me
out to many exhibitions which appealed to me very much. The
best was a reconstruction of the naval triumph at Zeebruge, with
model ships tussling amid explosions, flashes of light and smoke.
Granny probably did not like war exhibitions, but she had very
good judgement about what I would like.

About this time I began to feel that perhaps my parents were
not always right. Father decided I must be vaccinated against
smallpox and have my tonsils removed. That was all very sound
medicine (before he went to King's my father had been doubtful
about vaccination), but both the vaccination and the tonsil
operation were very painful. During the winter, we moved to a

smaller and depressing furnished house. I had begun going to school, but my parents were very worried about me and my mother took me to see the Head. I listened to their conclusion that I was depressed. But when spring came, everyone was more cheerful. My father enjoyed his work at King's, and my new sister was born. She was a cheerful, pretty baby, and my parents named her Jasmine because she reminded them of a jasmine bud. Fairly soon Eithne was brought home from hospital and we had a nurse living in to help look after her. I remember seeing Eithne lying on a bed in the garden and thinking that with splints on she looked like some strange insect that had got stuck on the ground. There was very little communication between us.

Soon, life took a turn for the better: by the summer, we were all cheered by talk about Birmingham, where my father had obtained a post as School Doctor. I was very excited when he told us that Birmingham was the biggest engineering centre in Britain — there, he said, 'they can make anything from a steam engine to a pin.' Having been torn out of our New Zealand Garden of Eden and temporarily dumped in furnished houses, it was a great relief when we found ourselves at last in leafy Wylde Green just north of the city. The milkman came round with his churns, a green-grocer brought a cart loaded with cabbage, potatoes and fruit, and the postman delivered the *British Medical Journal* to my father. It was home, and we soon felt we belonged there.

An important contribution to transforming our Wylde Green house into our home was my father's working in wood. Making a bookcase came first; and then a verandah, in New Zealand style, and a pergola for roses to climb on. He assembled a wooden shed and equipped it with a real carpenter's workbench and proper wood-working tools. During one particularly snowy winter Father built us a large wooden sledge, and fixed iron strips on to it so that it would slide well. To bend the iron he did a blacksmith's job, heating the iron red-hot in our living room coal fire with the aid of household bellows. In Sutton Park the lakes were frozen hard, and the whole family – even Eithne – squeezed on the sledge, slid down a hill and shot across the ice.

I went to school just around the corner at modest, benevolent Wylde Greene College, which was surrounded by horse chestnut trees – a useful source of conkers. The Headmaster, Mr Burd, was a tall, friendly man who gave geography lessons enlivened by his reminiscences of his home county of Lancashire. I also had a lot of fun with another Lancastrian, my good friend Harry Goodwin. Harry was a hero at school because his very special conker had won more duels than anyone could remember. When at last Harry's conker was broken in two, the boys crowded round to look inside the record breaker. Harry said it 'had been matured like good wine'. I enjoyed getting to know Harry's warm, good-hearted and sociable family. They were devoted to their Lancashire community, and never missed their summer visit to Blackpool. Their gramophone filled their home with humorous songs, such as George Formby, with his banjo, singing (with amusing innuendo) *When I'm Cleaning Windows*.

My family was happy in its own company. On Sundays in the summer we drove to some quiet shady place where we could sit comfortably, have tea (my father liked to make a fire and boil a kettle New Zealand style) and then wander about and explore. We made the long drive to Wales for our summer holiday at Aberdovey, and stayed in modest boarding houses close to a sandy beach where all the family could enjoy the sea. We could just make the journey in one day; and, following New Zealand custom, we strapped the suitcases on the car between the front mudguards and the bonnet, and Eithne and I sat in the dickey seat at the back, with bags and cases piled in beside us.

In Wales, we had days out in the car, and my father was good at finding interesting, restful picnic spots that were easily accessible for Eithne. Although she would be permanently disabled, she had made good progress back to mobility. But the most important part of my holidays was 'Worship of the Hills', which meant my father and I went climbing mountains. Our favourite mountains were wild, remote Trum Gelli and Taren Hendre, a short drive away from the crowds at Aberdovey. We liked to strike up the hillside with no track to guide us, through hummocks of grass, bogs and peat, up heather-covered slopes and past huge boulders. We delighted in the rough beauty of the mountainside and in anticipating the view at the top. When the weather was clear the view widened as we climbed, and when it was wet sometimes a sheep would suddenly loom up, seemingly magnified, out of the mist. We worked our way up, trudging, trudging, and getting very tired, finding our second wind and going on trudging. Then, at the top, high on the edge of a cliff, we would see the enormous gap below, and beyond it the wide valley, the plains and the estuary and another range of peaks in the distance. The suddenness of that view was like magic.

At home, the workshop was very important to me. I felt at home there, and it became 'my place'. Father showed me how to hollow out wood to make little boats; but I wanted to go my way. I liked to make things full of power, that could go whizzing along. If the wheels on my little cars did not turn, it did not matter: in my imagination I could see the cars darting about, and hear them roaring as they went faster and faster. One day at the newsagent, a magazine called *The Modern Boy* caught my eye. It was just what I wanted – all about power and speed and specially for boys like me. On the cover I read ' "FREE WITHIN" fine coloured METAL MODEL of the World Record-Breaking Car Major Segrave's 1000 horsepower Sunbeam.' I eagerly paid the price of two pennies, and I was never to forget how excited and happy I was as I walked home. I proudly carried the magazine with its bright orange and blue cover, showing Segrave streaking along at 200 miles an hour; and I carefully held the coloured, pressed-out metal sheet which was the wonderful free model of Segrave's Sunbeam.

Britain in 1928 was a world leader in making all kinds of powerful machines. When *The Modern Boy* proudly discussed the World's Greatest Locomotive or the World's Biggest Flying Boat, they were always British, because 'British was Best'. I was particularly excited about how power and speed came out of careful design and thinking. At 200 miles per hour, Segrave's car tyres would fly to pieces if they had not been designed well (a lesson in centrifugal force), and the whole car could fly off its track if the shape of the body did not let the air move smoothly by (a lesson in aerodynamics). I enjoyed reading about the heroic drivers and the new kinds of risks they took to break through the record barrier and on into the unknown. Major Segrave, at 203 m.p.h., was my special hero. With his dignified name and army title, he seemed like an Arthurian Knight on a Holy Quest. Compared with him, Captain Malcolm Campbell, at 206.9 mph, seemed too ordinary for his awesome role – more the kind of man one might see coming out of a pub. But his beautiful Bluebird with its Napier Lion 12 cylinder 875 hp aero engine was much more refined than Ray Keech's three-engined American block-buster. Segrave 'got to the top', like my father and me climbing in Wales. I was beginning to feel that science and technology had some almost religious qualities.

Many of the exciting new advances were very clear. Heroic men and women flew solo to Australia, and great airships with 100 passengers went to New York. Then rocket cars achieved over 400 mph! I got a Roman Candle firework and fixed it on a little model car. Better than I could have hoped, it shot off with a life of its own across a flat roof and disappeared into the distance. I knew a little astronomy and it seemed extraordinary that new Russian ideas about rockets might really make space travel possible. 'A Glimpse of the Future' on the cover of *The Modern Boy* showed a fantastic Metropolis where the dreams of architects and engineers had created a vast temple to science. Between towering skyscrapers with spires and domes, passenger aircraft wove their way under bridges high in the air, while down below streamlined vehicles sped along the ground. I eagerly looked forward to growing up in that marvellous world of the future where we would all be whizzing about and seeing the Universe from new angles. That was what 'modern' meant – there was lots of optimism then; given time, science was certain to give us a better world.

Normally my father left me to enjoy *The Modern Boy* with uncritical wonder. He helped me by buying tools, materials and books when I needed them. But Britain had just been through the General Strike, we were plunging into the Great Depression, and I often heard him using the slogan 'Poverty in the Midst of Plenty' as he talked and talked about malnutrition in the slums of Birmingham where he worked all day. When I made a drawing of the wonderful City of the Future and showed it to him, he surprised me by asking how the aircraft could fly with almost no wings. It was a good question. I think he had doubts about the over-fanciful *Modern Boy*, and was aware that science did not operate free from economic pressures.

When I was approaching 12 years of age, I began to lose interest in reading about exciting things in *The Modern Boy*: I wanted more direct contact with power and speed. I watched aeroplanes overhead as they flew to and from Castle Bromwich aerodrome, which was quite close to my home. A schoolfriend knew a man at the aerodrome and we were able to go into the hangar where planes were being checked and repaired by engineers. I was not allowed to talk to the engineers, but it was still very exciting to be in the same room with real aeroplanes. Back in my workshop, I made little flying planes. I had found a book about flying models and I designed and made one with satin walnut for the propeller, and silk, birchwood and piano wire for the wings. When I took it to the school playing field, during the school holidays when no-one was about, I was very pleased by how well it flew. It was a beautiful sight: the plane climbing with its outstretched wings against the sky and the propeller purring in the sunlight.

My scientific career owes much to a visit around this time from a Mr Manton, who was the headmaster of one of the schools where my father was school doctor. He called at our house to discuss some aspects of my father's work at his school, and they also talked about what I was doing in my workshop. Mr Manton seemed impressed, and he said I should go to Cambridge and do research in the Cavendish Laboratory. I had never heard of the Cavendish, but I always remembered it as a place that might suit me later on. The first step towards Cambridge was for me to go to King Edward's High School in Birmingham (and Eithne could go to the Girls' High School close by). As I reached my twelfth birthday, on 15 December 1930, I became eligible to attend King Edward's, and I sat the entrance exam and obtained a scholarship and a free place. In January the term began, but soon a severe bout of ear infection caused me to be rushed at night into hospital. The horror of the anaesthetic being pushed over my face never left me. I think that leaving the quiet security of Wylde Green College contributed to my illness: to get to that school I only had to walk round the corner under the leafy conker trees, whereas to get to King Edward's I had to travel seven miles to the centre of Birmingham on a crowded steam train, and get out at enormous New Street Station, in all the crowds of boys pushing their way to the enormous black stone school. It had been designed by the architect of the Houses of Parliament, and was just as awesome. All that black stone, in the freezing winter weather, and the boys streaming into the enormous entrance, was like a medieval picture of crowds of lost souls entering Hell.

After my operation I found the journeys to school much easier. Our gang of boys shared a compartment with some young businessmen who played cards. By joint agreement we left the 'card sharpers' to get on with their games while we were free to lark about, doing gymnastics on the luggage racks or unrolling toilet paper out the window to catch the attention of the girls sitting further along the train. I found that the nuts on the steam heating pipes could be easily loosened so that steam came out. Having left a compartment full of steam we were amused to watch a dignified passenger open the door and recoil in consternation as a great cloud of steam billowed out.

At school I admired the clarity of the teaching, and recognized the kindness of the imposing uniformed Head Porter, whose presence in the School Entrance had scared me at first. Our teachers, especially the older ones recruited soon after the

1914–1918 War, were very successful in building a sense of community. The good spirit of the teachers was illustrated by 'The Bish' (with clerical dog collar), who taught mathematics, and whose light-heartedness was accompanied by a quiet discipline. Mr Hare, a physics teacher, had great breadth of interests and clarity of mind. The practical physics class was divided up into pairs of students, and Hare visited each pair to check on progress. Once when he came to me he sat down and asked, 'What will we discuss? Physics and Chinese Philosophy?'

My most important friend when I started at King Edward's, the tall, handsome and wild Philip Marples, would not have thrown an ink bomb in the Bish's maths class because he respected him so much. But Philip and I sat together in a boring class on German for scientists, and I devised a way to fold a sheet of paper so that it formed a small container which I then filled with ink from the inkwell in my desk. When the teacher, who was too casual, was writing on the blackboard, I handed the ink-bomb to Philip, who stood up and threw it across the class. It hit the wall and the ink shot out, making great black dribbles down the wall. When the teacher asked who had done it, Philip immediately owned up and was given 100 lines – he knew which teachers gave light punishments. Unfortunately, he was expelled from school for setting fire to the Headmaster's study (I had no connection with that); but I would see more of him at Birmingham University during the War – he quietened down and made a career in calculating machines.

For several years I was a keen astronomer, using telescopes

I made in my workshop. Philip introduced me to a family friend, a young clergyman called Mr Wright, who was an expert maker of lenses. Wright also organized a remarkable Science Fair where a range of scientific developments was displayed. These included an early non-electronic television transmitter and receiver, but it gave miserable definition and did not impress me. Wright had some equipment for grinding and polishing lenses and mirrors, and he kindly lent me a steel tool for grinding a disc of glass to the correct curve to make a mirror for the powerful reflecting telescope I was building. I made a 7-inch concave mirror which gave a much better performance than my previous 3-inch lens. Later I made a 9¼-inch mirror, which was of a quality and power comparable to those used by experienced amateur astronomers. I had found an invaluable book, *Amateur Telescope Making*, written by F.A. Ellison, the director of the Armagh Observatory, which taught me how to test the accuracy of the curve on my mirrors. Strong metal supports were needed for these bigger telescopes, which were heavy – they were made of brass – and I got some very useful help from my local blacksmith, who said, 'with your brain and my brawn we could make anything'.

I was amazed to find, as I approached the Sixth Form, that there I could spend all my time on science. This sounded like Heaven. My friend Keith Gilbert gave me the very important advice that I should choose St John's College at Cambridge because its staff included specially able physicists such as Oliphant. Keith also introduced me to socialist ideas, encouraging me to read George Bernard Shaw and H.G. Wells' short stories about lonely people peering into new worlds. Wells' *History of Man* had a breadth of vision that excited me. Another important friend was Bob Cooper, who was keen on the science at school and had wide cultural interests. He took me to a cinema that specialized in top-quality foreign films, which was a great mind-opener. Even more inspiring was the Birmingham Art Gallery where we concentrated on the exceptional collection of Pre-Raphaelites.

When I was interviewed by a County of Warwick committee for a Cambridge scholarship, it seemed that, hearing I was advanced in telescope-making, the committee decided I was interested in nothing but science. They told me that I must study art and architecture, go to the theatre, and generally broaden my interests. I was, of course, pleased to think the committee would approve of the interests I already pursued with Bob Cooper, and I specially looked forward to increasing my reading in the excellent City Library. I did get a Warwick award, and with other scholarships most of my expenses were covered; but first I had to gain a place at Cambridge.

CHAPTER 2

FINDING MY FEET

On one of my visits to Cambridge to sit scholarship exams I walked out to the Solar Physics Observatory and rang the front door bell. I explained that I was busy making reflecting telescopes as well as taking scholarship exams. Roderick Redman, the Observatory Director, took me around the Observatory and told me that the next day Cyril Burch, who had exciting new ideas about making telescopes, would be having tea at his house and I ought to join the party. It was very exciting and I found the discussions with Burch very useful. Because of the rift between the Wilkinses and the Huttons, I knew nothing then about my grandmother Mary Hutton's many contacts with the Astronomer Royal at Cambridge.

After success in the scholarship exams and in my applications to the charitable guild the Worshipful Company of Carpenters (I preferred that to the Fishmongers), I was able to start at Cambridge. I was, however, disappointed that astronomy was only taught as part of a maths degree. So after some discussion I decided to take a physics degree with geology and mineralogy for the first two years. I quite enjoyed the geology, which reminded me of my climbing holidays in Wales, and the mineralogy which would turn out to be useful later when my research concerned crystal physics and X-ray diffraction. Despite my childhood interests, I found that I could drop astronomy without much regret: during my early months at Cambridge I had become much more interested in science that was directly related to the problems of human life. Student organizations spent much time drawing attention to the Nazi threat, the Spanish Civil War and the acute problems of Indian Independence, and I became so interested in Indian freedom that I wished I was Indian and could relate my life directly to that problem. All in all, I began to feel that astronomy was too much 'up in the clouds'. I no longer saw science as an escape from human problems: instead, I took the opposite view. I was not very interested in intellectually exciting science of any kind unless it had a real meaning in relation to some aspect of human problems. I was developing a greater breadth of interest like that of my Unitarian ancestors and my Birmingham friends at King Edward's School. In my enthusiasm for *The Modern Boy*, I had seen Major Segrave, holder of the Land Speed Record, as a Medieval knight on a Holy Quest. I raised the matter of a special mission in life when I was a new student at St John's College, and the great mathematician Arthur Eddington gave a talk there. The lecture room was very full, and I was sitting on the carpet at the front of the audience. Eddington was profoundly impressed by numbers, which seemed to him to have very special significance. At question time I asked him if he saw the kind of study he described as the most important kind of activity a human being could undertake. Eddington replied that he would not put it quite that way. Possibly he was embarrassed by my naïvety.

It was a privilege to be in St John's, which had so many distinguished staff. I was specially fortunate to have one hour every week of the undivided attention of my supervisor, the physicist M.L.E. Oliphant. Marcus Oliphant was from Australia, and was Deputy to the great New Zealander Ernest Rutherford, who directed the Cavendish Laboratory. Both men had a down-to-earth approach to physics, and believed that a physicist should make his own apparatus. This suited me well, since I had grown up in my family's workshop tradition. Oliphant continued in the do-it-yourself style after Rutherford died, and his staff had some dramatic accidents. The apparatus had become much bigger than in Rutherford's day, and eventually Oliphant had to bring in professional engineers. At our supervisions, he told me a lot about Michael Faraday's concept of tubes of force which, in the nineteenth century, had helped him to discover the relation between magnetic and electrical forces. In the twentieth century, tubes of force were only to be found in histories of Faraday's work, but the simple tube concept had helped Faraday to sort out the phenomena he studied. Later in my career, when I was studying electrons moving in crystals, Oliphant pointed out to me that simple mechanics could explain some phenomena normally seen in terms of quantum theory. His interest in choosing simple rather than more complex ways of analysing phenomena illustrates the different ways in which a scientist's mind might work, and may have helped him to handle political problems after retiring from science, when he became Governor of New South Wales. Altogether, Oliphant was very good to me. I felt we were on the same wavelength.

I felt the atmosphere at St John's to be warm and supportive. For example, although I found physics easy enough to understand, I had some difficulty with pure mathematics, and I was very grateful to my fellow student George Barnard for helping me. George went on to a distinguished career as a statistician and became well-known for his left-wing anti-establishment views. In my second year John Cockcroft was my supervisor. He was famous for splitting the atom, and was quite as distinguished a physicist as Oliphant. He was steadily supportive of me although he was rather withdrawn, and was a very great help when I had difficulty in choosing which research direction to take. Sir James Wordie, my Tutor, who acted as general adviser, was also very friendly and helpful. He had been a polar explorer and was ready to talk about boots and nails for climbing. In a similar way he gave me very practical advice in my final year and introduced me to the psychologist Dr Bannister, who would help me on several occasions. Wordie's waiting room nearly always had many students waiting to see him about some problem or other. Distinguished workers such as Harold Jefferies (author of the famous book *The Earth*) were always ready to discuss my questions when I knocked on the door. Keith Gilbert had been quite right to recommend St John's.

After my first year I was invited to join the Natural Science Club, where a small number of undergraduates and research students gave talks that were discussed by other members. These meetings helped me to understand some of the new research being done, and how research workers think about their work. My talk was called 'Seeing Structures', and I tried to explain the great Cambridge crystallographer J.D. Bernal's work in X-ray diffraction. Atoms in crystals will scatter an X-ray beam, and the pattern of scattered X-rays can yield useful information about the positions of the atoms within the crystal structure. Crystals have a simple, regular arrangement of atoms and so are relatively simple to decipher, but Bernal was trying to use X-ray diffraction to study the structures of proteins and viruses, which are very complicated. After my talk, Dick Synge, who was a biochemist, told me that he had been very excited by Bernal's ideas and thought he would give up biochemistry and use X-ray diffraction to study biological structures. However, when he began careful discussions with X-ray workers about the details of the Bernal's research, they mentioned what they called 'the phase problem', which he had not heard of before. This problem meant that analysing the diffraction patterns was extremely difficult. So Synge decided to stay in biochemistry, and was eventually to win a Nobel Prize. I was rather shocked by what he told me because, although I was doing a course including X-ray diffraction, I was none too clear either about the phase problem. I do not think it was just lack of intelligence on my part. I believe that the teaching was not being done by scientists who were actively involved in the new X-ray diffraction work. Bernal himself did little to raise the quality of the teaching: he gave lectures in the crystallography library and often arrived late, and without apology or explanation he would silently take books off the shelves and read them. When he had finished consulting the books he would begin his talk. We were much in awe of the great man – he was widely known by the name 'Sage' – and, apart from wondering what he had been reading, it did not occur to me, or, I think, any of the other students, to imagine that an atmosphere of awe was not conducive to education. Some of Bernal's fame derived from his awesome charisma, but he certainly had breadth of vision, which excited me and many others.

I had a rather luxurious College room, and quite soon a student knocked on my door and asked if I would join the Student Socialist Society, which was known as Soc-Soc. I was glad to hear an enthusiastic account of what Soc-Soc was doing, and I began knocking on doors too. That was how I met Morris Cunningham, a first-year philosophy student who was interested in modern art. Soon we had walked all the way along the Cam until we got to Ely Cathedral in the Cambridgeshire Fens; and at the end of the year we walked around Western Ireland and then took the train to Dublin where we stayed in one of my ancestor's homes.

The Irish tour, however, had too much slog along motor roads and little of the special uplift I had on the grassy slopes and rocky peaks on holiday in Wales with my father. There were so many things to do in Cambridge, and Morris and I drew apart. I moved into lodgings to save money. But Soc-Soc had made me aware of the political element in science, especially in relation to the prospect of war. I was led into the Cambridge Scientists'

Anti-War Group by John Fremlin, a PhD student. That contact I owed to Eithne, who was studying German at Somerville College, Oxford. Out of Eithne's many friends, John's sister Celia was one of the best. (She later told me that Eithne, in spite of her disablement, attracted so many interesting men students in Oxford that the women students were quite jealous.) John was researching at the Cavendish Laboratory, and when Eithne told me about him I quickly went to the Cavendish. It was very exciting to find John there surrounded by strange apparatus, and he was very warm and encouraging. I found that the Anti-War Group, CSAWG, was led by Bernal. We held informal weekly meetings to discuss policy in a basement room under a King's Parade café, and I was the only undergraduate member. (I was later to find that I had relatives who had been involved in anti-war activity: one of the Swanwicks had married the sister of the famous artist Walter Sickert, and she was a prominent campaigner, in the early days of the League of Nations, against the use of aeroplanes in warfare.)

The Spanish Civil War had begun and the threat of Germany attacking Britain was increasing. CSAWG felt it had to work to protect British civilians. The Government was very concerned that war might lead to poison gas attacks on Britain, and when conflict was imminent, gas-masks were issued to every citizen. CSAWG studied the masks and helped to get them improved. The Government also made plans for gas-proof rooms, and CSAWG made tests of such rooms. John Fremlin had a big room in Trinity College which he carefully sealed everywhere except around the door. He then filled the room with his CSAWG friends (including me) and sealed the door, and for several hours we measured the rate at which a harmless gas leaked out of the room. The basic idea was that the rate of leakage out should equal the rate of leakage in, and would help provide a realistic picture of how safe gas-proofed rooms might be. This experiment was not examined very carefully by members of CSAWG, in spite of the high scientific quality of the Group. It was the very wise geneticist J.B.S. Haldane, then working at University College London, who pointed out that the rate of leakage out of a room might be much higher than the rate of leakage in, since gases were likely to enter largely through only one wall on the outside of a building. That was the beginning of my admiration for Haldane, without whose help CSAWG might have published an unduly alarmist report. But there is no doubt that it was very fortunate indeed that the War did not escalate to the point of gas attacks, and I did feel that in many ways the CSAWG work was useful in helping to increase public awareness and encouraging improvements in air-raid precautions.

At the end of three years at Cambridge, when I had finished my degree exams, CSAWG asked me to check on an alarming story from Republican Spain about the damage that incendiary bombs could do to a multi-storey building. The report claimed that a single incendiary bomb would set fire to the top of the building, burn through the floor and then set light to the next room below. Thus one incendiary bomb might destroy a whole building. If this terrifying story could be verified experimentally, it could be a powerful propaganda tool exposing the terrible effects that the German air attack could have on the people of Republican Spain. The dreadful German bombing and burning of the little town of Guernica had been deeply shocking – the horror had been made clear by Picasso's painting *Guernica*, which had been exhibited to the world at the Great Exhibition in Paris just a few months after the dreadful event. W.A. Wooster, a leading member of CSAWG and a lecturer in crystallography, told me I could use his spacious back garden for experiments. I built an area of conventional floorboards and placed an incendiary bomb of magnesium metal and oxidizing chemical on the floor. It was easily ignited but in spite of much violent flashing and burning of the bomb, the floorboards burned very little. One difficulty was that masses of white powdery magnesium oxide tended to form an insulating layer under the burning magnesium. I tried changing the design of the bomb, but applying heat to the top surface of a floorboard was always a very ineffective way to burn a hole through it. Suddenly it seemed obvious that fire burns up and not down. Incendiary bombs alone would be slow to destroy buildings. Wooster was very disappointed when I told him my results. He said that whatever I did after my degree I 'should not try experimental science' (I took no notice – I had close contact with first-rate experimentalists like Cyril Burch who knew about my telescope-making). But evidently I had let the side down. Had the very scary stories about the power of incendiary bombs been true, and had my results confirmed that, my experiment might have had an effect even greater than Picasso's painting.

A few years later, during heavy bombing in Birmingham, I saw clear confirmation of my Cambridge results. In the street where I lived the roof of the doctor's house was burning, and the hoses drenching the outside of the roof did not seem effective. I went inside and saw that the ceiling under the burning roof was intact, and I broke a hole in it to put a jet of water directly into the roof space. But when I had finished making the hole I could see through it that the fire had already been put out. I felt embarrassed that I had damaged the doctor's ceiling. Then, further up the road, I saw another house with its roof burning. I went inside the house and again saw that the ceiling under the burning roof was intact. Given time, the burning roof timbers might well have crashed down and set fire to the whole house, and incendiary bombs combined with high explosive could be devastating. But clearly my Cambridge result that incendiary bombs alone had little direct effect on the ceilings and floors below the roof was amply confirmed. A more general conclusion can also be drawn from my incendiary bomb experiments and the CSAWG study of gas-proof rooms: in very emotive situations, scientists may not find it easy to stand back and view the facts objectively. I was to experience this again in tense times later in my career.

The CSAWG had a broad political membership, ranging from one Christian Pacifist to Bernal, who often visited the Soviet Union and seemed to be an open member of the British Communist Party. That Party gained wide support in Cambridge because it had a very vigorous anti-Nazi policy; in comparison, the Labour Party was very weak. Most of the intelligent left-wingers

I knew were Party members, and it seemed very natural that I join too. As well as the Nazi horror, the very serious economic slump of the 1930s encouraged interest in the Soviet planned economy. I did not know anyone who tried to keep their membership secret, and I was the same. Soon, however, Party members had to cope with the extraordinary Moscow Trials where many longstanding members of the Soviet Party were accused of trying to overthrow Stalin. At the trials a number of old Bolsheviks confessed and were condemned to death (years earlier, Trotsky had been eliminated). A leading British Party member who was a lawyer attended the trials and supported the Stalin line. I found the whole proceedings very disturbing, especially the confessions. It all seemed unreal; but most of the Communist Party members I knew eventually dismissed the whole affair and continued to support the British Party. If scientists like me had known how the Soviet government at that time was supporting Lysenko's unscientific plant breeding ideas and was condemning Mendelian genetics, we would probably have been much more cautious. However, looking back at those times when the Nazi threat was growing, it was very important to support the Soviet Government as a future ally in the war that Hitler was preparing. I respected Haldane for becoming editor of the *Daily Worker* and supporting anti-Fascist forces in Spain. When he found out about Lysenko after the War, he strongly condemned such anti-scientific policies.

Years after the War it was discovered that two Cambridge graduates had secretly been members of the Communist Party and had given classified British information to the Soviet Government. In my time, when the Nazi threat had become very pressing, I think the atmosphere was very stressful; but the many very enthusiastic Communists I knew were open about their enthusiasm. Some of this enthusiasm for dialectical materialism did not seem to me to be based on proper understanding. On the other hand when I studied Marx's work years later I formed a very high opinion of his materialist theories of history. I think that approach to history has been taken up quite extensively, but often without acknowledgement to Marx. His failure was not to find a way towards a humane non-dictatorial Communist society. However, I believe that Marxism certainly helped, in those tense years of the 1930s, to build up a united front against Nazism.

The Spanish War grew and gave more urgent signals of the need for democracies to build a defence against the Nazi threat. Volunteers from Britain joined the International Brigade to fight Franco's army. Few British students went to Spain in that way: lack of military experience was one deterrent, and another was the realization that staying in Britain and working to increase public understanding of the Nazi threat might be more effective in resisting Nazism. Among the few Cambridge students who went to Spain was tall, handsome John Cornford, the son of Francis M. Cornford, the Professor of Philosophy, and a well-known leader in the Cambridge Communist Party. John's death in the International Brigade was a great shock. Suddenly there was a sense of the enormous destructive forces in the world, which contrasted with the comfort and security of life in Cambridge.

My best friend in Cambridge shared my feelings about war. Arthur Hone and I had some very good times together – perhaps the best times I remember from my youth. What we did together at Cambridge was what many students did, under the cloud of war and Nazi horror: we went to meetings, demonstrations and sometimes big marches in London. And to keep our sanity, we went to films such as those with the Marx Brothers, and *Battleship Potemkin*. Arthur was a language student from the working–class East End of London. He told me about the indignities of poor families there. Men working in the street and eating lunchtime sandwiches in public was, Arthur said, especially painful. Working men still smoked clay pipes then, and Arthur was very fond of his. He had great hopes of a communist future free from bitterness, anger and injustice. We would sit on the grass by the River Cam as the punts went quietly by, and Arthur would talk about his hopes for the future. And when our time at Cambridge was ending, we gathered with other students and lay on the green of Parker's Piece, and watched desperate classmates tearing up their academic gowns and trampling them on the ground, so distraught they were to have to leave. Arthur was not, like some communist students, fascinated by dialectical materialism, but his mind was filled with intense dreams of a new, united worldwide society.

My sister Eithne, now a graduate in German, had visited Germany. I had never been on the Continent, and it may have been the prospect of Europe being enveloped in an enormous war that stimulated me to plan a Grand Tour including France, Italy and Austria. A student friend borrowed his aunt's car and with two young scientists we had a very enjoyable trip for three weeks in the summer of 1937. Two years later Britain was in the War, but on our trip I do not remember any unpleasant sight of Nazism or Fascism. My most intense memory is of sitting in the huge main piazza at Parma where small chamber orchestras played in each corner of the square. What is it about the world that it can be transformed so suddenly from a state of peace and beauty to one of war and destruction?

In my last Cambridge year, 1937-1938, academic studies continued as the threat of war increased. The flow of refugees from Nazism increased. Nazi policy was to sack Jewish academics even though they were often very distinguished and had international reputations. To its credit, the international academic community worked hard to find jobs for refugees, and many travelled far to fill a post offered to them. I was reading up on the theory of X-ray diffraction when I heard that Paul Ewald, the leading X-ray diffraction theorist, had arrived in Cambridge as a refugee and had been given temporary accommodation in the very overcrowded Cavendish. I was keen to consult Ewald on a point of theory. Without an appointment I indulged in my habit and knocked on his door. He was very kind and helpful; but I was embarrassed that such a tall, dignified man had been squeezed into such a tiny room after being driven out of a presumably imposing office commensurate with his status. I had a graphic sense of the Nazi ruthlessness. I have always remembered Ewald's friendliness and retain an image of his distinguished figure on a high stool in front of a narrow bench strewn with papers.

The dreadful threat of world war was increasing, and I was swept along by all the excitement around the very disturbing news from Europe. During these tense times, I met, through the CSAWG, a young woman called Margaret Ramsay. She was the only woman I fell in love with in Cambridge, but I was incapable of making a suitable advance to her. I felt like I had as a teenager, when I had been quite unable to act on my feelings for the girl-next-door. Sitting at the opposite end of my room from Margaret, I told her, as a bald statement of fact, that I'd fallen in love with her. After a short silence she got up and said goodbye. I felt helpless but not very upset. The ratio of men to women students was then 10:1 in Cambridge, and there were very few women physics students. The only one I knew was Eilleen White, who helped me with my incendiary bomb experiments and invited me to a tea party at Newnham College (she married my good Australian friend Dick Makinson). The only physical contact I had with a woman was when I bumped into a shop girl as she and I rushed around a corner in opposite directions. She was presumably in a hurry to get to her shop, and I was late for my 9 o'clock lecture. The remarkable softness, warmth and perfume was on a different plane from missing a science lecture. Years later I found out that my lack of experience with women had not been so unusual then, but I felt confused and helpless at the time.

About halfway through my final year at Cambridge, I ran into another problem. Although I felt fairly normal, when I sat down to revise for my degree exams I found I could not concentrate. I soon realized that I had to do something about this problem, and I was fortunate to have Wordie who, as my Tutor, was responsible for advising me. He sent me to see Bannister who taught psychology. After some discussion, Bannister concluded that I was suffering from depression. He told me that I was worried about my father having to earn extra to cover the shortfall in my scholarship funds. In the evenings my father drove to Coventry, 20 miles from home – a long trip in those days – where he had very suitable work, but in the dark winter my mother went with him after wrapping herself up in furs to keep warm. Bannister told me that my father was glad to do extra work to help me. Bannister was a wise man, and whether or not his diagnosis was right, I soon got down to my revision.

When I had finished my degree exams, I found myself facing a new kind of problem. As Mr Manton had said when I was a young boy, my intention was to do physics research at Cambridge. But what particular kind of research? There were so many different branches of physics and none them really satisfied me. Rutherford had died, and studying the structure of nuclei in atoms did not attract me because it seemed to make little direct contact with human life – like astronomy, it was too much up in the clouds of strange mathematics and weird ideas. In any case, with Lawrence Bragg, the pioneering X-ray diffraction specialist, replacing Rutherford at the Cavendish, it seemed likely that Cambridge physics would change direction, but no new direction attracted me.

It might seem that an obvious choice would be the study of the atomic arrangements in very large biological molecules. That meant 'seeing structures' with X-ray diffraction as I had discussed in my Natural Sciences Club talk. But Bragg was not using his X-ray diffraction techniques to study the complex macromolecules that Bernal was studying as a world leader. I had decided that the difficulties of such research were great, and the static structures that resulted might not be very interesting. Bernal had given me no encouragement to join his group: instead, he recommended the new Coal Utilization Research Laboratory. Edward Bullard, Cambridge's leading geophysicist, was very friendly and encouraging, and links between physics and geology interested me; but again, I felt study of the Earth's crust was not lively enough for me. But I was fortunate to have distinguished and broadminded scientists to advise me. Cockcroft suggested I go to the research library and thumb through the recent research published in the international journals. Like most students, I had read little about very recent research. After an hour or two I was struck by a study of thermoluminescence, which was something quite new to me. An electron could travel freely, as described by quantum mechanics, through a regular crystal, but could become trapped at an irregularity. Then, if the crystal were warmed, the electron would jump to freedom and emit light. The paper was written by a Dutch physicist called De Groot who was working at the famous Phillips lab in Eindhoven. Cockcroft's suggestion had opened up the whole world of science to me – I had never heard in Cambridge of electrons jumping about in crystals, and it all seemed very lively and exciting. For more than a century physicists had studied the movement of electrons in metal wires, inside atoms, and across the empty space behind television screens. Now physicists had begun studying the movement of electrons in the regular structure of crystals and in irregularities. The new quantum mechanics was needed to understand these electron movements. After the War, an important new industry was to develop to produce light from crystals bombarded by electric discharges. At around this time, William Shockley was using the movements of electrons in crystals in the development of the transistor – work that would lead to the revolution in information technology. Of course I did not know at the time in which directions my new interest in thermoluminescence might lead me, but I did have a feeling that there was something specially interesting in this research, and I resolved to pursue it. This was a key moment in my career.

Having made my choice of research I was, however, rather surprised that I achieved only a lower-second-class degree. Perhaps I would have done better if I had put less effort into the Anti-War group; Carmichael, who studied cosmic rays, had warned me against spending too much time writing about science for a Communist Youth magazine when my degree exams were getting close. I had also lost time to depression. I do not think I was very upset by getting a poor degree; I did not respect exams as a test of research potential, and I had enough inner confidence to feel that I would somehow overcome the disadvantages of my unimpressive grade. However, when I went to see Cambridge scientists, I found that none of them could or would find money for me to work as a postgraduate research student. My degree grade meant that I could not stay in Cambridge. That was a very big shock indeed, and for a while I felt as though my world had ended. But I soon came to realize that there were other universities in Britain, and I began to look around. It would turn out to be a stroke of luck that I was obliged by my poor degree to think beyond the small world of Cambridge.

With all doors closed to me in Cambridge, I began exploring possibilities in other universities. Carmichael had written a testimonial for me, and sitting in a train on one job-hunting trip I looked at the envelope he had given me and saw it was unsealed. I read what he had written. I knew nothing about testimonials, but I could hardly believe what I read. It certainly did cheer me up. However, after visiting several universities that might have had a suitable job for me, I arrived back at my home in Birmingham depressed after my dismal lack of progress – including my failure to chat with the young woman receptionist in an overnight hotel. The research I had seen did not impress me, and here I was back again in Birmingham after three years of Cambridge. It was good to be home, but I was beginning to panic: my life looked an all-round failure. I felt dreadful, and I was concerned about disappointing my quietly unobtrusive parents.

Then suddenly I had a thought – Birmingham had a University! And two years earlier, my first-year supervisor Oliphant had left Cambridge and taken over the Birmingham Physics Department in order to build the biggest atom-smasher in Britain. Why had I not thought of Oliphant before? More than a week must have passed since I had begun searching outside Cambridge. I rang the University Physics Department and asked for Professor Oliphant, and found it was he who had picked up the telephone. He seemed to remember me immediately, and when I explained that I wanted a research job on luminescence in solids he told me that an expert in that area had recently joined his Department and was looking for a research assistant. Randall was his name, and he was 'doing interesting things'. I went to see Oliphant like a shot. It was a remarkable piece of good luck: I had found exactly the research I'd chosen.

John Randall had had a successful and wide-ranging research career at the General Electric Company's leading industrial research laboratory. His biggest success at GEC had been on luminescent lamps and the electron processes that produced light by luminescence. He recognized the importance of the basic quantum mechanical processes in luminescence, and in order to concentrate on that he had obtained a Royal Society Fellowship that enabled him to work full-time in a University. Oliphant recognized Randall's distinction and provided him with space and facilities for a research laboratory. I met Randall there, at the start of his new career in the University world.

From the first moment I saw Randall he made a very good impression on me. He was a small man, upright, with clear bright eyes and a lively energetic presence. I sensed the 'go' in him. He was full of interesting ideas about luminescence research. When talking with him, I felt I was at the leading edge. He was actively in touch with the great Cambridge theoretician Neville Mott. Also, I liked the way he treated me as a fellow scientist and did not talk down to me. He chatted freely and seemed frank and open, even to the extent, later, of gossiping about personal problems. His neat bow tie gave the impression that he was well organized. I felt very lucky to find him, but my luck had come very much from my privileged position at Cambridge where I had known world leaders like Oliphant.

Randall's Luminescence Lab was a bizarre set of rooms in the teaching area and overlooked the new Nuffield research building where the big atom-smashing cyclotron was going to be assembled. One of the luminescence rooms was under the seats of the biggest physics lecture room, and when students were excited and stamped their feet we sometimes needed to readjust our equipment. But apart from that, the space was well suited to the needs of research. I was told by an awestruck colleague that when Randall had arrived from GEC he had many large vans filled with much equipment and a big collection of luminescent material. Lab space was found for spectroscopes and X-ray diffraction equipment, and a furnace for treating materials fitted well into a small room with a fume cupboard linked to a Gothic-type tower. Altogether, it was a very good place for creative scientific work.

I had two good friends who had been art students in Birmingham: Sven Blomberg and Raymond Mason. They came to the Luminescence Lab one evening and did some painting with Randall's luminescent powders. Using the powders like a pigment they painted a sunset so that one could watch the colour of the sky changing as the sun went down. I often worked late in the lab by myself, and the bizarre rooms and equipment stimulated me to make a drawing of myself in deep thought as strange ideas floated about me.

Having spent many years on my own in my workshop, it was marvellous to be able to interact with other staff. Oliphant had assembled a real community of research workers with a wide variety of skills. In the Departmental workshop there were many expert instrument makers, and a glassblower worked full-time making all kinds of equipment in glass – there were so many people with special knowledge and skills. I found it immensely satisfying to work in that environment. When I had worked by myself in my schoolboy workshop, I had felt that I was able to get a finger into a crevice in the great rock of science; in Oliphant's Department I felt I was part of an army of professional climbers swarming up the side of that rock and getting ready to change the world. There was a simple, positive attitude that science was going to benefit humanity.

In the Luminescence Lab, I was, at first, ready to have a go at anything, and I barely noticed the months slip by as I made equipment so that I could reproduce, in a form suitable for publication by Randall, a pile of not very interesting data he had collected before I arrived. At the GEC industrial lab where he had worked before, the jobs I was doing had been done for him by technical specialists, but I had to sort things out myself with advice from technicians. By the time I had finished that unrewarding task I was rather fed up, and when Randall then asked me to go to the workshop and make a standard type of apparatus to separate light of different wavelengths, I began to object. I pointed out that I had taken the job of research assistant to him (at a low salary) because I would be doing research for a PhD and I had seen nothing of that yet. Randall told me not to worry and that I would soon be doing research with the apparatus he had asked me to make. I felt he had exploited my ingenuous enthusiasm, but I went on with the work and much to my relief Randall soon began discussing a major programme for me which could lead to a PhD. Also he got extra funds and appointed a young technician, so I had more time to concentrate on the basic science. Things were looking up again; but I had learnt that I could not take it for granted that Randall would always act in my best interest.

The research programme seemed good, and I enjoyed very much the way it developed. It was a very satisfying experience. The research was about thermoluminescence – the process I had read about in the library at Cambridge, by which some crystals can store light for a long time and then give it out quickly when they are warmed. Crystals may also give out light spontaneously some time after they have absorbed energy; that delayed emission is called phosphorescence. What happened to electrons during that delay was very little understood. It was supposed that electrons in a crystal fell into traps, like a billiard ball falling into a pocket. If the crystal was heated, the electron would jump out of the trap and could emit light. A small amount of heat would be enough to free an electron from a shallow trap, and more was needed for a deep trap. Because electrons can stay in deep traps for thousands of years, archaeologists often use thermoluminescence to date the objects they study. Randall's idea was to measure how light was given out as crystals were gradually heated up. That would show the numbers of traps of different depths. Those numbers would tell us how fast phosphorescence would be, and allow us to form a picture of how electrons moved about during phosphorescence.

Although I felt very positive about doing 'real science' in the impressive professional community in Oliphant's Physics Department, I was distracted by wider interests as I had been in Cambridge. Each day, after lunch with Randall and my school-friend Harry Boot who also worked there, I would disappear for coffee in the Zoology Department where Lancelot Hogben was Head. He had wide interests and broad left-wing views, and was well known for his very popular book *Mathematics for the Million*. At coffee I met very interesting and lively young people connected with biology, and the large proportion of young women livened the talk in a way not possible in the Physics Department, where there were almost no women. There, Bill Bentley and his wife became my long-standing friends.

When I began working in Oliphant's lab I found I did not enjoy the tedious journey there from Wylde Green, through all the miles of Aston with its depressing factories and factory workers' 'slum' homes where my father worked with the poor school children. The University was on the other side of Birmingham, not very far out, and that was where the more educated people lived, such as the families of my widely cultured King Edward's School friends. There too lived the Newth family. My father had met H.G. Newth at a Poverty and Malnutrition committee. H.G. (as he was called) was a micro-dissection expert at the University, and he had been very helpful when I was making tiny pinholes for Cyril Burch's new testing of telescopes. Even more important was that I was able to lodge with the Newths, close to the University. I was especially welcome when they heard about my work with the Cambridge Scientists Anti-War Group and that I was a member of the Communist Party.

My year at the Newths' was very positive: to me the household was a microcosm of civilization where everyone worked to unite all humane, liberal and democratic forces against the horror of Fascism. Nan Newth was a school teacher who spent much time and energy working against war, Nazism and Fascism. She had found the Labour Party very lacking in energy and was glad to join the Communists with their far-sighted leadership in the Popular Front against war and Fascism. Many keen people interested in politics did the same, the exceptions being Jews who knew about

Russian anti-Semitism and did not like the Communist Party's connection with the Soviet Union. Nan was concentrating mainly on the Spanish Civil War, and had a wide range of friends working on refugee problems. I realize now that the progressive spirit in Birmingham then may have been passed down the years from the times of Priestley and my Nonconformist ancestors.

Eithne spent a night in the Newths' living room, and she liked to tell how, in the morning, Nan pulled back the curtains and called out happily that it was a beautiful day and the Republicans in the Spanish Civil War had advanced on the Ebro. That was typical Nan: the news was very cheering because the War had not been going well, and Nan was warm, hospitable and optimistic. Public meetings and demonstrations about Spain were always taking place, and remarkable people visited us. A special friend of Nan's was Professor Hyman Levy, a leading academic who had worked his way from poverty. The great Bernal stayed with us after giving an inspiring talk on science and society to a large audience in Birmingham. (Next morning I drove him to the University in the little Austin 7 I kept on Nan's front drive.) And there were University friends like the Peierlses, the physicist Rudolph and his wife Eugenia, and the Shapiros who, even though they were anti-Soviet, encouraged Nan's political work. I felt privileged to be there; and it only now strikes me that nearly all our best friends were Jews, in spite of their anti-Soviet views.

As well as all the serious activity, we had a lot of fun. Nan had two sons: David was a zoology student at University College London, and Anthony was studying Physics at Imperial College;

and there was also Thomas, of about the same age, who was the son of friends in Germany. We played table tennis in the basement and did small-bore target practice in the garden supervised by our housekeeper's husband. Nan and the housekeeper produced excellent food, and a friendly cat sat on our shoulders and reached for food as we raised it to our mouths. Both Anthony and David had been to King Edward's School and were very thrilled when they found that the legendary Philip Marples, famous for setting fire to the Headmaster's study, was an old friend of mine. Soon Philip was visiting us and joining in everything. He charmed us all. Though he was quite capable of indulging in Robin Hood-style thieving and all kinds of larks, he was very highly principled, and he vigorously attacked the Soviet aggression in Finland. Like so many others we knew, he had joined the Communist Party but, as at school, he was expelled for gross lack of discipline.

None of us liked the Soviet invasion of Finland, but it was understandable that the Soviet Union did not want to leave its frontiers so very close to Leningrad. That the Finns fought so valiantly made it all the more horrible. It was only years after the War that the extraordinary desperation of the Soviet defence of Leningrad became known. For example, the extreme shortage of food in the city led to frozen human bodies in the snow becoming a useful source of food. The British, not having been often invaded by land forces, often did not realize how frightful the War on the continent had become.

While my work on the programme of luminescence research continued steadily, I had not forgotten the important issues raised in the Cambridge Scientists Anti-War Group about the danger to civilians in air raids. The Blackout had begun so that people could get used to it: we had to learn to take care that light did not escape from buildings, so that night-flying bombers would not be able to see if they had reached their target. To protect civilians in air raids, trenches were being dug in parks and metal Anderson shelters were being issued to fit as roofs over holes people dug in their gardens. Such shelters would be safe if a bomb did not make a direct hit. However, Camden Borough Council in London had plans for a deep shelter with strong rooms like those that gave complete protection to the government ministers who formed the War Cabinet and other people of key importance. There had been no public discussion about deep shelters in Birmingham because political energy had been occupied with other issues such as the Spanish Civil War. But I saw trenches being dug in parks and thought that a public discussion about deep shelters was needed. I decided to organize a public meeting in Birmingham Town Hall, and with support from a group of young people it was all arranged. Air-raid wardens were invited because they were trained to deal with air-raid precautions. We met in a big conference room at the Town Hall, and, sitting at the platform, I was interested to see the room steadily filling. I was glad to see that many air-raid wardens were arriving. But as the number of wardens grew, I began to feel uneasy. I opened the meeting by outlining the need for deep shelters in addition to the trenches and Anderson shelters. I then threw the meeting open for discussion. I was surprised that one warden after another stoutly defended the Government's shelter policy and dismissed the Camden-type shelters as unnecessary. I tried to encourage pro-Camden speakers, but I had never been in charge of a public meeting before and I began to realize that the wardens had been instructed to make sure Government policy was firmly defended.

After the meeting my young friends collected in a Milk Bar (which had begun to be fashionable), and we tried to cheer ourselves up. I began to realise that my life in Cambridge, where many unconventional ideas were discussed, had led me to misjudge the possibilities of effectively challenging Government policies as war came nearer. The very important role of London Underground Railway stations in the heavy bombing of London would eventually show the soundness of the Camden ideas. But in the War it was probably right to give priority to boosting military strength to prevent an invasion of Britain, rather than making civilians safer in air raids: Nazi occupation would surely be so much worse than the risks of air raids.

CHAPTER 3

———◆◆◆———

IN A WORLD AT WAR

Through 1939, the British people wondered when their war would begin. Then, on 1 September, Hitler launched a great mechanized offensive that rapidly advanced into Poland. Appeasement was over, and Britain declared war. Reaching the north of Poland, the German army neared the frontier with Russia. The Red Army was said to have moved across its border into Poland, where it met the Germans on 17 September. There was great consternation in Britain among those who had seen the Soviet Union as the key ally in the war against Hitler. Had the Soviet Union moved into Poland in collaboration with Hitler? There were stories of German officers giving Nazi salutes in Moscow's Red Square. The publisher Victor Gollancz, of the influential Left Book Club, urged members of the British Communist Party to resign. His argument that the basis of our war was to defeat Fascism impressed me, and I resigned from the Communist Party. A fair proportion of members followed Gollancz, but Nan was not so hasty and stayed in the Party which continued to lead the Popular Front against Fascism. My decision to follow Gollancz caused embarrassment between me and Nan. We remained good friends, but she felt it might be better if I moved to the house of her Quaker friend Francesca Wilson, a very active refugee worker.

Before I moved from Nan's, on a peaceful Sunday afternoon we were startled to hear, for the first time, a siren giving us the warning of an air raid. Everyone quickly filed down the stairs to the cellar, and we stood together in the bare dark room. What would happen to us? All sorts of thoughts went through my head. Stanley Baldwin, when Prime Minister, had said, 'the bombers will always get through'. I had studied the effects of bombing, but I had no idea whether this was a real raid or a false alarm. There was a peculiar sense of anxiety as we stood there in silence, holding our Government-issue gas-masks – we did not know what would happen, or what it would be like. I think we felt the tiniest hint of what a Jew might feel, getting off the train and looking at the Death Camp in front of him. But soon the 'all clear' siren sounded, and we relaxed. Had it been a false alarm? We went upstairs again to the comfort of our rooms.

No air raid afterwards had the special quality of that first experience. We got used to the bombs and the noise of anti-aircraft guns firing (and were very relieved when there was no poison gas). The only person I knew who was killed in a raid was one of my fellow students at Cambridge, a political leader who got a first-class degree and had the privilege of staying in Cambridge for postgraduate work.

∞

Working at the University in Randall's lab, I was making good progress with the luminescence research. Fortunately, amid the turmoil, the British scientific community had prepared a well-designed survey of all scientists in Britain to help decide how they should be used in the war effort. Most scientists were reserved for war research. That planning was indispensable for winning the war. In contrast, the Nazis were guided by their narrow anti-intellectual vision and foolishly neglected the military potential of Germany's scientists, and allowed many to be called up for ordinary armed service. That mistake may have been decisive in leading to the Nazi defeat. I was very satisfied when I went before a tribunal and heard the wonderful words 'Reserved in a Civilian Capacity Only'. The success of the survey of scientists is illustrated by the case of Rudi Komphner, a Viennese refugee. He had been forced by his father to study architecture, and was working as an architect. Rudi, however, was a brilliant devotee of physics and in his spare time he did theoretical research on microwaves. He had published several papers, and these meant that Rudi was included in the survey of scientists. His work was drawn to the attention of Oliphant, who invited Rudi to visit the Birmingham lab. Much impressed by Rudi, Oliphant offered him a job immediately, even though it was the first time Rudi had been in a physics lab. Rudi had a British wife and we became good friends. After the war he was very successful at the Bell Telephone Lab.

The policy of reserving scientists was very sensible, but it produced some peculiar anomalies: I, like many other students of the same year, never met anyone who was killed in action.

Sometimes the old saying 'Wartime is career time' was true. In contrast, Cambridge students two or three years younger than me, if they were non-scientists, were selected to be fighter pilots in the Battle of Britain and were killed in large numbers. Sometimes I have felt a little uncomfortable that I seem to have had a charmed existence – not bullied at school and never exposed to violence (except bombing) during the war.

Oliphant was a big man in every sense, and with typical foresight and enterprise had secured for our lab the most interesting problem in the war research – how to generate strong beams of microwaves for precision radar. Even before war began nearly everyone from our lab was taken to a secret lab on the Isle of Wight to find out what had been done on radar. I was the only active research worker in the lab who stayed behind in Birmingham. I think that Randall had pressed Oliphant to make me an exception so that I could push on with the luminescence work. Having left his industrial career, Randall needed to establish himself more firmly in basic research so that after the War he could gain a good university job. It was therefore very important for him that I continue his luminescence programme. I much enjoyed working on my own through the summer, and the work went very well. As war work it began as part of a rather ludicrous programme for helping people to walk about in the Blackout, and included luminescent dog collars which gave rise to the joke 'What, for the clergy?' But soon my work was linked to the important problem of improving screens for radar. For almost a year after the war began there was no heavy air attack on Britain, but we were all waiting for it to begin, and good radar could enormously improve our chances of surviving. I was proud to go to London to sit on a committee with the experts who designed and made the equipment (like a television set) where an attacking bomber would appear as a bright spot on a luminescent screen. I visited other radar labs and was taken up in a bomber to see how a new screen would work in the air.

When everyone came back from the Isle of Wight, they all began working on Oliphant's radar programme. As a result, Randall had no more time for luminescence, and he worked full-time with Harry Boot who had been one year behind me at school and had just graduated. Harry had made remarkable electrical research equipment (quite as good as my telescopes) in his father's garage at home and was brilliant at getting unusual electrical things to work. Randall was not very good at technical things, and was very lucky to have Harry with his electrical 'green fingers'. And Harry, of course, was very lucky to have Randall because Randall had special originality and determination. The two of them formed a very effective complementary pair. They used to come up for coffee mid-morning in the luminescence lab where I worked, and later we would go together to the Students' Union for lunch. Randall preferred the informal Students' Union to the rather stuffy academic Refectory. Other physics researchers often joined us over lunch, and we would have exciting brainstorming sessions about U-boats and night bombers and all kinds of scientific schemes that might help to win the War. With many lively refugee scientists (mainly from Vienna), our discussions were often quite hilarious; but we all worked hard and long. Sometimes I used to discuss with Randall what I was doing on luminescence, but once he had begun working on radar I had almost no guidance from him because he threw all his energy into his cavity magnetron invention, which was a device for generating microwaves.

Randall gave an interesting account of how he had the key thought that led to his very important success with the cavity magnetron. He could see no way of giving a magnetron the huge power that was needed if radar was to work effectively, but on holiday in Aberystwyth, he bought a book in a second-hand bookshop that described how Hertz had discovered radio waves by making an electric current oscillate in a simple loop of copper. This led Randall to think that if a circular hole was made in the copper body of a magnetron, high current could travel round the hole as it had in Hertz's copper ring. With a number of circular cavities in the body of the magnetron, very high energy could be emitted. Randall's idea, with Boot's very practical skill, eventually produced a magnetron much more powerful than previous microwave generators.

I realized I had been really lucky not to have got a good degree in Cambridge. If I had, I would have begun research there and, when the War began, I might well have been sent, 'for the duration', to some isolated and possibly boring government war research lab. Cambridge physicists were dispersed around the country because Lawrence Bragg, who replaced Rutherford, did not have Oliphant's ability to think big and sell his ideas to the

Government. In Birmingham I had the luxury of many contacts in the University, and all kinds of civilian life in the town with its theatres, libraries, Art College and other cultural amenities. So although I was very keen on my research, I was also able to pursue my interests in social and political life.

Through the wall of my bed-sit at Francesca Wilson's house, I could hear someone playing a violin in the house next door. Through contact with neighbours over air-raid precautions, I soon found that the violinist was Brita, a pretty young woman who played in the restaurant at Lewis's Stores, the largest shop in Birmingham. We went cycling in the countryside, and even dug part of an air-raid shelter together. Our relationship was very prim because my feelings were confused and I could not express them. After a while I decided I had fallen in love with her, but I had very little idea of what I should do. Eventually, I repeated the strategy that had already failed with Margaret in Cambridge: sitting at the far end of Brita's room, I simply announced to her, as though I were making a philosophical statement, that I was in love with her. I imagine she was discouraged by my unromantic approach, for she did nothing to help me out of my difficulty. I retreated frozen with horror and despair, and spent the evening in my room playing gramophone records of emotional operas. I was quite incapable of pursuing Brita any further, and decided to give up my Love and immerse myself in higher things – I had a muddled memory that Spinoza gave up his Love and began grinding telescope lenses. Thus I began intensively reading about quantum mechanics and luminescence. I soon had a reasonable grasp of the subject and found that some of Randall's ideas, though in the right direction, needed tightening up. I began to feel more confident and in control of my life. I was not just being enthusiastic about science, and not just learning about it – I was really doing it. I do not know what Brita made of our time together, but after a little while I realized that she had made a crucial contribution to my career.

At the lab, Randall became more and more absorbed with Harry in developing their immensely important cavity magnetron for radar. I thrived on being left alone with luminescence, using the rich collection of equipment and luminescent materials that Randall had brought with him from the GEC. I rapidly began a wide-ranging study showing how phosphorescence arose from electrons moving in and out of traps. It was a big step forward, and took two years. I wrote it all up in the form of two papers for publication. Clearly the first paper had to be published under Randall's name as well as mine. However, the second paper seemed to me to be all my work, Randall's suggestion being covered in the first paper. I therefore thought it should be under my name only. But when I raised this with Randall he insisted he should be joint author because he had defined the problem and had made suggestions about the whole research. He was unyielding. From his time at the GEC he must have learned that authorship problems can cause rows, mainly because careers depend so much on publications. On the other hand, knowing little of the world of professional research, and having lived my life of amateur science, I felt he was being unjust. I was rather unworldly, and wanted the recognition more to confirm my considerable sense of personal achievement rather than to advance my career. There had always been a strong sense of justice in my upbringing, and I was very disturbed by Randall's attitude. Finding no peace of mind, I went to Cambridge to see Dr Bannister, who had helped me overcome my depression when I had been a student.

It was an unusually beautiful summer's day as I made my long, slow, wartime railway journey to Cambridge. But it was 22 June 1941, and the radio news was echoing in my head: Hitler had launched his vast attack on the Soviet Union. It was a very awesome day, but I was cheered that the War might be entering its decisive and final phase. Looking out at the flat expanse of peaceful Cambridgeshire, I knew that the German tanks were, at that very instant, roaring across the plains of the Eastern Front. I imagined the explosions and flames in massive battles, but because I was conditioned by years of ghastly war news, I did not think of terror in the villages and the shrieking of children. Instead, as the whole world shook I was preoccupied with what names should head my research paper, and I wondered what Bannister was going to say to me. In the event, he advised me to let Randall have his way because my career could depend on keeping his goodwill. That seemed to me good pragmatic advice, and I accepted it. Looking back, I think Bannister was even more right than I felt at the time: I had not realized how much Randall's career could depend on his list of publications, especially when the work in question was of special quality. Randall would have known that more publications would strengthen the case for his being elected a Fellow of the Royal Society (which would greatly improve his career prospects). Having moved from a secure position in industry to a temporary position at Birmingham, Randall needed a long-term appointment to satisfy his research needs, and to support his wife and child.

I had written every word of the two papers, and, after consulting Oliphant, I linked them together with a few sentences, added an introduction and submitted the whole as a PhD thesis (seldom was a thesis written so readily). The distinguished Cambridge physicist Neville Mott was external examiner, and thought well of it. Thus, in less than the usual three years, I had a PhD and had formed a very good basis for a research career. I have always been very conscious that my rapid advancement was due to Randall giving me a good research problem; many research students fail to establish careers because their supervisors give them poor problems, and they lack the experience to make good choices on their own. Randall, together with Oliphant, helped me to eclipse my lower-second-class degree. Most young scientists at that time had to do war research, much of which was not suitable for a PhD thesis. I was lucky because the needs of the War, and the career interests of both Randall and me, required that I did fundamental research. Optimum afterglow in radar screens was important, and my PhD work helped to clarify the problem, though no big improvement was achieved.

In the radar lab, during the first few months of the War, Randall's creative intuition, combined with Harry's great technical skills, produced a highly efficient cavity magnetron. It was enormously successful, greatly increasing power output and making radar much more effective. It did more to win the War than any other scientific advance (the atom bomb would come too late to be decisive). Looking out of my lab window at the Nuffield building on 21 February 1940, I saw a peculiar metal horn projecting through the roof above Randall and Harry's room. I was told that such enormous electrical power poured out of the magnetron that filaments of unconnected lamps glowed brilliantly and burned out, and cigarettes burst into flame. The power was so extraordinary that many of our scientists could not believe that it really came from radar wavelengths; but Randall and Harry soon proved that it did. The idea of radar in any case was almost unbelievable – shine radio energy into the sky at some distant plane, and when a tiny fraction of that energy is scattered back, expect to pick it up and locate the plane? But it did work. The magnetron was a staggering breakthrough, everyone could see it would transform radar. 'Getting things done' was one of Randall's strengths.

But it took months of intensive struggle before a magnetron was ready for testing. Oliphant felt the military-scientific establishment was reacting too slowly, so he and his staff built the Dog's Breakfast, a rough but complete set of microwave radar equipment in a big van covered with microwave antennae. He took it and demonstrated it to the Armed Services. Also Oliphant wanted to make direct tests at Birmingham, so he got a big metal-lized balloon and filled it with gas outside the Nuffield building. As the radar staff stood around, a gust of wind blew the balloon up into the air. I saw Oliphant grab hold of it, but he was pulled up into the air. For a moment I thought he was in danger, but the staff seized hold of him just in time.

Two months after the magnetron first worked, the military lull suddenly ceased and the Germans seized Denmark and Norway. Then, in May, the Blitzkrieg swept through Belgium, the British Forces escaped at Dunkirk and the French capitulated. We all wondered when it was going to be our turn in England. It was also clear that U-boats in the Atlantic were sinking so many supply ships coming to Britain that we would not be able to continue the war for very long. But I have few memories of how we faced that awful threat of invasion. I had a childish image of standing outside the Nuffield building holding a Home Guard rifle as German infantry advanced towards us. Obviously the enemy would sweep all resistance away. I spent my evenings in libraries reading up on short-wave radio and vaguely hoping there might be some way to hide an illegal radio station. I con-cluded that to operate such a station would almost certainly lead to torture and death. Really we had no choice but to go on working as we always had, and just hope that some way, somehow, Britain might not be invaded. Then, in August, the invasion barges were building up in the Channel, and the Germans launched a big air attack on our invasion defences. At first I could not believe that the German losses were as great as our propaganda machine

claimed. But largely it was true. The British had carefully prepared pre-magnetron radar which was accurately locating the
enemy planes even as they took off on the Continent. As a result
our relatively small force of Hurricanes and Spitfires could
quickly find the enemy and shoot them down. When the magnetron got into service we knew that we should do even better. It
was enormously encouraging for us scientists, and all the more so
when, after a few days of heavy losses, the Germans gave up
attacking our invasion defences. Instead, the bombers turned
against London and other cities. It seemed clear that the invasion
of Britain was postponed.

There was still work to do on the magnetron. The difficulty was
that it was unstable, and kept switching from one frequency of
radiation to another. Jim Sayers, a very clear-thinking physicist
from Cambridge, and about the only member of staff with real
experience of radio, was largely responsible for getting rid of the
magnetron instability. That led to intense rivalry developing
between him and Randall. The excitement of those magnificent
months was spoiled for me by that rivalry, and by Randall's frequent complaint that Oliphant was not giving the magnetron
enough support (which I found difficult to believe then, but
which hindsight shows may have been partly true). I was shocked
to hear that the 'rivals' kept their rooms locked when they were
not in them. Why should they want to keep secrets from each

other? Should not they share their results when we were in a life-and-death struggle with the Nazis? With my limited experience, I naïvely thought that science always advanced in an atmosphere of openness and cooperation – apart, of course, from the fact that secrets had to be kept from The Enemy, and commercial secrecy and competition were unavoidable in industry. Even if I allowed for Randall's ten years in industry, I still felt that he was unduly competitive, and that linked with the ruthless way he had some-times treated me. He seemed too concerned for his success as an individual, rather than as a member of a laboratory. With hind-sight, I think I did not make enough allowance for the extra-ordinary excitement of the magnetron race: there was not only scientific excitement, but also the great tension due to the threat of a Blitzkrieg sweeping through Britain. We all worked hard not only because the science was an interesting challenge, but also because we wanted to help to win the War.

There were quite a few refugee scientists with us, as well as Rudi Komphner, and their presence gave us a special encourage-ment. In my family we learned much from refugees. For many years, Aunt Lizzie's careful reading had kept us informed about the dangerous increase of Hitler's power, and before the War began my mother, at our home in Wylde Green, was being helped to keep house by Helen Mendel, a very good person who was a refugee from Austria. Fairly soon Helen's husband was able to join her. Helen remembered him as a big strong man with lots of dark hair, but when he arrived at our home Helen was horrified to find him thin and frail, and with white hair. He had been in a concentration camp, digging graves for Jews, and that worried my father who was in the middle of digging a hole in our garden for an Anderson air-raid shelter. My mother heard from Helen how her husband had suffered – which was not the kind of thing Mendel wanted to speak about, except to Helen.

We also met Ernst Kaiser, a novelist who was a refugee from Vienna. Jews had been allowed to leave Austria during the early stages of Nazification if they could leave large funds behind. Ernst had been busy helping Jews to work through the official channels. When the risk of being sent to a concentration camp became too great, he left Austria and managed to travel from one country to another until he arrived in England. He was not able to find out what happened to his family, but he carried a locket with a photograph of his beautiful young sister. Ernst shared literary interests with Eithne, whom he courted with much success; and his steadiness was a great asset in their very happy marriage.

My landlady Francesca, who worked with refugees, gave me an opportunity to spend a holiday with some Czech refugee trade unionists, who were living in her country cottage in a very charming and remote part of the Cotswold hills in South-West England. I invited my good friend from my student days, Arthur Hone, and with his working-class background and political enthusiasm he helped to create a very positive feeling in our isolated community. The Czechs were a remarkable group, working hard in the fields. They lived together in one large room, cooking, talking, and playing darts – all in a warm, friendly way. When the Czechs were getting ready for bed the jollity reached its peak.

Arthur and I, having returned to our separate little bedroom, could hear the Czechs in bed creating music from a combination of laughter and farts. I remembered that when I was a boy I had slept in one room with my cousins Roddy and Paul, and lots of farts and laughter had helped us to go to sleep. But that was on family holidays, whereas the Czechs had been driven out of their country by Nazi invasion. Once again, I found much to admire in the refugees.

I continued to enjoy the company of my artist friends Sven Blomberg and Raymond Mason, who had come to the luminescence lab. Their lives were uplifted by a very remarkable and attractive young French lady who was employed to delight the dull wartime lives in British cities with a travelling exhibition of modern French painting. In succession she lived with Sven and Raymond, and then moved across the Atlantic. Certainly the charming French lady was completely out of my reach; but I had made a small but, for me, significant move in that direction. After the fiasco with Brita next door, I was helped by my good friend Philip Marples. Philip had a young sister Biddy who was glad to meet me. Like Philip, Biddy was friendly and warm. She helped me to make, for the first time, bodily contact with a young woman. Biddy's gentle exploration was a success except that Francesca's housekeeper was annoyed because I had not been available to eat her excellent supper. My relationship with Biddy was so successful that I took her home to Wylde Green. But I think my mother expected Biddy to be as tall and handsome as Philip, and the visit was not encouraging.

Fear of invasion often led Jews to move across the Atlantic in search of safety. Thus 'Ship' Shapiro, a lecturer in English at our University and a good friend of Nan's, had sent his wife and children to Canada while he continued at the University so that his salary could support his family. Ship was left with several empty rooms in his elegant house near the centre of Birmingham. He was looking for congenial lodgers, and I decided to move there. Ship and I had a lot of interests in common, mainly in literature and art. His attitude to science interested me – during our discussions, he often commented: 'But Maurice, that is not very scientific.' We both very much liked Bill Blotz, who also lodged at Ship's. Blotz was a Canadian psychologist supervising a group of Canadian young women who were helping to solve wartime problems of children in Birmingham. With an excellent housekeeper and cook (Austrian again), we had a very good time at Ship's.

While I was at Ship's, air raids began on Birmingham. Most of the bombs were incendiary. Ship was busy at nights on the roof of the Arts building of the University in central Birmingham, extinguishing the fires that were started by the raids. In houses near Ship's, I had useful experiences with fires that confirmed my Cambridge experiments of a few years earlier. But the bombing raids made it difficult for me to sleep at night, and I felt tired at the lab. For a while I moved out to Wylde Green where risks from bombs were much less than in central Birmingham. Even so, the anti-aircraft guns made a great noise and the journey across Birmingham took much time. Sometimes I joined my father in his car and I remember the roads covered with fire hoses and debris. I then moved to the home of the Nunn May family, fairly near the University but with much less bombing than at Ship's. The Nunn Mays had advertised for lodgers who wanted to be clear of bombing. Their son, away on war work, was a brilliant mathematician and a former pupil at King Edward's. The Nunn Mays were high-minded and intelligent people, but I did not find them as congenial as Ship. So I moved to a quiet Quaker student residence full of young people and close to the University.

There was a real risk that the Nazis (who had many distinguished physicists) might find a way to make an atom bomb. If they did that before we did, the Nazis would almost certainly win the War. I thought about this, and decided that if I worked on war research it must be on something 'big'. I remember using that word – I meant something which, by itself, could defeat the Nazis and bring the War to an end. Birmingham University was a leading centre for atomic physics research, and Oliphant had a team working on the atomic bomb. We had a very important lead in the research: two brilliant Jewish refugees from Nazism, Rudolph Peierls and Otto Frisch, had come to Birmingham, and they had calculated that making a Bomb would take less uranium than was supposed at the time. That was very important indeed, as it meant that such a bomb was a practical possibility. I decided I would ask Oliphant if I could join the team.

I was very pleased when Oliphant found me a job working on how to evaporate uranium metal. It had never been done before, but it was thought that evaporation and diffusion could be a way to separate out the particular uranium isotope needed to make a bomb. The lecture theatre above the luminescence lab had the highest ceiling of any part of the Physics Department, and was therefore the best place to set up very long vertical tubes to study the gaseous diffusion of uranium. The tubes were in full view of the students at lectures, but I do not know if any student knew that the tubes were part of the Bomb project.

The Birmingham Bomb Lab became very important, and that was how I met the great nuclear physicist Niels Bohr, who had escaped from his native Denmark in a rowing boat and was flown by the Swedes to England. Bohr was as big a physicist as Einstein. I met Oliphant and Bohr walking in the lab passage, and Oliphant, in typical democratic style, stopped and introduced me to Bohr. Oliphant, I think, told Bohr that I was trying to evaporate uranium metal. (Later I was to find that before the War, Bohr had been at the roots of the study of DNA, mainly by holding small meetings for geneticists to meet specialists in X-ray diffraction.)

Oliphant had visited the University of California at Berkeley, where the physicist Ernest Lawrence (another big man) had made a cyclotron atom-smasher twice as big as Oliphant's. When Oliphant came back from California he said it was a 'New Civilization'. Oliphant sent Peierls and Frisch's calculation about the amount of uranium needed to make a Bomb to Berkeley, but when he was next there he found the calculation had been put in a safe and not shown to the relevant scientists. Once the implications of the calculation were realized, the US Bomb project speeded up; and it was decided that Oliphant and all his associates should be moved to Berkeley. That included me.

What a wonderful surprise – after years of war-time Birmingham, living like troglodytes in the inescapable oppressiveness of the Blackout! The only bright lights in our streets were from roofs set alight by incendiary bombs. I knew something of Californian life from reading the novels of John Steinbeck, and there was so much to look forward to in Berkeley. Apart from our families, we were not to tell anyone about our leaving for the USA. My parents knew where I was going, and understood that they might not see me again until the War was over. We were to disappear in the night. At the Quaker residence, I had met a charming Polish refugee student called Zosia, and I was very glad that Biddy had taught me how to kiss a girl goodbye. I told Zosia that I would not see her again for some time as I gave her a cuddle in the Quaker's bushes.

My colleagues and I crossed the Atlantic in February 1944 on the *Queen Elizabeth* – the biggest passenger liner in the world, and so fast that by zigzagging unpredictably, it was never attacked. I watched for whales; and I caught flu and was glad to find the ship's hospital more comfortable than the cabin in which I was crowded with colleagues. Arriving at New York I had to get dressed and walk off the ship in order to escape being kept on Ellis Island in quarantine. After resting for a few days in the hotel I was able to explore New York. The lights everywhere at night seemed quite extraordinary, but I was even more moved by seeing oranges and bananas once more, even in trash cans. What a feeling of freedom and delight! The height of skyscrapers also pleased me – I could not think why Le Corbusier had grumbled that they were not high enough. A visit to the Museum of Modern Art was my best experience: it held a marvellous collection on an enormous scale, and there were no crowds preventing me seeing so many of the great works that I had read about. At the Museum I was mainly by myself because none of the other British scientists was interested in art. I visited my Birmingham colleague, Rudi Peierls, who was now in New York with his very lively Russian wife Genia (she tried teaching me to dance on an icy road), and Claus Fuchs who had lived with them in Birmingham. Fuchs had helped me with my PhD studies and was, as ever, smiling pleasantly but saying very little. Genia called him the Penny-in-the-Slot Man because he would seldom say anything except in response to something said to him. The Peierlses and Fuchs went to Los Alamos where the Bombs were prepared for testing. I do not think I ever saw Fuchs again, and it was many years after the War, when he was working on Bomb design in England, that he was convicted of giving secret information to the Russians. All who knew him in Birmingham were very surprised to learn that he had been a spy.

After two or three weeks in New York we were put on a train across the USA to Berkeley. I contracted a severe ear infection, and when Harrie Massey, an excellent Australian physicist, met us at Berkeley, he found me a bed in a good hospital. I spent seven weeks there having holes drilled in my head (no penicillin for me, only for fighting men). I always felt confident in the hospital, which was not far from the great cyclotron lab, and I was surprised by the smart hairstyles of the ladies sweeping the floors – very different from our Mrs Mops back in England. I could see why Oliphant had seen Berkeley as a New Civilization.

When I had recovered from the infection, Oliphant very kindly took me out of the hospital and drove me around so that I could see what Berkeley and the great Bay Area were like. Visitors to the hospital who came to see me had not been able to give me an adequate idea of the extraordinary world outside. Seeing the Pacific coast had a very special significance for me, because when I was a child I had been very happy on the Pacific coast in New Zealand, where Wellington had a great Bay Area too. It was like a dream, full of memories of happiness with Eithne. I had not seen a eucalyptus tree for decades. Because I was convalescent, Oliphant offered me a room in the University, but I wanted to be in contact with the local community and was found lodgings with University students in the house of Mrs D, a retired high-school teacher. It was a very pleasant, quiet house with fruit trees in the garden, and I was well able to convalesce. But when I went to the cyclotron lab I was not able to do much because I kept blowing fuses and burning out switches. I seemed to be in a romantic dream where everyone was very cheerful and energetic, and even the noisy jukeboxes seemed enchanting.

I was beginning to get my feet on the ground in the comfortable reality of Mrs D's when I met Ruth, an art student, who was another lodger. I had been looking for the household radiogram, which Ruth used for listening to chamber music. I was rediscovering the world of music that I had shared with my father. I was also very glad to find that Ruth had political sympathies like mine and was a voluntary worker helping the blind and opposing racism. We shared many interests. She was cheerful and attractive and her friends often came to Mrs D's. The most interesting friend was Burt Tolerton, who was a 'perpetual student' of anthropology, with whom I am still in touch in Berkeley and London. Burt and Ruth were both very able at introducing me to life in California, and Ruth and I became close.

Life in the cyclotron lab had strong international qualities. One day I noticed a scientist standing quietly, and I commented that he looked rather sad. Yes, I was told, he lost all his family in Germany. I felt humbled. How lucky we British had been so far, only having ordinary high explosives dropped on us, and not being occupied by the Nazis! There were many refugees on the team who gave us a special sense that we must make sure the Germans did not make the Bomb first and enable the Nazis to rule the world. The attitudes of most of the Bomb scientists were much the same: the Allies had to get the Bomb first. But some attitudes about what would happen after a Bomb was exploded were very different. One man shocked me by his lack of concern. He said we would be safe in nuclear wars because we could live miles underground. He did not seem to be sad that we might not see the sky again. A distinguished German woman scientist gave a talk about the possibility that a nuclear explosion might cause the whole of the Earth's atmosphere to burn up. But that did not seem at all likely. Another colleague, the Australian Eric Burhop, had known people in the pre-War Cambridge Scientists Anti-War Group where I had worked. Eric was a fine representative of the very many scientists who campaigned, after the War, for international agreement that all nuclear weapons should be banned. David Bohm, an American of Austrian descent, had similar views – he later became a long-standing friend in England. We three enjoyed a holiday together at Burt Tolerton's cottage on Lake Tahoe, and Dave and I went on to Lake Pyramid to climb the famous pyramid-shaped rock there. Eric and Dave combined their enthusiasm for scientific progress with a sensitivity and concern for the problems of human life more generally.

My research job was to continue looking for a way of vaporizing uranium metal. The vacuum pump I was given was more than 10 times the size of the one I had used in England (things were big in Berkeley). Even so, I did not seem to be making much progress. Then, one day, Lawrence, the head of the lab, suggested I should try sputtering uranium instead of heating it. That meant having an electric discharge between two pieces of uranium. I tried this, but I had no experience of making electric discharges. Then Lawrence took over the controls, and turned them like a racing car driver. Soon he got a very big discharge, and a lot of uranium evaporated. It was very exciting watching him work. After that success, Lawrence arranged for my apparatus to

1   'Skerries', 30 Kilburn Parade, Wellington.

2   Maurice, his sister Eithne, and their father Edgar, in 1917.

3   Edgar showing Maurice and Eithne how a watch works, *c.* 1919.

4   Eithne and Maurice, 1919.

5　Maurice, Eithne, and Jasmine Wilkins with their mother Evelyn, 1927.

6   Maurice in 1929 with scale model Hawker Fury aeroplane (which still hangs in his bedroom today).

7   Maurice skipping, 1930s.

8   Maurice in 1934 with home-made 'hot box' solar energy panel (in front of shed) and home-made astronomical telescopes.

9   Edgar and Granny Wilkins ,1931.

10   Edgar and Evelyn
      Wilkins during the
      Second World War.

11   Maurice: self-portrait, 1930s.

12   Anti-war demonstration in London, 1936 – 'scholarships not battleships'.
Maurice is in the foreground, with his back turned toward the camera.

13 Maurice during experiments on gas-proof rooms carried out by the Cambridge Scientists Anti-War Group, Trinity College, 1937-8.

14 Maurice during experiments on incendiary bombs carried out by the Cambridge Scientists Anti-War Group in W. A. Wooster's garden in 1938.

be used in his 60-inch cyclotron. We needed two teams, one for day and the other for night. I led the day team, and Douglas Allen, who was also British, led the night team. At the end of each shift we discussed how the work was going, and prepared for the next shift. For the first time I shared research completely, and I enjoyed it very much. It strengthened my belief that in science, the greatest pleasure is in sharing knowledge and working together.

When the Germans were halted by the Red Army and the Japanese were pushed back in the Pacific, we scientists began to think about what we would like to do after the War. Some scientists were enthusiastic about continuing the Bomb work, and they went on to make bigger bombs as well as the hydrogen bombs that were much more powerful than our uranium bomb. Although some scientists saw nuclear power giving 'free' electricity, I was uneasy about such ideas, which I felt were rather unnatural. I felt that solar power was much more attractive. All in all, I was certain that I did not want to continue nuclear research after the War.

I much respected and liked Oliphant and Massey, but they did not seem to have any ideas for post-War research that especially attracted me. Then Randall offered me a job at St Andrews University in Scotland, where he had been appointed Head of Physics. He wished to explore links between physics and biology. I had depressing memories of Randall's biological interests – he had done some experiments with horse's blood at Birmingham – and I turned him down. Then Massey, seeing I wanted to find some new direction, lent me a new book with the rather ambitious title *What is Life?*. It was written by Erwin Schrödinger, the celebrated quantum physicist. As a student I had liked Schrö-dinger's contributions to quantum physics because he expressed his ideas in the form of wave motion which had a down-to-earth character, like Einstein's thoughts about how a boy would see the universe if he were sitting on a light wave. He was thinking in terms of physical reality rather than mathematical abstractions.

I was attracted by Schrödinger's thinking in *What is Life?* because he linked the extremely important biological idea of a gene with the rather strange world of electrons moving in crystals. He wrote about a gene being an aperiodic crystal, and that con-nected directly with my PhD research where electrons moved freely in perfect crystals but could be slowed down and trapped when the crystal had irregularity. It seemed to me that 'aperiodic' referred to the local irregularities in which the genetic message was written, against a periodic background. But the main impact of Schrödinger's book was that it set me in motion. It was not just what he wrote, but how he wrote it. Ruth often said 'it is not what you say that matters, but the way that you say it.' Schrödinger used the language of physicists and that stimulated me, as a physi-cist, to persevere with his book and its introduction to genetics, and to decide that this was the general area that I wanted to explore, as a 'biophysicist'. Such thoughts led me to accept Randall's second invitation to join him in Scotland (and the increase in salary he offered must have helped too). My feeling was that set-ting up biophysical research on the very important and funda-mental area of genes would need the wide imagination and business-like management skills that I felt Randall possessed.

The war with Japan went on and on and the military decided to drop an atomic bomb. Only a few top scientists at Berkeley knew that a Bomb had been successfully exploded in a test in the desert. Most of us only knew that the Bomb really did work when the dreadful explosion at Hiroshima was reported in the newspapers: *Japanese City Destroyed*. Almost everyone in our lab, it seemed, was filled with a joyful sense of achievement. Year after year the great project had struggled on, and now we knew we had at last reached our goal. All work stopped, and everyone was milling around filled with a great sense of relief: the War was over. The streets of San Francisco were filled with wild people, especially the men from the armed services who now knew that they could stay safely at home, and no longer needed to face the threat of death.

In the evening I went to the home of Ken Simpson, my philosopher friend and colleague with whom I had often talked about big questions over a sandwich lunch, looking across the Bay at the Golden Gate. I cheerfully rang his door bell and waited. I was a little puzzled when he opened the door: he did not look very happy. He said 'This is Black Monday – I always hoped it would never work.' I felt rather small, and gradually the penny dropped. I said 'Yes, you are right.' That summed up the end of my work at the cyclotron lab.

Without our intending to bring it about, Ruth had quite soon become pregnant. When she confirmed this I immediately said that we should marry and keep the child. Ruth took over a very large house and we lived in a community of young people, mainly University students. She knew that I planned to work in Scotland after the War, and when I warned her that it rained a lot there, she cheerfully replied 'I like rain'. I admired Ruth's positive attitude, but we should have examined much more carefully the real difficulties of our position, which were like those of many wartime marriages. We had too little time to consider our relationship. I had made a mistake in not discussing the implications of marriage more thoroughly with Ruth. We should have discussed all aspects of the situation – social and legal attitudes to marriage were very different in England and California. I was driven by my family's rather old-fashioned view and did not imagine that it might be questioned. In the big house we had little experience of living as a married couple, and after a few months Ruth divorced me. This came as a great surprise: Ruth told me one day that she had made an appointment for me with a lawyer, and when I arrived at his office I was shocked to hear from him that Ruth wanted to end our marriage. Shortly after our divorce, Ruth gave birth to a son, whom I visited in the hospital. Ruth was to leave Berkeley to begin a new life in the Pacific North-West, and we made contact occasionally in the years that followed. But in July 1945, I returned to England alone.

CHAPTER 4

RANDALL'S CIRCUS

I arrived back in England in August 1945. I found the nation very exhausted, like someone after a severe bout of flu. That was quite a shock after energetic California, which in comparison had been barely touched by the war. I hurried to Wylde Green to see my parents and younger sister Jasmine. They would have got my letter only a few days before, telling them that I would be alone – I had hesitated to give them news of my divorce. I realized that I had made a great mistake in sending the letter to my father at the school clinic where he worked. I had done so in order to protect my mother, but it must have been hard for my father to undertake his day of work after receiving such news. I had tried to be kind, but had not judged the situation well. Nevertheless, at home my parents seemed quiet and normal, and they did not assail me with questions. I ate excellent porridge again. My father was trying to finish writing his book about poverty and child health, and he surprised me by being more upset by my divorce than was my loving mother.

I looked at the wartime vegetables growing in our family garden, and I inspected a new 'Prefab', one of the prefabricated houses that provided accommodation for families whose homes had been destroyed by the bombing. I felt a thrill of optimism about the post-war growth of peace. The university term was soon to begin, and I was due to start at St Andrews. The horror of the nuclear bombs destroying Japanese cities had not been strong enough to drive me out of science and send me to seek refuge in art with my painter friends in Paris. My Californian dream of wife and child living with me on the Scottish coast had faded away, but I looked forward to exploring a new world of science where non-living physics interacted with the biology of living things. It was as though a button on a Time Machine had been pressed, and I was now in a new future where studies of the living and the non-living were coming together in interdisciplinary science. I felt that there was a good chance that such work might bring not only fascinating science, but also some real benefit to people's lives.

As the summer ended I headed north to St Andrews, a quiet little Scottish town on the North Sea coast. The University was ancient like Oxford and Cambridge, but the old stone buildings were on a smaller scale than the magnificent King's College Chapel I had known at Cambridge. On my first morning in St Andrews I looked out of the window and felt a sentimental warmth when I saw a familiar little red van delivering the Royal Mail at the ancient University. It felt good to be returning to the quiet decency of British life. However, I found it sad that there was little liveliness in the University: isolated on the east coast of

Scotland, it had suffered badly from wartime stagnation. The staff Common Room was like a recreation area in a prison, with inmates exchanging stories about lucky escapees who had disappeared into the world outside.

But soon new life was flowing into St Andrews. Randall's success in rapidly building up his new Physics Department was very impressive. Sweeping away post-war somnolescence, his energy and enterprise were really making things tick. It was what I had been looking forward to. He had established himself well in the University and was admired by the Principal. He had acquired new staff, and a new building for research, and was negotiating for Government funding. The programme of research was very wide, on all kinds of cell studies linking physics and biology. I wanted to work on genes and chromosomes – aggregates of genes that could be seen under a microscope – because I saw that as central to biology, but I knew very little about them. It took me months to decide where I should begin my research: reading about biology was like learning to live in an unfamiliar culture.

Then my father became ill. He had heart problems, and I travelled back to Birmingham several times to see him as he quietly faded away. In the hospital as my father died I wondered about the new tools physicists were providing for doctors – I remembered the electron microscopes that had impressed me when I read about them as a student at the Cavendish. My father was only 57 when he died, despite his very vigorous youth when he had been a champion athlete, and our long treks when he led me to the peaks of Welsh mountains. His work on child health in the Birmingham slums led him far into understanding the relationship between poverty and ill-health, and he made many connections with leading figures in nutrition, economics and sociology in his study of the many factors contributing to health and well-being. Forty years later I would meet a PhD student working on hunger in the developing world, and she asked me: 'are you the son of E.H. Wilkins who wrote so many excellent letters to the British Medical Journal?' I was proud of my father, and of his book, *Medical Inspection of Schoolchildren*, which was published shortly after his death. He had been a wonderful father, and it seemed almost unbelievable that he was gone.

During my father's last days, I missed an extremely useful conference on DNA, deoxyribonucleic acid, a substance found in chromosomes. Pioneering work was presented at the conference, including the X-ray studies of DNA that had been done at Leeds University by the crystallographer Bill Astbury. At the time, it was known that DNA had a very high molecular weight, and so must be a very large molecule. It was thought that its structure was like a long thread. Chemists had determined its composition, so we knew that it contained phosphate groups, sugar rings and nitrogen bases. But we did not know the three-dimensional organization of these components within the thread-like molecule. Astbury's X-ray work was beginning to address this mystery – X-ray diffraction could give important insights into molecular structure. Most scientists believed that DNA was something to do with genes, perhaps in a supporting role, accompanying a protein that carried the genetic information. But it was clear that the genetic material itself would have to be a very extensive molecule indeed if it were to contain enough information. I should emphasize that at the time, almost no-one thought that DNA might be of genetic interest – it was thought to be associated with genes in some way, but it was not the genetic material.

I found the excellent Charlotte Auerbach, a geneticist in Edinburgh University – one of the few British universities that were interested in genetics – and it was probably she who told me about the American biologist Herman Muller's important work using X-rays to produce mutations. I wondered whether another kind of physical agent might be used to alter genes. Such altering might cast light on how genes worked. No-one seemed to have tried strong high-frequency sound (ultrasonics) on chromosomes, and I decided to have a go and see what happened. It was a way of starting; I could do it on my own and it might help us to understand how genes worked. A few months after I decided to study the effects of ultrasonics on genes, Muller was awarded a Nobel Prize for his X-ray work; but my ultrasonic experiments were much less successful, and I was never to get very far with them.

My post at St Andrews involved some teaching, which presented some unexpected challenges. As a student in pre-War Cambridge I had always seen lecturers treated with respect, but at St Andrews the students could sometimes be rowdy. I was surprised to hear silly interruptions and noisy voices coming from a lecture hall while a physics lecture was in progress. Towards the end of one of my lectures I heard students making noises like a bomb dropping. I realized that the noises would grow into a general racket if I did not stop the interruptions at my next lecture. I spent an anxious weekend making a plan to 'stop the rot'. On the Monday my lecture was orderly at first, but then I heard the bomb noises. When the noises were loud enough for the whole class to hear, I said that since students were clearly interested in the War I would tell them about my bomb work at Birmingham and about the physics of the bombing noise. After a few minutes of this I stopped and said that students with questions could see me at the end of the lecture. I continued my original lecture with no further interruptions.

Apart from my teaching, I was able to press on with constructing a high-power ultrasonic generator. Meanwhile Randall visited the USA to wind up some wartime collaboration, and he took the opportunity to visit US biologists who could advise him on his programme of research. I had been out of the USA for almost a year, and although I corresponded with American workers, I felt cut off and was keenly looking forward to hearing what Randall had found out. But on his return I could hardly get a word out of him. I knew he had been at the Rockefeller Institute in New York where there were very interesting people working on the chemistry of genes. He knew the biochemist Alfred E. Mirsky there, who opposed the idea that genes were DNA. I knew nothing then about the extraordinary war Mirsky waged against the medical researcher Oswald Avery at the Rockefeller, who was obtaining proof that DNA really was the gene material. Mirsky's attacks on Avery could well have confused Randall and made it difficult for him to give me any clear news. He would tell me nothing. I was resentful; if he had found nothing interesting he could at least have told me so! He simply would not tell me anything. Refusing to put his cards on the table seemed to me to be against the whole spirit of us working together. After leaving his luminescence work I had been across the world and widened my research experience. It was not right that he should treat me as a mere underling. I had not been aware of that kind of difficulty with him before. We had quite a row.

Looking back, I see that my expecting Randall to tell me all the interesting things he had found in the USA could easily have stirred up jealous feelings towards me. There was I, back from exciting years on the Bomb Project, probably the largest science project ever! And all that was in the USA where he (as he later wrote bitterly), the inventor of the extremely important cavity magnetron, had, in contrast, never been invited. So many leading British scientists had been in the USA during the war. It was strange that he had not been involved in planning war-time magnetron production. And, although he was given two US prizes for his invention, some US experts seemed to dismiss his work.

My row with Randall soon blew over. One reason was that I had begun looking in London for a better research base. Although Randall was building things up very well in St Andrews, it was clear that the environment was too limited. The Professor of Zoology, D'Arcy Thompson, had an extremely distinguished past – as well as being an accomplished classicist, he had pioneered the use of mathematics in biology – but he knew little that was relevant to our interests in genetics, and in biology at the level of cells and macromolecules. The Professor of Botany was even less use: when I asked him how big a nucleolus is (it is a small body inside a cell nucleus), he replied, 'as big as the full moon', which may have been poetic but was hardly science. I do not think we understood each other. The Medical Research Council was the leading British agency organizing and funding biology research related to medicine, and it was quite rightly doubtful about giving us a big grant for research in isolated St Andrews. We needed to be in a very big centre like Cambridge, or even better in London, where we could interact with a wide range of scientists working in many areas relevant to our interests. It became clear to me that new kinds of interdisciplinary research grew best in a very widely-based environment.

Although D'Arcy Thompson was unable to help much with my research, I enjoyed his company enormously. He was then over 80 years old, and we had fun at the Circus, where he called loudly for 'the young lady in the short frilly skirt' who would stand on the horse's back and whirl round the Ring. I also enjoyed touring the pubs in nearby Dundee with the University architect's daughter (like most of my girlfriends, a prize dancer). I lived in various rooms where entertaining was difficult, and I once annoyed Randall by serving a dinner in the lab: he brought a visitor to see the lab the next morning, and I had not yet got around to clearing up after the meal. I doubt Randall or his visitor expected to see the debris of a dinner party on the lab bench. I also remember well some very impressive performances of music and theatre in St Andrews – especially one performance of Shakespeare stripped of the usual seventeenth-century costumes and flamboyance, where the language and insight into universal problems shone through with great clarity and feeling. Most exciting was watching, time and time again, the superb Scottish dancing at social events. San Francisco was proud of Isadora Duncan and modern dance; but Americans just watched dancing whereas the Scots did their traditional dancing themselves. But from a social point of view, St Andrews did not really suit me. When I had accepted Randall's invitation to St Andrews I was expecting to go there as a married man with a wife and small child. As a family we could have very much enjoyed living in a small seaside town. But as an isolated divorcee wanting to build up a new life, I needed a big and active cultural centre. I had vivid memories of the liveliness of San Francisco and New York. In Britain, the obvious place for me was London.

Nan Newth had moved to Ealing Broadway, a pleasant western suburb of London, and she gave me a base there. I enjoyed very much being with her. I contacted scientists in many places, particularly at the John Innes plant genetics lab, which was just south of London and specialized in agricultural problems. My closest contact there was Mick Callan, a zoologist who was about my age and had been led by radar work to become interested in physical approaches to biology, especially genetics. Mick loved science (and was, like Charles Darwin, a keen hunter), and I was especially interested in his emphasis on science as a craft. That down-to-earth idea of craft expresses the need of the scientist to understand and respect the material on which he or she works (and that idea has more meaning in it than loads of philosophy of science). Mick and I investigated various labs where we might work. At University College London, A.V. Hill was keen on applying physics in biology, and had a Nobel Prize for work on contracting muscle. But he used nineteenth-century physics, which did not inspire me (at least, his book *Living Machinery* had left me cold when I read it at school). In contrast, Schrödinger's quantum physics was very modern and exciting. In any case, Hill could not give me a job because he had high principles and did not want to poach: he regarded me as 'Randall's man' (which was rather frustrating). Mick and I discussed the possibility that, if Randall was not able to get a good lab going, we might ourselves apply for funds for a joint programme. In hierarchical Britain, research money almost always came through senior members of the scientific establishment like university Heads of Departments, but our plan was to bypass all that and obtain our own money direct from government funding agencies such as the Medical Research Council. We faced two challenges: we had to find a university willing to house us in its physics or biochemistry department, and we needed the Medical Research Council to agree to give us the money for our research.

We did not get far with our plan because news of Randall's impressive impact on St Andrews spread around the universities and, just in time for me, he was offered the distinguished Headship of the Physics Department at King's College London. King's was one of the founding Colleges of the University of London, and had very strong departments of physics, chemistry, biology and medicine. My father had taken his Diploma of Public Health there. Randall was confident that it was a good place to start a programme of biophysics research. He and I resigned from St Andrews and I began work at King's before I had a salary – I had no doubts that Randall's plans would go well. Mick admired the spirit of our lab and helped to get things going. But by strange coincidence, he soon became Head of Zoology at St Andrews and enjoyed life there with his wife and family.

Randall's appointment as Head of Physics at King's came in the wake of the arrest of the likely internal candidate for the post, Allan Nunn May. He was one of the sons of the family with whom I had briefly lodged in Birmingham. The story circulating at King's was that the police had waited outside the door of the lecture theatre while Allan was teaching, and had arrested him as he came out. He had been in contact with atomic scientists during the War, and had been passing confidential information to the Russians. Allan admitted to passing the information, but successfully protested that since the Russians had been our allies at the time, his activity did not constitute spying. He was, however, convicted of breaking the Official Secrets Act, and was sentenced to 10 years in prison. There were claims that if Nunn May had not been arrested, he could have been appointed to the Chair of Physics, and Randall's career at King's would never have happened.

In London, as in St Andrew's, the post-War recovery took time. The College had been exiled to the countryside during the War, but was settling slowly back into a normal routine. Randall took me to see the College, which was in an excellent location: it overlooked the Thames and Waterloo Bridge to the south, and opened onto the Strand to the north, which was and remains a busy street of shops, restaurants and theatres. As Randall proudly pushed into the College's elegant entrance hall, we were stopped by a nervous, short-sighted porter who asked what our business was. Randall replied that he was Professor Randall, the new Head of the Physics Department, and somewhat doubtfully the porter allowed us to proceed.

That meeting with the porter symbolized Randall's reception by some sections of King's. College bureaucrats were disturbed by Randall's long-distance telephone bills, and stuffy academics were offended by his unusual plan to mix physics and biology (traditionally very separate) and by what they saw as his pushy style. However, Randall was soon in a position to display his almost genius-like talent, and he quickly gained approval for his plans, and a great deal of money. When beginning at St Andrew's an adviser had told him he had asked for too little money, and Randall never made that mistake again – people were amazed at how much money he got. Government committees, remembering the importance of new kinds of research during the War (including Randall's magnetron), allocated new funds for research that did not fit with the established University structure. That helped Randall's new plans and he got a good slice of the

money. The Medical Research Council made him D.
Biophysics Research Unit and paid for biologists to w.
physicists in the Physics Department, and for physicists li. me
who wanted to work with the biologists. Money was also supplied
for new equipment. The MRC did not know that Randall had
earlier applied to the Rockefeller Foundation for money to buy
equipment. This Foundation was based in New York, and was
very wealthy, and it had enlightened policies on the allocation of
funds to new areas of scientific research. After the MRC grant,
the Rockefeller grant came through too, and the MRC read about
it in a newspaper and felt they had been manipulated. Randall
explained that the US grant was for his College Department and
the MRC grant for his MRC unit. That sounded logical and indicated the skill Randall developed in handling his affairs. (If there
had been a fault, it was the failure of the MRC to check Randall's
funds.) The advancement of my own research depended on
Randall having entrepreneurial skill which was something I (like
many scientists) lacked. Impressed by our financial progress, the
College authorities agreed to use a big bomb crater in the College
quadrangle to house new labs for our influx of researchers. So
Randall's lab grew out of a bomb crater, and the supportive staff
who collected round him were inspired by his success.

I was, at that time, Randall's right-hand man, and as his
plans for research kept expanding, we had many discussions about
them. I became more aware than before that, although Randall
was extremely zealous in advancing research close to his own
interests, he was also ready to act disinterestedly for the general

good of academic and scientific advancement, and sometimes he even under-estimated his own interests. I respected him for that. I had to push hard to prevent him allocating space in the new building to physics research that was not related to our biophysics. Randall also benefited the College by finding top quality people to fill important vacancies, such as biological professorships. He was unusually knowledgeable about top-rate scientists, and a good judge of form. Also, he was one of the few leaders in British universities who saw the need to make links between the various traditional branches of biology such as botany, zoology and biochemistry. He put King's in the forefront of important university developments by persuading the departments to connect their teaching and form a School of Biological Sciences. During years of struggling on committees towards that goal, Randall, emerging from an exasperating meeting, rather out of character let slip to me that he did not know why he put so much effort into that struggle. It could not have done much to increase his personal prestige; he just *did* care. It was like his almost religious enthusiasm for gardening. Research was the same, except that it had the seductive aspect of leading to personal recognition and fame.

Especially during his early years at King's, Randall's bold modernizing created jealousy. Archives show that when Randall had his lab working well, the Principal of King's (presumably under pressure from jealous Department Heads) asked the MRC to cut its support for Randall because it was creating imbalance in the College's research. That seems to have had no effect. Ironically, it was probably the very success of Randall in the College that caused him to have to wait fourteen years before he was honoured by election to the College Fellowship – two more years and he had his Knighthood. The committee dealing with Fellowships did not represent the College, and, as the years went by, the College, with its many distinguished academics, increasingly appreciated Randall and the lustre he brought to King's. In our second decade at King's the Principal claimed Randall had the most incisive mind in the College; and a later Principal told me that Randall was 'more than an academic' – which I thought was a very good compliment.

In our lab Randall, in Napoleonic style, could certainly make his staff 'go hop' (as a collaborator once said), but very largely he gave staff freedom to pursue their research and organize themselves into their own groups. That helped to generate enthusiasm, and our lab had a very good creative, non-hierarchical, democratic spirit. There were many good scientists, nearly all young, in the rather mixed bag that flowed into Randall's Circus, as it was called in College gossip. The combination of freedom and good funding gave rise not only to enthusiasm, but also to friendliness and good work. Randall added to the good spirits by holding parties after the annual cricket match (in which he played vigorously), at his home, and in the College at Christmas. He was obviously proud of the community he had created. A visiting scientist from Naples, who had encountered many British scientists at the Zoological Station there, was delighted with an opera and other hilarities at our Christmas party. He exclaimed he had never known that the British were capable of such extraordinary light-heartedness. Randall's party was like a scene from Orson Welles' *Citizen Kane* where Kane celebrates the success of his great newspaper by joyously leading his dancing staff across the stage. Though Randall did not dance, he roared with laughter at our office-party jokes.

The general community spirit that showed so clearly at our laboratory parties was also apparent in the day-to-day working of the various research groups: friendly, cooperative relations between the members of a group helped the progress of research. I think an important factor in this friendliness was that the staff had been attracted to Randall's lab because they liked the idea of new kinds of interdisciplinary research and were exploring areas that were new to them. We tended to be amateurs in the best sense. The scientists, working with new kinds of equipment or techniques, wanted to break new ground.

Randall's non-conformist Lancashire background encouraged not only his enthusiasm for cricket, but also (as with my non-conformist family) a welcoming attitude to women in science. The unusually high proportion of women on his staff added to the lively social spirit and scientific cohesion. Many of the biologists were women, which was a new experience for me because there had been almost no women in the labs I had worked in. I had long talks with Margaret Preston, a research student who had come with Randall and me from St Andrew's, and I enjoyed finding out from her how an intelligent young biologist looked at science. Marjorie M'Ewen, entertaining and, in her physics, very rigorous, was another of the St Andrew's staff whom Randall had brought to King's. Jean Hanson, a zoologist, took the main role in helping our physicists and biologists to work together (after Randall retired, she became Director of our MRC Muscle Unit).

The spirit of Randall's lab was dynamic and positive, but relations with Randall were not always happy. He occasionally showed the rather baffling, negative side I had sometimes seen in Birmingham and St Andrew's. Every year or so he and I had a stand-up row, and nearly always he would give in (and often he brought me a plant from his garden the next day). When we had such a good row we were open – we said what we thought and we heard what was said. Randall had bouts of self-pity because he wanted more time for research, and he had once explored the possibility of having a smaller lab in New York where he would have more time to do research himself. But Randall's occasional indulgence in complaining that staff did not show enough gratitude for what he did for them did little to spoil the positive spirit; and when any irritation arose, Jean Hanson, who was very sensible, shared the problem with me. When Randall was on sabbatical he emphasized that we must not worry him about problems. As a result, when a proposal was made by St Thomas' Medical School, a distinguished school just opposite the Houses of Parliament up-river from King's, that we should form a joint research group with them, we investigated it ourselves. In spite of careful thought the situation became muddled; but all was cleared up when Randall came back and the plan was dropped. Randall's ability to sort things out showed clearly.

If I had had more understanding of Randall, I might have eased some of the difficulties I had with him. After he died I wrote a Memoir for the Royal Society about his life and work. The Society is the premier scientific academy in Britain, and it confers a Fellowship on distinguished scientists. Randall was a Fellow, and as such merited an official obituary, the Memoir. Fellows are asked to deposit notes in anticipation of this Memoir, for the use of the eventual author – in Randall's case, that would turn out to be me. So some years later I saw the excellent notes Randall had left for the Society where he, very much out of character, revealed much about himself. I think his openness derived from his respect for the Society. Calmly and objectively he described his early difficulties. His lower-middle-class Lancashire family was poor and had little education. But its good nonconformist liberal principles made common ground between Randall and me. Our main difference was that Randall's life had been much harsher than mine. To help his father's struggling horticulture business, he drove the family lorry to market each morning before school, and formed a lifelong habit of working from five o'clock in the morning (whereas I liked to lie in bed late). His family taught him to revere education and urged him to succeed at school. But with no aptitude, he wrote, except substantial capacity for hard work, he failed to reach the famous Manchester Grammar School. That seemed to hang over him all his life. At Manchester University, he survived on part-time teaching (like my grandfather William). Randall set his heart on physics research; but even with a first-class degree and Prize of the Year, he failed again. Lawrence

Bragg – the X-ray diffraction expert who became Director of the Cavendish, but who was at Manchester in Randall's day – did not recognize his academic potential, and sent him to the GEC to do industrial research. After a year there, Randall was advised to go into school-teaching. But he tried research, and went on trying.

Gradually he learned to do research, and to choose good problems and good collaborators. Pressures were great and competition rife, but he learned to be versatile and played his cards close to his chest. Thus he built up his power and, I was told, was respected as a 'dark horse'. And, after painful years, he had lived down his Lancashire 'rough edges' and had learnt to manipulate the Establishment. In time Randall became a leader of research. But he was not satisfied. He wanted to study fundamental science. So he made the difficult move from industry to University and began again. I believe it was through his failures that he learned and gained his somewhat ruthless wisdom, Napoleonic determination, and ultimately intuition and self-confidence. He had to sink or swim; like learning on an assault course.

After retiring from King's Randall moved to Edinburgh, because it was good for gardening, and set up a small research group. This required frequent visits to the neutron lab at Grenoble. Dieter Middendorf, a member of Randall's group, wrote: 'I think of him arriving at the great neutron lab at Grenoble where he was engaged on several research programmes. I heard that young scientists there were inspired by the sight of the "small, dapper, smartly dressed elderly gentleman … smiling and carrying a suitcase … full of samples that needed immediate attention."' Randall continued research until he died in 1984 aged 79. I admired and respected him, but I can not really say that I found him very likeable.

Randall made my life difficult, but most of the time I was carried along by the excitement of DNA. After three years in our bio-physics lab I was, like the lab as a whole, riding high on a wave of success. Under Randall's leadership, the lab had established itself as a world leader in the important new science of molecular biology, which pointed to a new understanding of biology; and my own work had been a significant part of our laboratory's success. I remember my naïve thought that, if I were a million-aire, I would not choose to be working in any other way than in our lab. It had been a wonderful idea to move out of straight physics into research that made a new synthesis of physics and biology. I found living things marvellous with all their exotic forms and strange mechanisms and movements. New biophysical techniques fascinated me, and the scientists I worked with were very helpful and encouraging, especially the biologists who had come to support us physicists who depended on their advice.

   In moving into a kind of science that was new to me, I was fortunate in many ways. For my first year I continued trying to get mutations with ultrasonics. A geneticist in the King's Botany Department was a great help, but the results were not encourag-ing. As a result, when Randall asked me to take over the research he had begun into how DNA moved and grew in living cells, I was quite willing to make a change. The general idea seemed a bit vague but it was about DNA in cells and involved optical technology related to my schoolboy experience of making astronomical telescopes. It was a very pleasant coincidence to get high-grade help from Cyril Burch of Bristol University. He was the eccentric genius who had inspired me as a schoolboy. Burch had invented new reflecting microscopes that we used to study DNA in the lively proliferating cells that Honor Fell, our MRC Senior Biological Adviser, grew so skilfully in tissue culture. It was a great privilege to work with her – such a distinguished scientist doing beautiful work, and such a good, kind and shy person. She directed her own lab in Cambridge and spent one day a week with us. Our aim was to find out more about how genes made copies of themselves and how they controlled the growth of cells. Since DNA absorbed ultraviolet light we could, by using ultraviolet microscopes, follow the way DNA moved in cells. However, it was a great help if the microscope also worked with visible light. Burch's brilliant microscopes were very refined but were designed only for visible light; my main success at that time was to develop a simple reflecting microscope that worked well for visible, ultraviolet and infra-red light. Our studies helped to make clear that genes were DNA. My work received strong support from the MRC and I was made Assistant Director of their Biophysics Unit.

Most of the staff of the Biophysics Unit were from outside King's and had been attracted by Randall's reputation as the inventor of the magnetron. Also attractive was the fact that our main research funds came from the Medical Research Council, a prestigious body with broad interests. We took a long view into the future. We had an interesting, loosely attached group of scientists working with microscopes of special kinds. Peter Walker was a zoologist with special engineering experience, and he was able to make a refined machine that automatically measured the opacity of photographs of living cells, so that the distribution of matter in them could be determined. In that way, the amount of DNA could be measured in cells as they grew and divided. Thus it was confirmed that the amount of DNA doubled when cells divided, which fitted with the idea of genes being DNA. John Kendrew came from Cambridge to measure X-ray photographs of proteins, and the accuracy of his measurements helped the elucidation of the protein structures. Howard Davis had been a hospital physicist, and was a very dedicated scientist who excelled in using ultraviolet microscopes to measure directly the distribution of DNA in cells as they grew in tissue culture. He was, like Peter Walker, a very co-operative colleague, and his passion for precision led him to electron microscopy of chromosomes in cells, thus approaching the problem of gene structure and organization. It was a great pleasure to work alongside colleagues like Peter and Howard, and to co-operate with and learn from them. They shared a room that was next to mine, and we three often lunched together in the Men's Senior Common Room. Upstairs from the Common Room, overlooking the river, was a comfortable room full of big leather armchairs where we drank coffee.

These rooms were for male academics only – women academics and other staff took their meals in a room along the corridor, and when we lunched in a mixed group we would all go to this other room, or to one of the many cafés on the Strand (the men-only rule would very soon be abolished). We often talked about research at lunch, and one day in the Common Room when we were very absorbed in our conversation, a College bureaucrat who had been sitting at our table got up saying 'I don't want to hear anything more about microscopes', and moved to the next table. I thought he might have expressed himself more politely, but we were at the early stage where the College tended to regard us as Randall's Circus.

Shortly after I started at King's, while I was still struggling with my ultrasonics experiments, I received a visit from a physics graduate called Francis Crick. Crick was very keen to do interdisciplinary work and use his knowledge of physics to explore living processes, but did not know where he might find a job that encouraged such work. He had already enquired at University College London in Bloomsbury, where Harrie Massey who had looked after me in Berkeley was now working. Crick had met Massey while working on magnetic mines during the War. Massey could not think of a place for Crick at UCL but he knew what we were trying to do in Randall's lab, and so had sent Crick across Covent Garden to see me at King's. I found Crick very bright and lively, and suggested to Randall that he be offered a job with us. However Randall was not keen – he had decided that Crick was rather boisterous and talked too much. Crick went to

Cambridge and found a way into biological research there, but he and I became firm friends. He thought I was wasting my time on DNA, and he told me one day, as we sat by the Thames in the Embankment Gardens just outside King's, that he could not understand why I did not concentrate on something useful such as proteins.

The Medical Research Council did not look as favourably on Francis Crick's ambitions as it had on ours. It rather unimaginatively suggested that he learn about biology by working on living cells in the Strangeways Laboratory at Cambridge, which was directed by Honor Fell. But Francis could not settle at the Strangeways Lab – he thought it was most aptly named. He did however spend two years there, and described the very complex cells he explored as 'Mother's Workbasket', which well expressed the great tangle of substances and structures such as one might see in a sewing basket. Francis was then able to move to the biochemist Max Perutz's lab where they were working on protein structures, which he found much more rewarding.

Among those who did join us at King's was Keith Norris, a research student whom I supervised. He was a very good Yorkshireman – very skilful: I probably learnt as much from him as he did from me. We developed ideas from Burch which helped the study of DNA in living cells. Bill Seeds worked with us: he was Irish–Swiss and entertained Randall with his wit. During a study Bill and I made of the lining up of atoms in live virus particles, we were very amused to find that Bill's measurements contradicted those of Adolf Butenandt, who had won a Nobel Prize in 1939.

We checked our work extra carefully, and made sure we were right. But I did not think Bill was right when he boasted of having seduced Jean Hanson after a lab Christmas party – I respected Jean too much to believe that.

Although our lab was full of women technicians and research workers, the only woman I worked with closely was the excellent young sister of Rudi Komphner who had done so very well in Oliphant's lab during the War. The large number of young women in our lab and the friendly spirit led to several marriages, but none of my friendships there showed any signs of leading to marriage. Once I was settled at King's I left Nan's house and went to live with my sister Eithne and her husband Ernst in Hampstead, a leafy north London suburb which I liked because it was full of artists, intellectuals and refugees from Nazism. I had enjoyed drawing since I was a child, and in Berkeley I had taken art classes (and singing lessons from an excellent Welsh teacher) to lift my spirits after my divorce from Ruth. Now I took art classes again, and found painting and drawing a satisfying way to relax after a day in the lab. I also visited galleries that exhibited recent work, and one day in Bond Street, a smart street in the West End of London where many galleries exhibited and sold works of art, I was attracted by the work of a painter called Anna. I rang her up to ask if I could see more, and she invited me to her studio. I much enjoyed meeting her – like many of my most interesting friends, she was from Vienna – and soon we had a close relationship. Anna lived in a studio flat in South Kensington, and was well known in artistic circles. She had beauty and wisdom, but I very much wanted a family and children, and that wasn't going to happen with Anna. She was 40 years old – ten years older than me – and I knew she had been involved with many men. She had sympathetic feelings for children (I still have in my study a painting of hers showing happy children flying through the sky), but she was sure she was unable to have children herself. After my father's unexpected heart problems I had found what I thought was a reliable doctor, and when I noticed one of Anna's paintings in his office and remarked upon it, he shocked me greatly by recounting tales of her many relationships. So it seemed that she was well known as someone with no intention of settling down to family life. Within a year I had given up on any thoughts of a long-term relationship with Anna, and when she heard that I had been out with a friend of hers, she ended our relationship. So we separated, which saddened me greatly.

I had long been interested in Freud and, after my experiences with Ruth and Anna, it seemed that Freudian analysis might be useful to me. After a year of daily 8 a.m. visits to a Freudian woman therapist, arranged for me by the official Freudian organization, I was thrown out because I reported thinking (I thought according to Freudian rules) 'that woman will never get anything out of me'. Having been officially assigned to the analyst I thought the Freudians would try to help me, but I did not hear from them. First Ruth, then Anna, and now the Freudian woman! I was in very low spirits. I was living in a top floor flat in Soho that had been vacated by friends of Francis Crick – a strange place, like Caligari's Cabinet, with the floor and walls all cock-eyed. I felt a bit suicidal, but I thought of my loving mother who had recently lost my dear father and did not want to cause her any more grief.

When I was not absorbed in the lab I explored in libraries and discovered the philosophers Simone Weil and Søren Kierkegaard, who both had a great breadth of vision and helped keep me going. I also joined the London Fencing Club, thinking that a new activity might cheer me up; I had lessons from an Italian instructor. After the lessons the club members would fence with each other, and one day my opponent pointed out in exasperation that all I was doing was copying his every move. Actually I was not particularly interested in fencing itself, and I was certainly never any good at it – it was too quick for me – but I enjoyed the lessons and the exercise, and the deep bath that filled with hot water in just a few minutes, and going after class with the Italian instructor to little family-run Italian restaurants with their excellent food and friendly atmosphere.

After the Freudian débâcle, I did try psychoanalysis again. I went for advice to Dr Bannister in Cambridge – I found him digging the garden – and he recommended a Jungian who specialized in marriage breakdowns. Having learnt about the Unconscious from Freud, I was now very interested in Jung's ideas about thinking and feeling, and I found a very helpful analyst whom I was to visit for many years. I was determined to be positive. Happily, some good news about DNA was soon to lift my spirits.

CHAPTER 5

CRYSTAL GENES

Then came the very big news that DNA was the gene material. For about two years our lab had a special advantage in knowing this; the scientific community as a whole was still living in the belief that DNA was little more than an accessory to the proteins that were the basic element of genes. DNA had seemed much too simple to be gene material. We obtained this very important understanding of DNA because our lab had research students who were not weighed down by the authority of older scientists (Honor Fell, though an authority, did not throw her weight about). The crucial person was research student Geoffrey Brown, who was very bright and enquiring. He had graduated in 1946 in our Physics Department and had begun PhD work with Randall on the spectroscopy of cells. Geoffrey went to many conferences to learn about genetics and biochemistry. He also learned biochemistry from Dermott Taylor in the King's Biochemistry Department. Taylor had worked in New York, and knew Avery, who had strong evidence that genes were DNA and not protein. Geoffrey gave us this extremely important news two years before the results of Avery's group's work were published. This stimulated us very much to study DNA as important in itself, and not as a mere component of genes. However, I was fascinated by studying living cells with microscopes of various new types, and the MRC liked such work. Both Randall and I, in the first years at Kings, had been attracted by the beauty and fascination of living things. Having given up the somewhat inhuman study of physics, we were disinclined to make physical study of the seemingly nonliving, static structure of DNA. I was distracted by making new kinds of microscopes to study living cells. It took me some time to overcome my distaste for studying static structures and to move on to DNA structure. But if DNA really was the stuff of genes, then that was where my work should concentrate. I should have confronted the fact that it was Schrödinger's vision of a gene being like an aperiodic crystal that had persuaded me to study genes and to give up physics. I would give up microscopes and concentrate on DNA.

Apart from Geoffrey Brown, we had another key colleague: the young visiting American Gerald Oster, who was lively, stimulating and full of fun. His sister was a well-known actress. Jerry had the advantage of being closely in touch with exciting new American work, and was able to stand back from the stream of work in Britain and judge it from the outside. He was in contact with the biochemist Wendell Stanley in California, who was studying the structure of crystalline viruses with X-ray diffraction – the fascinating area that Bernal had pioneered while I had been a student at Cambridge. That work on crystals had led to an interesting new view of the relation of living and non-living matter. Jerry encouraged me to think about X-ray diffraction, and showed me how to grow tobacco plants, infect them with TMV, the tobacco mosaic virus, and study with microscopes the virus crystals that grew in the leaves. We measured the length of living, rod-shaped particles for the first time and were able to show that all those tiny living things had exactly the same size. A leading TMV expert, clinging to conventional views, did not believe us. Alec Stokes, one of our physicists at King's, gave us very valuable help in understanding the banded appearance of the TMV crystals. He pointed out that the TMV particles might join up and twist in a helical way.

I faced criticism of my reflecting microscopes: at a conference I described the microscopes and their use with ultraviolet and infra-red light, and a somewhat competitive member of the audience then took the floor, criticized our designs, and finished by asking if someone more expert than him could come forward. I immediately stood up (which made the audience laugh), and offered a rebuttal of the criticisms. We had a good laugh, and I was pleased to be able to stand up for myself.

Jerry was excited by our microscopes, but urged me to use them to study the arrangements of atoms in living molecules, rather than the location and movement of DNA in living cells. That meant I should study molecular structure with the microscopes; and thus Jerry helped to lead me towards the more powerful X-ray study of DNA molecules. Swedish and German workers had shown that the flat bases (groups of atoms that later were seen to be the basis of genes) lay perpendicular to the length of DNA molecules, and I began using our microscopes to study this kind of orientation in DNA. Our special microscopes had given me much enjoyment studying living cells, but now they helped me get to grips with gene structure.

I then had a very special stroke of luck. At a big scientific meeting in London, the biochemist Rudolph Signer from Berne, who had worked with Swedish scientists who were studying the shape and size of DNA molecules, stood up and, in the true spirit of science, held out glass phials containing his latest preparation of DNA which he generously offered to any research worker who wanted to study it. He was proud that he had used very gentle methods to extract and purify the DNA, and he believed that it was in almost pristine form – almost the same as in living cells. No-one else from our lab was in the queue for DNA, and I was very glad to get a phial full of it. I found out much later that Signer had been a research student of Hermann Staudinger, the great German chemist. Staudinger was an organic chemist at the University of Freiburg, where he worked on many different substances including rubber, insecticides and synthetic flavours. During the 1930s he developed the concept of macromolecules – molecules extending through hitherto unimagined distances and containing many thousands of atoms. Despite the strong evidence for his claim, Staudinger at first faced much opposition from chemists – he was shouted down at conferences by scientists who could not believe that such enormous molecules could form and hold together. But Staudinger's work was accepted eventually, and in 1953 he was awarded the Nobel Prize for his discoveries in macromolecular chemistry. His student Signer, understanding that the DNA molecules he was trying to isolate might be extremely large, handled his samples with extreme care in order to preserve their structure. So Signer was right about the quality of his DNA – it was in very good condition; and I was very lucky to have it.

Signer's DNA looked like a bundle of tiny white threads when it was dry. I thought that in a living cell the DNA would be wet, so I decided to keep the DNA moist. When it was wet, it formed a sticky blob that, Jerry Oster once remarked, looked like snot. In order to study the structure of the DNA molecules – or at least to find the way in which the chemical groups were aligned in them – I took the damp DNA, smeared it into thin sheets and used one of our microscopes to measure how polarized ultraviolet light was absorbed in the sheets. The Signer DNA was very different from other DNA I had used. I was intrigued to find that the sticky blob of DNA seemed to dislike forming sheets, and instead tended to form very long thin fibres like those in a spider's web. When I looked carefully at the fibres with a microscope, I saw that they were extraordinarily uniform and transparent – there was a perfection about them which led me to a strong intuition that the arrangement of the molecules in the fibres might form a regular pattern. If the organization within the fibres were regular, then they were crystalline, and could be examined by X-ray diffraction.

Such intuitions are not very logical and often lead nowhere, but they can be very important, and this intuition proved very fruitful indeed. If I was right, the fibres should give sharp X-ray diffraction patterns, and that might tell us very much more about the molecular structure of the DNA than was possible by using light microscopes. I knew little about how such X-ray analysis might be done, but I was excited by the idea of finding more about the structure of DNA because that could tell us about the structure of genes. Nothing in biophysics could be more important than that! But I did not dare to think that quite soon all the essential features of DNA structure might be known. That seemed a rather incredible idea. I used to sit and ponder in an old wicker armchair in the corner of the basement laboratory that I shared with Bill Seeds. I was not as audacious in my thinking as some of the other scientists on the trail of the DNA structure, but I was going in the right direction.

I was quite right in thinking that fibres of Signer DNA would help us to understand DNA structure. But I soon found a very peculiar thing about the fibres. They did not stretch uniformly. When I applied tension to them they suddenly gave way, and a long neck pulled out until the fibre was almost twice as long. The stretching process took place at a shoulder that was between the stretched and unstretched parts, and during stretching, the shoulder travelled along the fibre. When I examined the stretched and unstretched parts of a fibre with a polarizing microscope, I found that the flat bases in the DNA, which were normally at right angles to the fibre length, had lined up along the length of the fibre as it stretched. This reminded me of my student days when I had learned that some protein fibres can be stretched and the chemical groups in the protein rearrange themselves. It had amused me that permanent waving of hair depended on such a change: when α-keratin changes to β-keratin. But DNA was much more exciting than the hair on our heads. Could the strange flipping of structure in DNA fibres tell us something important about genes?

I had just got to this stage when Francis Crick sent me a note that he and his French wife Odile were coming down from Cambridge and they would like to visit me in the strange Soho flat that Francis had found for me. I was very glad to hear from Francis but I wrote 'We were on the trail working "til we drop".' Bruce Fraser, a research student in our infra-red spectroscopic group, was making infra-red studies of the structure. But it would be good if they came for dinner, and it would be good too if they brought 'some nice young woman' to prevent Francis and me talking about science all the evening and boring Odile. I was happy with the idea that they bring someone, as I was trying hard to find someone to marry. And I very much enjoyed the company of Odile, who was artistic and interesting company (I had no wish to try to separate her from Francis).

As far as I remember, Francis did not visit me then, and by the time I saw him we were disappointed that the stretched DNA gave only a weak, diffuse X-ray diffraction pattern, which meant that DNA was not like keratin, and stretched DNA was an irregular muddle. Others have tried since to understand stretched DNA, and no-one has been able to clarify its structure.

It was not easy for us to follow up the invitation the DNA seemed to be offering. Randall had had plans at St Andrews to buy X-ray equipment for studying diffraction from sperm, but such research was not on his 1947 MRC programme for King's. As a result, the only X-ray equipment we had was an ordinary diffraction camera designed for routine study of single crystals that were much larger than our tiny fibres. Indeed, Randall seemed to have forgotten about X-ray work until 1950, when he asked his student Raymond Gosling to take some patterns 'to complement the studies' of sperm he was making with his electron microscope. I was friendly with Raymond and had tried to help him because he only got poor diffraction patterns from the sperm. He asked me for some Signer DNA for comparison, but smeared lumps of DNA only gave diffuse patterns. He was very glad to try DNA fibres instead, but the fibres were so thin that they would diffract X-rays only very little. I therefore made a little frame of tungsten wire (which I knew well from my Berkeley days – it is the wire used for the filament in light bulbs, and is used hot in physics experiments) and, after a struggle, I managed, with watchmakers' tweezers and quick-setting glue, to stick a dozen or so fibres fairly parallel across the frame. I was not very patient – Astbury had once got a research student to line up several thousand tiny chromosomes for X-ray study, but their results were not encouraging. Our results, however, from the dozen DNA fibres on the wire frame were very promising.

It was very fortunate indeed that Randall had learnt at GEC that weak diffraction could be seen much better when the air in the camera, which scattered the X-rays, was replaced by the very light gas hydrogen. That was a very important new tactic, but making the camera hold in the hydrogen was not at all easy. It was impossible to seal the bottom of the camera, but we sealed the top with Plasticine and fed hydrogen in at the top, hoping that, being very light, it would displace the air downwards (I had done hydrogen arc-welding that way). Another difficulty was that the X-rays entered the camera at the side through a tube that had to fit loosely so that its position could be adjusted. But I found that part of a condom made a good flexible seal (and that seemed to amuse people). Our apparatus could be seen either as a real bodge-up or a brilliant improvisation. The important thing was to get some results.

The key factor leading to our success was the feeling, which I had picked up from working with live tissue culture, that DNA should not be treated as though it were inert and non-living. DNA was a sensitive part of living things, and its structure would depend on how it interacted with its environment. While we bombarded the DNA with destructive X-rays we should at least do our best to keep it, so to speak, in as healthy a condition as possible. Signer had taken great care in preparing his DNA and we should expose it to the gentlest treatment possible. I had noted that when DNA fibres were kept in moist air they swelled and the ultraviolet-light-absorbing groups lined up to the greatest extent. I remembered too, from my student days, that Bernal had obtained the first really sharp X-ray diffraction patterns from protein crystals by keeping them in the 'mother liquor' out of which they had grown – which made it sound almost as though they were alive. I was impressed too that when Honor Fell looked at the cells she was culturing so carefully, she spoke of them as her 'little dears', which nicely expressed her care and respect for living things. Her great success in tissue culturing derived from her sensitivity to the subtle needs of the cells she fostered – she was like a gardener with green fingers. Such thoughts led me to believe that the fibres being X-rayed should be carefully preserved in a moist atmosphere of hydrogen. They should certainly not be allowed to dry or be treated with alcohol as some workers had done – all of them had failed to get the results they had hoped for.

Keeping these points in mind, Raymond and I very soon obtained diffraction patterns of DNA that were much sharper and more detailed than any before. X-ray diffraction pictures are not like medical X-rays in which one's bones are clear for all to see: instead, they tend to show patterns of spots from which the internal structure of the subject can be inferred by a lengthy sequence of calculations. But the more regular the structure, the sharper the diffraction pattern will be. The pictures Raymond and I took consisted of dozens of well-defined spots on a clear background, which was a very good result: it showed us clearly, for the first time, that DNA was truly crystalline, and we could be very hopeful that its structure could be derived from X-ray patterns. The great community spirit and co-operation in our lab had produced this valuable result. I had discovered the extra-ordinary properties of the Signer DNA fibres; Raymond was building up experience of X-ray diffraction; and Randall had recommended replacing the air in the camera with hydrogen to make the patterns much clearer. Thanks to all these contributions, Signer's excellent pristine DNA was, so to speak, shouting at us, 'Look how regular I am!' On the other hand, we knew genes had to be very complicated and therefore DNA had to be complicated. That paradox presented us with a very important challenge in our thinking about the structure and function of DNA.

Meanwhile, having swollen the DNA with water to form a regular structure, we also removed the water in stages and observed the structure crumpling and the regularity fading away. One advantage of the big, unwieldy camera was that it had room in it for the steam-heated box that I had designed to surround the DNA. In that way we were able to dry the DNA thoroughly and to follow how its regularity decreased. When completely dried, the only diffraction from the DNA was from the holes that had been previously been filled with water. I did not publish these preliminary results and interpretations, and they were published three years later by Raymond and his new supervisor, Rosalind Franklin.

Raymond was good-natured and full of jokes and fun. As a young research student who had made a slow start, he must have been very cheered when the work went well. We would often work late in the long summer evenings. The war-surplus X-ray tube soon burnt out, but the Chemistry Department had a big

Raymax set that they let us use. It was deep in their basement, below the level of the Thames, and to get there we had to walk through long passages in the dark. But before going down the stairs we passed a window looking across the Thames, where I liked to catch a glimpse of a big illuminated sign that spelled out 'OXO' in bright lights high on a tower. I liked the OXO sign (which is still a part of the Thames skyline opposite King's) because it made me think of the popular brand of Oxo gravy; but it also had a dramatic impact on me like that from the lights flashing in the sky in a production of the dance *Le Jeune Homme et la Mort* that I had recently seen. I had been disturbed when I had watched the energetic, healthy young dancer (in that pre–AIDS era) being pursued by Death; but possibly the dance reminded me that not long before I, an energetic young scientist, after my divorce, had sometimes had the idea of suicide flitting through my mind. Fortunately, I had grown to feel more positive about life, and had been encouraged by DNA reacting, so to speak, in a friendly way to our scientific enquiries. I would have felt even more positive if I had known then that the big X in OXO presaged the famous X pattern that would appear in our X-ray photographs of DNA, and provide a crucial clue to its structure.

Raymond and I often worked late into the night, and after those long days he would give me a lift home on the pillion of his motorbike. That was invariably rather scary; but I much enjoyed our hilarious times together.

By 1950, X-ray diffraction had only provided fibre structures of fairly simple polymers. No fibre as complicated as DNA had been solved, and there was almost nothing to guide us. We went to the ICI laboratory, where they were developing synthetic fibres to make textiles, and met the chemist C.W. Bunn, who was the leading figure in X-ray studies of fibres. He tried hard to help us, but his polymers were so much simpler and clearer than DNA and he had little advice to give. He did, however, suggest that we looked for double orientation in the fibres. Such an effect would be given by lop-sided molecules and would help to separate over-lapping diffraction. We did not find that effect.

One advance at that time was made by Raymond who, with our colleague the physicist Alec Stokes, measured the position of all the spots on the DNA pattern and deduced that the DNA molecules were in a monoclinic crystalline arrangement (that is, skewed in one direction only). Raymond confirmed that the molecules packed together along the length of the fibre as cylinders, like a stack of pipes, as I had inferred. Stokes then came up with an enormously important idea. He had experience of diffraction from zig-zag and helical structures when we had been studying virus crystals. I knew that chromosomes, which were largely DNA, were often spiralized, that is they had well-defined helical forms. Stokes, pondering on the DNA pattern, noticed that there was no diffraction in directions on, or close to, the fibre direction, and he realized that this absence of diffraction suggested that DNA might be helical. Knowing about chromosomes, I was very interested in Stokes' helical idea. We were so much at sea with the problem of interpreting the DNA pattern that we felt it was very important to consider any simplifying hypothesis, and the helical idea seemed very useful indeed.

While we were in some respects uncertain about how to proceed, we were very clear that we must pass out of the stage of preliminary experiment with a borrowed generator and a 'bodged-up' camera. Being in a Physics Department, we paid special attention to having good physical equipment. We had to obtain equipment that was suitable for the particular type of work we needed to do. We considered a rotating anode X-ray generator to give a very powerful beam, but decided instead to use a new, fine-focus X-ray tube, designed by the brilliant Werner Ehrenberg and Walter Spear of Birkbeck College, which was designed to concentrate X-rays on very small specimens. I felt that we should work with micro-specimens consisting of only one fibre, or only a small number, selected for uniformity and perfection of crystallinity using a polarizing microscope. A special micro-camera would be needed. In that way we would be much better equipped for DNA work than most long established X-ray labs. More and more of my time was being spent on X-ray diffraction and DNA. My microscope work was less and less on living cells, and was becoming more of an aid to the X-ray work. My rather cold attitude to X-ray diffraction was disappearing as I studied gene structure.

I also thought that we needed more staff on DNA, especially an experienced X-ray worker. By the summer of 1950 I knew that Randall had appointed a new X-ray specialist to work on protein solutions. Her name was Rosalind Franklin, and she had been working in Paris studying the structure of coals. She had no experience of really crystalline materials, but was an expert in X-ray techniques. Protein solutions seemed to me an unpromising field and, since the DNA work had gone so very well, I thought Randall might agree to Rosalind being transferred to DNA. Generally I had difficulty persuading Randall to change his decisions, but when I saw him I was surprised that he agreed very readily to my suggestion, with merely the proviso that Rosalind would have to be consulted about the change. Randall wrote to her, outlining a new programme of work, and I heard that she had agreed to it.

I was away from King's when Rosalind arrived, on holiday with my new friend Edel Lange. She was the very beautiful *au pair* to my painter friends, the Dachingers, and she came often to my Soho flat. Our relationship soon became very close. I was surprised to find that her father was the Lange whose name I had heard in my pre-War luminescence days: he had developed photovoltaic cells. Before returning to the lab after Christmas 1950 I had taken Edel on a short holiday in the Welsh mountains. The mild winter sun shone clearly on the peaks covered with snow. We had fine walks, and in the evenings we read Jane Austen together. The beautiful atmosphere seemed to clarify my thoughts, and I remember very well how, one morning after breakfast, I stood looking at the mountains in the distance and thoughts of research drifted into my mind. I suddenly came to see that my interest in following with microscopes the movements of

DNA in cells was based on vague ideas. What were we really aiming at? I could see no way in which my fascination with microscopes and living cells could lead to a meaningful programme of research. I had been dragged into reflecting microscope work because Randall thought my telescope background would help. It had helped; my work was respected and I had a very successful and pleasant team; but I saw that I should now concentrate on my initial interest: genes. And, as a physicist, how could I do that better than by concentrating on the X-ray study of DNA? I had to face that – it came to me clear and strong, and my mind was made up. I must give up completely the microscope work and concentrate full time on X-ray structure analysis of DNA.

While I was away, Rosalind Franklin had taken up her new post at King's. Randall had held a routine staff meeting with Rosalind, Stokes and Raymond to discuss the DNA research. I was interested to discover what kind of person Rosalind was, and as soon as I got back I went to our basement where she was temporarily located. Our new building in the bomb crater was not quite ready and she had not yet been moved with Raymond into the nice big room with large windows that Randall had used as Head of Department. I had arranged for Raymond to work with Rosalind because I thought that as a research student he should be supervised by an X-ray expert. It also seemed sensible that Rosalind should be put in the picture as soon as possible, and Raymond was well qualified to do that. The big room was somewhat separate from our new main lab, but Randall and I had felt that Rosalind and Raymond would have peace and quiet there for making the laborious calculations, involving a system of cards, that were necessary, in those pre-computer days, for turning the patterns on X-ray diffraction photographs into the three-dimensional structures of molecules.

When I found Rosalind in the basement, she was sitting with her back to me at a desk in a corner of a poky little room. When she turned round, I saw that she was quietly handsome with steady, watchful, dark eyes; but, more importantly, as we discussed research it was clear that she knew what she was talking about. She gave an impression of quiet confidence. After we had talked for a while she stood up, and I was a little surprised that she was not quite as tall as I had expected. Possibly that was due to her appearing somewhat authoritative. I suppose we were both trying to size each other up. Another time, when I stood talking at the door of her room, she rather brusquely beckoned me into the room so that she did not need to turn in her chair. She gave me the impression that she was a little tense, but I was confident that she would make a good colleague – for four years men and women had joined our staff and all had fitted in, except the bright if dreamy young student Margaret Preston, who wanted to save humanity and so became a nurse. Rosalind, however, did one thing I had not noticed other women do in our lab: she placed a small mirror on the wall so that it faced her as she sat at her desk. It seemed too small to allow her to see who was behind her at the office door, and at the time I wondered whether she was anxious about her appearance.

Rosalind told me that before she could begin working on DNA, she had to finish writing up some research on coal that she

15 Birmingham University Luminescence Laboratory: 1939 (with a sloping ceiling, under the seats of the lecture theatre).

16 Laboratory sketch by Maurice. The strange creatures in the air are ideas.

17   Ruth.

18   Berkeley: the Magnetron team,
      August 1945. Maurice is fifth
      from the left.

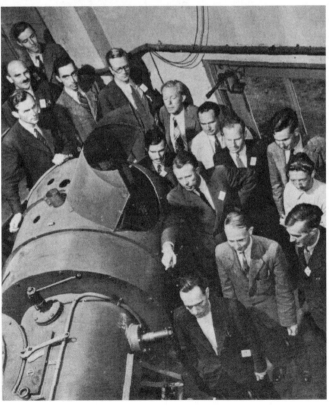

19 Excavating the quadrangle at King's College for the new Wheatstone Physics Laboratory. This major expansion of physics at King's was achieved by John (later Sir John) Randall following his appointment as Wheatstone Professor in 1946 and allowed, with support from the MRC and the Rockefeller Foundation, the development of a unique Biophysics Research Unit. The excavators completed what a German Second World War bomb had begun, providing a cavity large enough for a building on two floors.

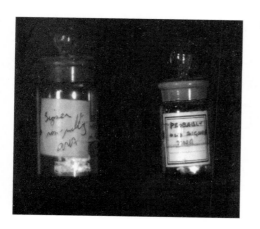

20 Two bottles containing DNA used in the X-ray work in the early 1950s by Wilkins and Gosling and by Franklin and Gosling. The DNA supplied by Rudolf Signer gave particularly well oriented fibres. The DNA is the white fibrous material in the lower part of the bottles.

21　Phillips micro camera used in the early 1950s for recording X-ray diffraction patterns from fibres of DNA. X-rays entered the camera through a central pin hole in the front face of the camera. The flat film was located on a holder at the back of the camera and the pipe at the top right of the camera allowed humidified gas to be passed through the camera to control the water content of the fibre.

22　Cylindrical camera used in the 1950s for recording an X-ray diffraction pattern from a fibre of DNA. The pattern is recorded on photographic film inserted on the inside of the cylinder and the fibre is mounted on a goniometer at the centre of the cylinder. The vertical central axis of the cylinder is at right angles to the X-ray beam which is about 0.1 mm in diameter. The humidified gas (originally hydrogen, but from the early nineteen sixties helium) is passed through the cylinder to avoid air scattering and to control the water content of the fibre.

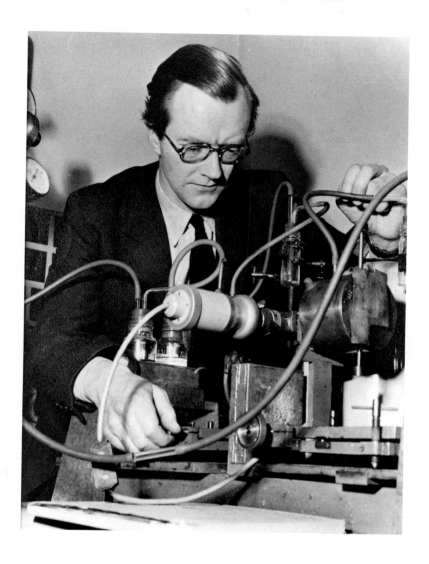

23   Maurice adjusting the position of an X-ray camera to maximize the intensity of the X-rays incident on the specimen. This camera was one of a number constructed in the King's workshops in the mid-1950s. The rubber pipe in the foreground carries humidified gas from the humidifying bottles in front of Maurice's right hand to the camera. A piece of lead has been placed on the back of the camera to absorb the part of the incident X-ray beam not scattered by the DNA fibre.

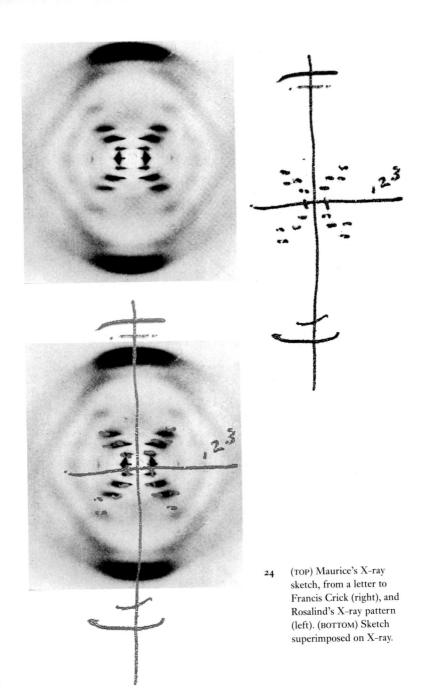

24   (TOP) Maurice's X-ray sketch, from a letter to Francis Crick (right), and Rosalind's X-ray pattern (left). (BOTTOM) Sketch superimposed on X-ray.

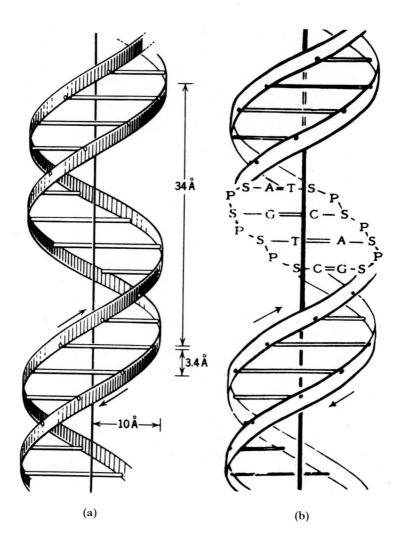

34 Å

3.4 Å

10 Å

P–S–A=T–S–P
P–S—G≡C—S–P
P–S—T=A–S–P
P–S–C≡G–S–P

(a)   (b)

25 Diagram based on the figure in the original paper by Watson and Crick describing
the DNA double helix showing the essential features and dimensions of the DNA
double helix i.e. the two sugar-phosphate chains running in opposite directions
linked together through hydrogen bonded base-pairs stacked on top of each other.
The separation of the base-pairs is 3.4 Å and there are 10 base-pairs per helix pitch
of 34 Å. In (b) A, C, G, T, S and P refer respectively to the bases adenine, cytosine,
guanine and thymine and to the sugar and phosphate groups.

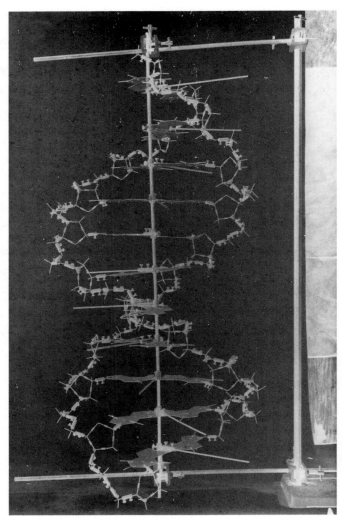

26 Wire model of the DNA double helix in which the base-pairs are represented by flat metal plates with wires representing the bonds to atoms in the sugar-phosphate chain. Atoms in the sugar-phosphate chain are represented by intersecting wires where the point of intersection represents the centre of the atom and the directions and lengths of the wires represent the covalent bonds formed when they are linked to other atoms by barrel connectors. The 5-atom sugar rings can be readily seen. Models of this type were used by Watson and Crick in their representation of the original double helical model of DNA and were used extensively in the mid-1950s at King's in the refinement of the original Watson and Crick model to account for the detailed X-ray data recorded from fibres of DNA.

had been doing in her previous job in Paris. That kind of tidying-up was quite usual when a scientist moved from one lab to another, and I did not have the impression that Rosalind's writing would take long. I was writing a short paper with Raymond entitled 'Nucleic Acid – An Extensible Molecule?' In this paper, we described how our DNA stretched, changing from one length to another as a shoulder passed along the fibre. We said that this suggested that the bases in the DNA molecule were perpendicular to the length of the molecule, and that they slid across each other and tilted so that they were parallel to the length of the molecule in the stretched DNA. We published this alongside Bruce Fraser's account of his infra-red studies on DNA, where he described various bonds in the atomic structure of the DNA molecule. I acknowledged discussion with Rosalind in my paper – she was fully informed about what we had done. Having got that paper off to the editor of *Nature*, I began to study more thoroughly how DNA fibres lengthened and swelled as they absorbed water. We thought that the ways in which the fibre changed when it was wet might tell us more about its structure, and help us to make sense of the X-ray results.

Because Rosalind did not begin DNA work straight away, we did not at first spend much time discussing it. I saw her mainly on Saturdays when a fair number of biophysics staff, especially those who were unmarried, came in to do research. Edel generally worked on Saturdays, and I would stroll through Soho buying food at Italian family grocers and then settle down mid-morning in the peace and quiet of our largely empty laboratory. Those of us who continued their work in the afternoon went to lunch together at the Strand Palace Hotel, just along the street from King's towards Trafalgar Square, where there was a good, inexpensive buffet. Rosalind often worked on Saturdays, and would join in the lunch. Geoffrey Brown and others were often there, but sometimes Rosalind and I were the only two. Our discussion was fairly general, and we talked about various topics other than science. I can remember little of the detail of our conversations, except that I was very interested in what Rosalind said about Neutralism. I was not keeping up with political thinking, but after my Bomb experience I was very concerned about the threat of nuclear war. I think Rosalind had read about Neutralism in *The New Statesman*, or had heard about it in Paris. It was clearly silly to think that neutral Britain would be unharmed if nuclear weapons were to fly over us *en route* to the USSR or the USA, but the idea of not taking sides in the Cold War seemed well worth looking into. I found Rosalind pleasant to talk to but occasionally a small spikiness would show. For example, after we had eaten fruit salad and cream, I remarked that the cream had been good. Rosalind replied coldly, 'But it was not real cream.' I was amused but said nothing, not having had the advantage of living in post-war Paris where food was not rationed as it had been in Britain. I seemed to have forgotten what real cream was like.

I did not feel there was any great meeting of minds in those discussions over lunch on Saturdays, but looking back now I realize that apart from very bright young Geoffrey, Rosalind had a greater breadth of interest than any of my colleagues, especially those in my own age-group. I knew then almost nothing about Rosalind's family, but I realize now that her background was very similar to mine – broad interests in education, culture and social justice. Rosalind's father was much occupied at the Working Men's College founded by F.D. Maurice, who had close links with my family. Apart from religion – the Franklins were Jewish while the Wilkinses were non-conformist Christians – there was little difference between our families, except that my family might be seen as more dedicated than hers to higher education for women. Most of my friends then were non-scientists, but if I had wanted a friend of about my own age in the laboratory, I realize now that the interests I shared with Rosalind could have encouraged such a friendship. My rather juvenile attitude towards women caused me to seek special liveliness in beauty, spirit or artistic interests, specially in 'shy young women' (as Eithne called them), and that for me ruled out any romantic interest in Rosalind. In any case my interests were fairly heavily occupied by Edel, whom I visited that summer at her family home in Berlin.

Stokes had got the new fine-focus X-ray source working by the autumn of 1950, but Rosalind, as the incoming experimental expert, was to carry out our plan of attaching to the new source a camera suitable for small fibres of DNA, or even for a single, selected fibre. At first, over the range of swelling I used, the increase in fibre diameter and length happened to be the same, and I thought that the swelling might not correspond to changes in molecular structure. My caution may have derived from my over-optimism about my stretched DNA – doing science requires a subtle combination of caution and optimism. Later, I increased the hydration and found that the fibre diameter increased greatly as more water went between the molecules, but the length of the fibres would not increase beyond about 20 or 30%. When I had only preliminary humidity data for DNA in our adapted camera, I was led in the wrong direction by the swelling results and I began to push the idea that DNA consisted of only one helical chain (which would have been sufficient to contain all the genes). Rosalind was able to demolish that idea as soon as she began using a proper camera. She then showed that the lengthening of the DNA fibres was the same as the increase in the periodicity of the diffraction pattern. Neither she nor I nor Stokes realized how the lengthening of the DNA molecule and of the whole fibre were related, though with hindsight it all seems so obvious. The change of fibre length resulted from the helices of DNA partially uncoiling and lengthening. When that was recognized, it would turn out to be an important step towards the DNA structure.

I was occupied for some weeks with swelling DNA. Rosalind had given me helpful advice about how to ensure that the hydrogen gas we used inside the camera was thoroughly humidified by salt solutions. This was important for keeping the atmosphere moist around the fibres. I had been reluctant to use salt solutions because spray might be carried over to the fibres, and I knew that salts could have big effects on DNA (later work confirmed this very strongly). Rosalind knew the best salts to use for various humidities, and in spite of difficulties from spray she was right to urge use of salts. This was a very helpful contribution to our DNA studies.

After Rosalind had been in our lab a couple of months or so, I was puzzled that she still had not begun work on DNA. She told me that she would soon be finished writing up her Paris research, and I should not worry about the DNA work because she was a quick worker. By Easter she was busy rebuilding the X-ray set with the fine-focus Ehrenberg X-ray tube that had been set up by Stokes and Raymond. Also she tried using the special X-ray equipment she had used in Paris, but she found it unsuited for DNA work.

I was very lucky in the spring of 1951: Randall asked me to go in his place to two important conferences abroad, one in Italy and one in the USA. I could make very helpful new contacts with outstanding scientists, and collect important new material for X-ray study – it was all very encouraging. The first conference was at Naples, where I was very glad to find a special beauty associated with science. This aspect of science had been very important for me: when I began my research before the War, I chose luminescence in crystals because I saw beauty in the light, in the forms of crystals, and in the strange elegance of the quantum mechanics of electrons moving in crystals. (Elegance was never apparent in my laboratory which, like many labs, was muddled and disorderly.) The Naples Stazione Zoologica was unusual in its display of beauty. I had left London in the famous Blue Train to Italy and I had felt sad as I left behind the green Kent woods with the bluebells in their prime. But the beauty of Naples was a very encouraging surprise. The Stazione had big windows and balconies so that visiting scientists could admire the view of Vesuvius and the Bay of Naples. Inside the Stazione was a splendid collection of living creatures out of the Mediterranean, and some stunning specimens were displayed in an underground aquarium: the flashing lights and changing colours were extraordinary. Upstairs, the Stazione library was well lit and packed with scientific tomes, and it was sometimes enlivened by performances of chamber music. The beauty of the young women in Naples was breathtaking – I was reminded once again of my feelings as a teenager when I was fascinated by a beautiful girl who came briefly to live next door.

I had planned to use my visit to Naples to collect sperm from *Sepia*, one of the squid family. The sperm had heads composed largely of DNA molecules arranged parallel and close together. Bruno Baltaglia, a skilful zoologist, very helpfully brought me a tank full of *Sepia* and extracted sperm from them. The *Sepia* were very strange looking creatures, but it was a joy to watch, through a microscope, myriads of scintillating sperm swimming together in large groups. It reminded me of how I was inspired as a schoolboy when I watched through my homemade telescopes the beauty of a myriad of stars, and was filled with wonder at seeing so far into space. In contrast to my solitary wonder as a boy, I had a very good opportunity at the Stazione to share my experiences with the community of scientists in the lab. The Director, Rheinhardt Dohrn, looked in on the progress of his visitors, and I reported on the good progress made with Bruno's help. I also mentioned that I was not very happy to see, in contrast to the beauty of the birefringent sperm with their DNA lined up, the very strange, rather ugly appearance of the *Sepia* themselves. Rheinhardt Dohrn, tall and dignified, replied with much wisdom and consideration for a newcomer to his lab. He spent some time helping me to see the beauty in the strange animals. It was quite an education: presumably he felt that recognizing beauty in the creatures would help me to respect them. I formed a special friendship with Rheinhardt's son Peter, who helped with running the Stazione: he had very broad interests in art and science and had somewhat wild spirits like my father.

At the Conference I spoke about several topics, but I think that the high point was showing the first really clear crystalline X-ray pattern of DNA that I had produced with Raymond Gosling. The pattern spoke for itself. I was glad that Bill Astbury was there, who had pioneered X-ray work on DNA: he seemed genuinely warm when he said our pattern was much better than anything he had got. I was very glad to meet him because he seemed a real human being. He liked making little jokes: for example, he published an X-ray study with 'boiled eggs' in the title which was literally true but sounded like a joke. My friend, the Cambridge chemist John Kendrew, told me he got to know Astbury best over a bottle of whiskey when Astbury discussed his love of playing the violin.

In Naples I also met Jim Watson, a young scientist from Chicago. He had trained as a zoologist, and had a keen interest in genetics. He had recently completed his PhD at Indiana University in Bloomington, where he was very much influenced by Herman Muller – the geneticist whose work had been recommended to me by Charlotte Auerbach at Edinburgh University, and who had produced mutations using X-rays. Another key figure for Watson was Salvador Luria, a microbiologist. Luria had supervised Watson's thesis, which was a study of the effect of X-rays on the reproduction of bacteriophage. Bacteriophages are viruses that infect bacteria. They are inactive until they meet a bacterium, when they bind to its surface, break through the cell wall and inject their own genetic material. This material makes the bacterium reproduce the bacteriophage, and the new virus can infect further bacteria. The process involves a good deal of DNA, and seemed to be one that might be a good basis for studies of genetics. Luria was a close colleague of the physicist Max Delbrück, who, like me, had started thinking about biology during the war. Delbrück had been a student of Niels Bohr, who had encouraged him to think about the physics and chemistry of biological systems. He and Luria ran a series of courses and summer schools on bacteriophage biology at the California Institute of Technology and at the Cold Spring Harbor Laboratory on the opposite coast of the USA, and Watson was a member of their group. He was very excited about my presentation when I showed our photographs that showed that DNA was crystalline, and he decided to work on the structural chemistry of nucleic acids and proteins. Later that summer Luria was able to arrange with John Kendrew for Watson to work at the Cavendish Laboratory in Cambridge, and he started research there in October 1951. But at the Naples conference, I did not understand much of what Watson had to say. He talked to me about genes and viruses, but I did not know much about bacteriophages and could not make much sense of what he was telling me. Watson was one among many interesting new people at this exciting conference, and I did not spend much time with him. His sister was with him, but I do not remember seeing her – in any case, I was somewhat intoxicated by all the beauty around me! Later on, in calmer environments, I was to find Jim Watson very clear and interesting.

CHAPTER 6

——◆◆◆——

GO BACK TO YOUR MICROSCOPES!

The prospects of our DNA X-ray work brightened as summer began. At Naples I had been encouraged by Astbury's warm response to our crystalline DNA pattern, and by my success in making X-ray specimens with sperm heads all lined up. Back in London, it was good that Rosalind had begun reconstructing our new X-ray equipment. While waiting for that, I made do with the old set-up we had used a year before for our breakthrough in understanding the crystallinity of DNA. I began thinking about the basic biological importance of the DNA pattern, and wondered if the structure of Signer DNA (which was made from calf thymus glands, sold as sweetbreads by butchers) was basically the same as that of DNA in other living things. Was there just one universal gene structure? If so, our sharp Signer pattern could have a very wide (and big) significance. Mary Nicholls in our lab had extracted DNA from humans and herrings as well as calves, and I decided to compare the diffraction from her DNA with that from the DNA from the *Sepia* sperm that I had brought back from Naples. I found that none of the new DNA would form beautiful Signer-type fibres, but by smearing and stretching I lined up the DNA sufficiently to give rough patterns.

I was very encouraged to find that DNA from the various sources all gave patterns that were basically the same. That could be very significant biologically; and it could mean that structure work would be much simpler than with proteins, which had very many different kinds of structure from one species to another. Also, although the patterns were very diffuse and rather different from the sharp Signer pattern, it was exciting that they all showed fairly clearly a central X. That feature, as Stokes had urged, was a strong sign of a helix. It fitted in well with his first idea that absence of diffraction along the length of the crystalline DNA fibre indicated a helix. I discussed these results in a talk I gave in Cambridge in July 1951, at a meeting of protein X-ray workers organized by Max Perutz (I had reported our results on the stretched Signer DNA fibres there a year earlier). Bill Seeds came with me, and sat in the back row with Francis Crick while I described how it seemed that all DNA had the same unique, universal structure which was twisted regularly into a helix. We were thinking in a new way – in terms of the overall shape of the molecule rather than, as Astbury had, in terms of the periodic sequence of its chemical components. The angle of the X on the patterns was about 45°, and that was the angle of ascent of the helix (like the slope of a spiral staircase). The sharp Signer pattern gave the diameter of the staircase as 20Å, and the distance ascended in one turn was about 27Å (Å stands for ångströms – there are one hundred million ångströms in one millimetre). The *Sepia* sperm pattern showed that we were looking at the structure of living DNA. Everything fitted together; and if DNA really had the simplicity of a helix it might enormously simplify the problem of finding the complete structure. But I did not at that stage dare to suggest that the elucidation of the structure might tell us how genes worked; in fact, I barely dared to think such thoughts – one thing at a time was enough for me. But the new results certainly made me more committed than ever to pushing on with DNA X-ray work.

My talk provided a coherent story. Jerry Oster said that a scientific lecture needed to tell a story, and, like a theatre performance, the clapping at the end was a measure of its success. I was clapped; and later in the tea queue, I heard Perutz say to the man next to him that my talk had been interesting, and I was embarrassed that he might turn round and see that I had overheard him. I had an extra satisfaction in giving my talk: 15 years earlier, as a first-year student, I had listened in that same lecture theatre to the great Rutherford giving lectures on physics (though I do not remember comparing myself to Rutherford!). However, as I left the building I found a surprise waiting for me. Rosalind Franklin came up to me and announced, quietly and firmly, that I should stop doing X-ray work. She concluded with the instruction: 'Go back to your microscopes!'.

I was shocked and bewildered. I had just reported encouraging progress. Why should she want me to stop? What right had she to tell me what I should do? Could she not see that the new progress would contribute to her work as well as to mine? I had never met such a negative reaction in my whole career – apart from the awful time when I had walked into a lab at King's and was angrily turned out by a professor who was (I was told afterwards) doing an illegal experiment on a live cat. I knew that there had been high tension at Birmingham after Randall and Boot had invented their epoch-making magnetron, but otherwise the research labs I had known had seemed, on the whole, to have been suffused with a spirit of enlightenment and comradeship. Rosalind's approach filled me with disbelief and shock. She had been in our lab for more than six months, and I had found her friendly enough, apart from sometimes being a little sharp with her tongue. She seemed a high-principled, civilized person. I felt that there might be something about my talk (possibly its success) that had disturbed her; but I did not know how to discuss her new attitude. I do not think we had any discussion then; I only remember that Rosalind wanted me to stop X-ray work. Then, after a day or two, I began to wonder whether I had taken what she had said too seriously, and that if I took no notice the crisis might simply blow away and things might become normal again. But that was not to be.

Rosalind's upset after my talk derived from a letter that Randall had written to her shortly before she came to our lab, outlining the change that I had suggested in her programme of work, from proteins to DNA. I had heard that Rosalind had agreed to the change, but I did not see the letter itself until many years later, when it was found among her papers after her untimely death from cancer at the age of only 37, and after Randall had retired. This letter made clear why Rosalind had believed I would leave X-ray work – a belief I had inadvertently reinforced by missing Rosalind's first staff meeting at which Randall had discussed DNA research with her, Stokes and Raymond. I was confident of my position in the lab and I did not think for a moment that any harm could come from my not having been at the meeting. However, years later, Raymond told me that his impression was that the meeting without me had indeed obscured my role in the X-ray work. As I was eventually to find out, Randall had told Rosalind, in her letter of appointment, that Stokes and I were leaving X-ray work, and my absence had only served to confirm that view. Thus the relationship between me and Rosalind began on an extremely unfortunate basis, thanks to Randall's letter. Dated 4 December 1950, it read as follows:

> *After careful consideration and discussion with the senior people concerned, it now seems it would be a good deal more important for you to investigate the structure of certain biological fibres in which we are interested, by both low and high angle diffraction, rather than continue with the original project of work on solutions as the major one.*

That was in line with our agreement that Rosalind should work on DNA and drop protein solutions. Although it was I who had persuaded Randall to switch Rosalind to DNA, and was the key person involved in the X-ray work as well as being Assistant Director of the MRC Unit, I was not mentioned in the letter, except to introduce Raymond Gosling, who had got good results working 'in conjunction with Wilkins'. Also, Stokes, who had been very effective in our X-ray work, was swept from the scene:

> *Dr. Stokes, as I have long inferred, really wishes to concern himself almost entirely with theoretical problems in the future and these will not necessarily be confined to X-ray optics. It will probably involve microscopy in general. This means that as far as the experimental X-ray effort is concerned there will be at the moment only yourself and Gosling, together with the temporary assistance of a graduate from Syracuse .... Gosling, working in conjunction with Wilkins, has already found that fibres of desoxyribose nucleic acid derived from material provided by Professor Signer of Bern gives remarkably good fibre diagrams. The fibres are strongly negatively birefringent and become positive on stretching, and are reversible in a moist atmosphere. As you no doubt know, nucleic acid is an extremely important constituent of cells and it seems to us that it would be very valuable if this could be followed up in detail. If you are agreeable to this change ....*

Randall has written that it was he and not I who suggested the change. Possibly he had decided the change was desirable before I raised the matter with him. He seems to have wished to be closer to the DNA work: it was clearly implied that Rosalind would be responsible for continuing it, and Randall may have hoped to achieve that closer link with Rosalind since she was directly responsible to him as Head of the Physics Department, whereas I was Assistant Director of the MRC Unit and only loosely attached to the Department. That Randall intended to manoeuvre me out of the work was amply confirmed by a correspondence we had the following summer, 1951, while I was at the Gordon Conference in the USA, when he advised me that the MRC had expressed the view that I should concentrate on microscope work.

To get a proper view of Randall's attitudes that underlay his letter I should emphasize that he quite frequently complained to his staff that they did not recognize the extent to which their success in research depended on his giving a great deal of time and energy to building up the laboratory and, as a result, depriving himself of time to do research. He was quite open about that. This passion to be personally involved in experimental science and in DNA structure in particular was an important factor in his strange behaviour. Randall had written a book on X-ray diffraction while he was at GEC, and then in 1941, during his radar work, he received a letter from a young geneticist, Horace Barber, who was also working on radar. Barber wrote enthusiastically about *Sepia* sperm, which he thought would be interesting to study with X-ray diffraction (Barber's two-page letter was one of the few I found in Randall's great pile of papers at Churchill College, Cambridge after he died). When, after the War, Randall began his biophysics venture at St Andrew's, it had been envisaged that Barber would collect *Sepia* sperm at the Plymouth Marine Biology Station and bring them up to St Andrew's. But Barber had decided to build a post-war career in Australian universities. Randall told me nothing about Barber until Rosalind came to King's, which is understandable given that Barber's disappearance to Australia was a shock and disappointment for Randall. Both he and Barber knew a leading British geneticist, C.D. Darlington, who had been at Niels Bohr's pre-War meeting where the idea of studying the molecular structure of genes was likely to have come up. When Raymond and I had got the first clear evidence connecting genes and crystals, Randall for the first time began talking about Barber. It was a peculiar time: every time I happened to meet Randall in the lab, he would tell me yet again how Barber had planned to get *Sepia* sperm. I could understand that he was disappointed by Barber, and probably I should have encouraged him to talk more about it.

Randall's lab, especially in its early years, was rather casual about organizational boundaries: if something exciting came up, we got on with the science and did not pay much attention to what group we were in. Raymond was Randall's research student but was now working with me. Raymond and I, sharing our DNA X-ray triumph, were also getting involved with Randall's personal research with his electron microscope, which he was using to study ram sperm (which did not have its DNA aligned). I had discovered the remarkable properties of Signer DNA with Raymond, and Stokes had opened up the route to helical DNA. Randall, it became clear, wanted me to stay on microscopes and stop invading X-ray diffraction territory. Rosalind had agreed to come to King's to study what seemed to me an uninteresting topic: the denaturation of proteins in solution. When I suggested to Randall that she should work on DNA I was surprised that he agreed unusually quickly. His rapidity had puzzled me, but it seems obvious now that he hoped I would move off X-ray work and he could move in.

It may well be that Randall's idea that I would move away from X-ray work was derived from remarks I had made to him. It is true that I had often said that I found more joy in microscopes and watching living cells, whereas X-ray study of static structures was rather a bore. But I certainly never said to Randall that I was going to give up the DNA X-ray work. Ever since my student days at Cambridge I had been clearly aware of the difficulties in X-ray work and would never, for example, have wanted to join Max Perutz and John Kendrew in years and years of important struggle to define a static structure, as they had to do for their proteins. I certainly expressed such views to Randall. But DNA was not static – it was 'alive', and I felt the life in it in much the same way as I enjoyed the liveliness of electrons in the quantum mechanical structures I had read about when I was a student. Whether I made my feeling about 'dynamic DNA' clear to Randall I do not know, but I always assumed I had.

My opinion is very clear: that Randall was very wrong to have written to Rosalind telling her that Stokes and I wished to stop our X-ray work on DNA, without consulting us. After Raymond and I got a clear crystalline X-ray pattern I was very eager to continue that work, and on holiday had decided that I must continue full-time on DNA X-ray work and stop all other research. If Randall really believed the idea that I did not wish to continue my DNA X-ray research, he had deceived himself – perhaps because *he* so strongly wanted to be involved in DNA research. Randall had enormous enthusiasm for research, and this sometimes led him to be ruthless. He may have kidded himself that he could persuade me to drop out of DNA X-ray work: what would he lose by trying? But how much did Rosalind and I lose by the 'Wilkins and Stokes are leaving' story? If Randall had not barged in it might even have been that Rosalind could have worked happily alongside Stokes and me, and her professional X-ray approach could have combined fruitfully with our techniques and theorizing. In retrospect, my general conclusion is that Randall wished to take over DNA structure work, with Rosalind and Raymond's full-time help. This conclusion is endorsed by Randall's abrupt letter which reached me when I was in Naples, declaring that he would be in direct charge of the sperm X-ray work, and his later claim that the MRC wanted me to concentrate on microscopic work.

Trying to understand 'what really happened' when a very admirable scientist models himself on Napoleon is not easy. Later, when Randall was due to retire, King's College commissioned a portrait of him, and my efforts to understand him were shared by the artist. I told the artist about Randall's enlightened leadership and outstanding determination, and he was very surprised: he said that Randall had seemed to him so frail and uncertain that he was anxious about his ability to attend the next sitting.

All this discussion about what happened when Rosalind moved to King's may seem unnecessarily complex, but it has one very clear message: Randall was not open. His secret letter to

Rosalind was not representative of my relations with him generally – it was very damaging, to her and to me. It was a pity too that Rosalind did not tell me about the letter. It is quite possible that she thought I knew about Randall's letter – after all, I was Assistant Director of Randall's MRC Unit. She may have believed that I was involved in the deception. Scientists, more than people in other occupations, need to be open.

After the shock of 'Go back to your microscopes!' my relations with Rosalind seemed to quieten down and become fairly normal. I was going to a conference in Leicester, and we agreed that Rosalind would give me a slide showing some of her graphical data so that the conference would get some idea of how she was approaching the problem of DNA structure. I was still, after several years, seeing my Jungian analyst (whom I found quite helpful), and he suggested I should invite Rosalind to dinner so that we could get to know each other better. Our routine Saturday lunches at the Strand Palace Hotel had petered out, so we did not have many occasions to relax and get acquainted. I went to see Rosalind on a very warm afternoon, and found her in a large lab where she was busy fitting together the electrical wiring for the Ehrenburg fine-focus X-ray tube. She was sitting on the floor in a labcoat and seemed quite willing to talk. The work must have been hard, for she was sweating in the heat, but she did not seem to mind the very close atmosphere in the lab. In those days before deodorants we were all used to smelling rather bad after some physical exertion, but in the stifling lab I found myself quite unable to imagine sitting down to dinner with

Rosalind that day. I very much admired her hands-on approach to the work, and respected the effort she was making, but I could no longer face the challenge of a sociable evening with her. I seemed to forget that our dinner was meant to be the means to a very worthwhile end: that of developing a better relationship about our research. Instead, I drifted away.

The second conference that I attended in Randall's place that summer was the important Gordon Conference, held every year in pleasant rural New England in the USA. I wondered vaguely whether domestic problems might be preventing Randall going abroad – his wife had persistent health problems – but I now wonder if keeping me away from our lab might have helped him to make contact with Rosalind and DNA. But it was interesting for me to return to the USA for the first time since the War, and to make my first airline flight. Meeting the biochemist Erwin Chargaff, from Columbia University in New York, was the most important event for me. He was very friendly and helpful, and seemed very interested in our X-ray studies of DNA. He had analysed the nitrogen bases in DNA, and had found that of the four bases, guanine was present in the same quantity as cytosine, and adenine in the same quantity as thymine. But he did not suggest that these 1:1 ratios were achieved by pairing, which would be the accepted explanation a few years later. He empha-sized the negative effect of the authority of the American analytical chemist Phoebus Levene, who had argued for decades that DNA could not be gene material because it only contained four bases, which would, he claimed, make it far too simple a compound to contain the genetic information. I think this negative effect of analytic chemistry made Chargaff, who was clearly very intelligent, over-cautious in not suggesting that the bases might be paired. On the other hand, Chargaff had found complex base sequences in DNA, and pointed to this being clear evidence of DNA being the gene material.

Altogether Chargaff impressed me greatly, and, since many biochemists were dismissive of X-ray techniques, I much appreciated his interest in our work. But my considerable respect for Chargaff may have led me to misinterpret his caution about base-pairing. Respecting a scientist can lead to a negative attitude, and I think that was why I was very slow in connecting the 1:1 ratios with base-pairing. Nevertheless, at the Gordon Conference, Chargaff was very helpful indeed in inviting me to his laboratory and giving me specimens of DNA from various sources. The ability of his DNA to form fibres for X-ray study was very encouraging. I was also glad to meet my friend John Kendrew at the conference, and I discussed my problems with Rosalind with him. He said it had not taken him very long to learn X-ray diffraction methods; but that didn't help me because I did not want to carry out X-ray work by myself. DNA needed a group, working together.

Randall had been applying more pressure on me, and it was while I was at the Gordon Conference that I received his letter claiming that our funding agency, the Medical Research Council, wanted me to give up my X-ray studies of DNA. At that time, some members of the MRC committee quite possibly may not have realized how much strong evidence was becoming available that genes were DNA. I replied to Randall while I was in the USA, referring to Chargaff's latest results on the complex sequences of bases in DNA, and other new results strengthening the evidence that genes were DNA. Also I drew attention to Chargaff's having prepared human DNA. Also, since the MRC might prefer me to work on living cells rather than purified chemicals, I pointed out to Randall that I did X-ray studies on *Sepia* sperm. DNA research was beginning to break down the distinction between the living and the non-living, and that made the work hard to classify. But there was so much new data on DNA that I was not worried that the MRC might continue to press me to go back to microscope research.

I returned from the USA very cheerful, very positive and possibly a bit cocky. Important talks with leading DNA people, much interest in what we were doing; it had been very good for my ego. It had been exciting flying the Atlantic, and after a week I would be flying off again, to Berlin, to stay with beautiful Edel in her family home, where I would discuss solar power with her father, the photovoltaics expert. Then I had to go with Randall and others in our lab to a conference in Stockholm, which focused on microscopy and other biophysics techniques; and that meeting was to give me further information that confirmed the correctness of my decision to continue on X-ray diffraction, and not to 'go back to my microscopes'.

Back in London in September, burdened by jet lag, I found it good to be in our lab again and to report on my travels. I found Rosalind, and excitedly began telling her about Chargaff's evidence that there were complex sequences of bases in DNA that could be the gene structure itself. But she interrupted me, and said something about having got new results while I was away. She was now using the new equipment, the fine-focus X-rays and the microcamera very much along the lines we had decided a year before, and which had been chosen for the study of a small group of DNA fibres or a single fibre. Rosalind was skilful in handling the fibres, and not surprisingly she had soon obtained important new results. I tried to finish what I was saying, because Chargaff's evidence seemed so basic to our work, but she stopped me again by remarking, in a cool, amused way, that it seemed that I did not want to hear what she had to tell me. I was rather taken aback, but, on considering what she said, I had to concede there was probably some truth in it. I was not very happy that she seemed to have detected in my behaviour something of which I had not been conscious. Her quiet air of confident superiority disturbed me. I stopped talking and asked her to tell me what she had done.

Rosalind had discovered a somewhat different type of X-ray diffraction pattern when the DNA was very wet – about 92% humidity. She showed me the new pattern, which we called B-DNA, which was similar to but much clearer than those we had made before. B-DNA looked set to lend itself to fruitful analysis. The DNA that gave the crystalline pattern, which we now called A-DNA, was not as wet as Raymond and I had thought – the humidity was only 75%. Clearly, Rosalind said, the DNA molecules could exist in two different structures, and changing the humidity from 75% to 92% caused the structure to change from A to B. It was clearly an important discovery. But she put so much emphasis on what I had got wrong that I could barely take any pleasure in it.

I felt frustrated not only because Raymond and I had been mistaken about the humidity of A-DNA, but also because Rosalind's step forward deserved praise, and it was not easy to give that praise when she seemed to be pleased by our mistake. I realize now that getting the humidity wrong was very good luck because it led directly to our getting the first clearly defined crystalline pattern of DNA, which impressed the audience at the Naples conference and was the basis on which the DNA X-ray programme at King's was built. So sometimes mistakes can lead to important discoveries. I had, in my ten years of research, made many mistakes, and had had to deal with their consequences. These were, of course, on the whole unhelpful, but sometimes they were unexpectedly productive. Science can be like that – sometimes a mistake can lead to a scientific advance.

The full importance of Rosalind's improved pattern was only recognizable after we had the fully crystalline pattern. It was a pity that Rosalind and I did not spend more time discussing the importance of her discovery and what it might tell us about the nature of DNA. Her air of cool superiority – a look I have never forgotten – temporarily undermined my self-confidence, and gave me a brief feeling of panic. It was an extraordinary experience.

For an hour or so – or was it only a moment? – I felt the air of our laboratory become chilled, and the warm sense of community seemed to disappear. Years afterwards, I wrote about my deep feelings of alarm at that time. I recalled the very popular pre-War cartoons of Bateman, of 'The Man who had Done ~ ~ ~', where a little man was cringing in front of a contemptuous crowd. I also had a nightmare that reminded me of a horrific dream I had had in hospital after my ear operation in Berkeley. In the nightmare I was a fish on a fishmonger's slab: 'Would you like a nice filet Madam? Or would you like it on the bone?' Rosalind could be terrifying.

Looking back, I continue to be puzzled by how Rosalind managed to work when our Head of Department's secret letter was so clearly contradicted by the reality of me and Stokes giving no sign of moving off DNA. It must have been a great burden for her, and I continue to be impressed by her fortitude. I can only guess that while Rosalind was setting up our new generation of X-ray equipment, she developed stronger feelings of confidence in the work she was doing. She was also reported to take very seriously the authority of laboratory Heads, and she was, after all, doing the work she had been told to do.

Another aspect of this situation is that it illustrates that scientists often become very strongly attached to their research. I did, and I think Rosalind did too. What the poet Coleridge said is still true: the scientist loves the material on which he or she works. For science to function for the benefit of society, this point should be kept in mind. Mountain climbers risk their lives to reach their goal, and scientists have strong feelings too. A single climber cannot reach the top of Everest without support from others. Centuries ago a single scientist could make much progress on his own, but today working in a group is almost essential, and so skill in building relationships is increasingly important.

For us, the question remained: how could our X-ray work be organized so that we could proceed in a reasonably friendly manner? My intention was not to do anything that might create bad feeling between me and Rosalind. I was still very excited by Chargaff's work, and I suggested that I should study the DNA that formed fibres that Chargaff had given me; and that Rosalind should continue with Signer DNA. I had designed a new camera that could be sealed up like a microcamera, but would give a somewhat larger X-ray pattern. Our excellent mechanics could make my camera in a few weeks. As a temporary matter I was prepared to use the old Raymax X-ray set that Raymond and I had used a year before. Rosalind had exclusive use of our new fine-focus X-ray tube. She agreed that I should try the Chargaff DNA while she and Raymond continued working with the Signer. Why did I not ask for a share of the Signer DNA? That was a mistake on my part. Signer had, after all, handed it to me in May 1950. If I had asked for a share, that would have been a contradiction of Randall's letter to Rosalind, and while I would not have known that, Randall and Rosalind's reactions to such a request from me might have brought the situation much more into the open. My self-effacing manner was probably not pro-ductive, and may not have impressed Rosalind. Randall, as Head of the lab, should have helped in theory: he called Rosalind and me to a meeting and suggested that Rosalind continue to work on the crystalline A pattern, and I could work on the B pattern. That seemed sensible, but his manner of telling us did not help matters: he said he wanted to be fair to both of us, and that made me feel like a naughty child.

Our situation was much altered in the summer of 1951, when the great chemist Linus Pauling published a paper on the protein α-helix. Pauling was working at the California Institute of Technology, and had been encouraged in the early 1930s by a grant from the Rockefeller Foundation to work on the structure of biological molecules, especially proteins such as haemoglobin and antibodies. This was a great challenge: protein molecules seemed to be far too large to investigate using X-rays, and they were very difficult to handle without damaging them. Pauling had a two-pronged approach to the problem, which involved thinking about the much smaller and simpler components of these enormous molecules, and then building models of them. So to find the overall structure of the protein, Pauling and his colleagues first worked out the structures of several amino acids, which were the basic units of the larger molecule. The physical and chemical properties of the amino acids would determine how they linked to each other, and Pauling saw that rigid bonds between them would hold them in certain positions relative to each other. He used his quantum mechanical theory of chemical bonding and the latest highly accurate data on bond lengths and angles to determine what these relative positions might be. Thus, from this understanding of the bonding between the amino acids, the bigger structures of the proteins could be deduced. Pauling built three-dimensional models of possible structures, to see how the different components might fit together into a physically and chemically stable molecule. In May 1951, he wrote seven papers giving the atomic arrangement within the molecular structure of many proteins, including the structure of the most important fundamental form of protein: a helical chain known as the α-helix.

Pauling had made this important advance in a fundamentally new way, by both thinking about the known details of inter-atomic bonding, and making large-scale models of possible molecular structures. His breakthrough is an interesting example showing how new thought and an increase of experimental data may create new ways of doing science. To put it into perspective, we can note that Bragg, Kendrew and Perutz had made a serious effort to find the very basic α-helix structure of protein, and had published a long, thorough study that failed to solve the problem. Pauling used a new approach: he used his quantum-mechanical theory of chemical bonds and his knowledge of up-to-date accurate data on inter-atomic bond lengths and angles, and brought these together as a three-dimensional model. In the case of the α-helix, this approach gave clear results. Pauling's success also depended on considering helices that did not contain integral numbers of amino acids per helix turn. He quickly obtained new structures which were shown to be correct by Perutz using X-ray diffraction. Clearly model-building had been put on a new scientific basis, and many scientists were stimulated to try it. I encouraged Bruce Fraser, in our lab, to try out his ideas in a model. Rosalind dismissed our excitement by saying that model-building is what you do after you have found the structure. Her position was sensible given the state of science before Pauling developed his new approach; but after his success with the α-helix, the situation had changed. A new way of exploring had come into being.

When I had finished reading Pauling's α-helix paper I was puzzled that he seemed not to have a way of calculating X-ray diffraction from the structure. I discussed this with Stokes, and our co-operation on this question was very fruitful: the next day he produced a Bessel function calculation of diffraction from a helix. He had worked it out on the train to London from his home at Welwyn Garden City. It was drawn on one sheet of paper and, with his quiet humour, he had called it 'Waves at Bessel on Sea'. I pinned it on our laboratory notice-board. The calculations confirmed Stokes' thoughts of a year earlier, that diffraction near the fibre direction would be very weak if DNA were helical. What was really exciting was how well the plot of calculated intensities corresponded with Rosalind's new B diffraction pattern. Stokes and I had a real feeling of scientific uplift, and we felt we must share this with Rosalind. We did not wait to think about it, but hurried along the corridor to show Rosalind how very informative her pattern had become. When we came to the room where Rosalind was working, all I can remember was seeing her standing in the room listening to us trying to explain what we saw as very important good news. Then suddenly she angrily exclaimed: 'How dare you interpret my results!' We were flabbergasted, and did not know what to say. It was the only time I ever saw Rosalind lose her temper. After a moment Stokes and I retreated, quite at a loss to know what to do.

The clearest memory I have of the whole incident is of seeing a continuous straight grey line on the diffraction pattern photograph. The intensity variation along one line corresponded to one of the waves of the Bessel function. Stokes had a clear memory of Rosalind's B pattern, and the theoretical results matched very well. We were carried away by the scientific excitement and did not stop and think about how best to approach Rosalind to discuss the very encouraging agreement of theory with experimental fact. Possibly it might have been best, with the new result, if Stokes by himself had gently drawn Rosalind's attention to the interpretation of her B pattern. He was very quiet and friendly as well as very intelligent. It did seem that Rosalind had a strong sense of personal ownership; whereas in science it is important to develop a sense of shared ownership so that members of a research group can co-operate. I had certainly much enjoyed co-operating on a fairly equal basis in our light microscope work with excellent scientists like Howard Davis and Keith Norris, and research students like Raymond Gosling (though I did not see much of Raymond after Rosalind arrived). I felt strongly that friendly co-operation was a very valuable and important aspect of science. If we had proceeded more carefully in this very important situation we might have found a way of co-operating with Rosalind.

I certainly felt that Rosalind's vehemence meant that nothing would persuade her to have a discussion. I realized later that I may well have been wrong. It was wrong to retreat. When we were dividing the work I had tried to appease and mollify. By not standing up for myself I may have lost Rosalind's respect and encouraged her to be aggressive. Stokes, more than me, had a quiet, non-aggressive style. We were not used to confrontations. We should have worked hard to clarify our ideas and then gone back to Rosalind to try to discuss them. If she sent us away, we should have made it clear that we would not give up and that she should choose a time when we could all sit down and argue back and forth to understand each other's position. If we really thought the matter was very important, we should have tried. It was unfair on Rosalind not to have done so. It left the door closed on almost any constructive interaction between us. It is only recently that I have seen this clearly, and I was interested to find that Anne Sayre, Rosalind's first biographer, described her liking of hot and heavy dispute. I cannot imagine Stokes in hot dispute, but maybe quiet persistence would have done.

In October 1951, quite soon after that confrontation, a laboratory colloquium was set up to survey the DNA X-ray work in our lab. We had planned this as an opportunity for open discussion; and when Jim Watson asked if he could attend we did not hesitate to say yes. In his new post at the Cavendish Laboratory in Cambridge, he had met Francis Crick, and they had formed a powerful team. They shared enthusiasm for Pauling's new model-building and for Stokes' Bessel function calculation of diffraction from helical molecules. Francis's interest in X-ray diffraction as a fundamental biological tool complemented Jim's enthusiasm for bacteriophage genetics. Together they formed a very effective complementary pair for the study of DNA structure.

I opened the colloquium by repeating the talk I had given at Perutz's meeting in Cambridge in July. I went through the X-ray evidence that DNA from a wide range of species gave a basically similar 'cross-ways' X-ray pattern indicating the same helical structure. I regretted that I had little new to say, but I probably mentioned Chargaff's important results. I didn't discuss the new helical evidence. Stokes then described his Bessel function description of diffraction from a helical structure, but I do not think he attempted to link his work with Rosalind's new B pattern. Rosalind then gave a first-class account of various likely aspects of DNA structure. She presented clearly reasons why the phosphate groups should be on the outside of the molecule, and the importance of understanding the role of water in DNA structures A and B. Rosalind's notes for this talk were discovered after her death, and include a discussion of helical structure. I certainly do not remember her discussing helical structures; and Jim Watson's recollection was the same. I think that after two talks about helical DNA it would have been surprising if Rosalind spoke along similar lines. To have done so would have given the impression that she agreed with the helical ideas of mine and Stokes. Clearly Rosalind wanted to work with Raymond, and she did not want to be committed to working with Stokes and me. To ensure her independence it is not surprising that she dropped the helical parts in her lecture notes. I think she wanted to work in well-established ways.

Apart from tension over helices, our lab was at that time very well placed indeed to discover the structure of DNA. We had masses of new X-ray data. Rosalind was well versed in X-ray techniques and understood the physical chemistry of DNA. Stokes was a master of diffraction theory. We knew the X-ray workers at Birkbeck College who were finding the structures of the component parts of DNA. A Norwegian research student at Birkbeck, Sven Furberg, had sent us his PhD thesis about very important X-ray work on DNA. We were in touch with the various relevant chemical and optical groups in our lab, especially Bill Price's infra-red spectroscopic group. Jim Watson stimulated us with new ideas from the USA, Francis Crick was always thought-provoking, and we were inspired by Pauling's great success with the α-helix. All we had to do was to get on with the job.

The strength of our position was illustrated by a model of DNA that Bruce Fraser built. He was a research student in Bill Price's group and used infra-red absorption to study the chemical bonds in DNA. The interaction between Price's group and ours was another good example of the co-operative spirit in the lab. We had studied Furberg's helical DNA structure, but there was only one chain in the structure and very little to stabilize it. An important thing we learned from Rosalind's experience at the Paris X-ray lab was how to measure the water content and density of DNA fibres, and those measurements pointed towards DNA being a three-chain molecule. Fraser worked in the room next to mine and, soon after the colloquium, he appeared at my door with a mysterious smile and beckoned me silently. Following him into his room, I saw that he had built a helical model of DNA. Bruce had done a good job: the model was very interesting. The three helical chains had the right pitch, diameter and angle, and were linked together by hydrogen bonds between the flat bases which were stacked on each other in the middle of the model. But the three chains were equally spaced, and that was contradicted by the X-ray diffractions. There were also basic difficulties with the hydrogen bonding between the bases: the bonds could only exist for special groups of three bases. The structure did not fit with Chargaff's 1:1 base ratios.

The model was designed to follow estimates of the energy of binding between stacked bases, of hydrogen bonds linking bases and of forces between phosphate groups. Bill Price was well able to advise Bruce on those energies. The model represented well the general state of thinking in our lab. It was based on a broad background, including, for example: J.M. Gulland's work at Nottingham University showing that the DNA chains were joined to each other by inter-base hydrogen bonds; the nucleotide conformation found by Furberg at Birkbeck; phosphates on the outside as urged by Rosalind; and the outside diameter of 20Å that had been found by Gosling and me 18 months earlier. But the difficulty was that we just did not know what to do with the three helices. We found ourselves completely stuck. There seemed to be no use at all in trying to build more models unless we could find some idea to guide us; and we could not find that idea. Thinking that there were three chains had completely stopped us in our tracks.

Our main mistake was to pay too much attention to experimental evidence. Nelson won the battle of Copenhagen by putting his blind eye to the telescope so that he did not see the signal to stop fighting. In the same way, scientists sometimes should use the Nelson Principle and ignore experimental evidence. Rosalind did a very good job of measuring the density and water content of DNA, but we might have done better if we had not had those data because they always seemed to point to the number of chains in DNA being three. This impression was strengthened by Rosalind rightly stressing that DNA fibres were not completely crystalline, and that we should make allowance for the different water content of the non-crystalline part of the fibre. But she insisted (and I should have asked why) that the allowance should increase and not decrease the figure for the number of chains. Thus, a figure of two-and-a-half meant that there were three chains. None of us checked up on the allowance to be made, and it never occurred to me to question what Rosalind had said: she was an authority on the structure of coal, which contained crystalline and non-crystalline parts, and she could adopt a very professional manner. This is perhaps another example of the negative effect of respect: I did not question Rosalind's statement that the non-crystalline parts of DNA fibres would contain more water than the crystal-line parts – a matter that was extremely important in deciding whether DNA could have two or three chains. I respected Rosalind as an experienced X-ray worker, and as a result we ignored the possibility that the DNA molecule had two chains and not three. Too much respect led me not to think critically and creatively. We should have borne in mind that DNA was very different from most crystalline materials, and that what we knew about those may not be serving us well in the case of DNA. In science there are no firm rules; a subtle mixture of questioning and not questioning is needed, as it is in ordinary living. For Rosalind to use the helix idea was already like stepping into some-one else's shoes and then having to walk in them, which is not a comfortable way to go.

All this discussion of mistakes and muddles may lead non-scientists to believe that science is not reliable. Science can and does solve important problems for humanity, but it may take much hard work and hard discussion before the truth is pulled out of the muddle.

CHAPTER 7

HOW DOES DNA KEEP ITS SECRETS?

The history of DNA research certainly had its up and downs. Barber's ambition to bring *Sepia* sperm to Randall, Schrödinger's quantum mechanics gene, Mirsky fighting Avery, Signer's DNA crystallizing, and Randall writing his secret letter to Rosalind – all this drama led to our quiet, steady colloquium and Bruce Fraser's very noteworthy ball-and-stick model of DNA, which had several important features of the Double Helix. But X-ray diffraction ruled out Fraser's arrangement of three chains – Rosalind quickly pointed out that the diffraction showed that three was not possible. I do not think that was why Bruce would follow Barber to Australia few months later. Bruce had married Mary Nicholls, who had made us herring DNA (Mary had dinner with me, but Bruce's Scottish moustache won the day). The loss of Bruce and Mary was to break the very valuable link we had with Bill Price's group at King's, which specialized in infra-red spectroscopic and physical–chemistry approaches to the structure of nucleic acids and proteins. Although there was much we still did not know about DNA, if we had been able to make an imaginative leap so that the Fraser model had only two chains instead of three, we might have been able to move closer to the correct model.

The lack of co-operative contact between Rosalind and pro-helix Stokes and me was a very serious obstacle to progress. To try to build up this contact I drew Rosalind's attention to the fact that the protein researchers in the Cambridge X-ray diffraction lab had begun a new way of working. Perutz, the leading X-ray expert, had the main responsibility for their work, but Bragg, the X-ray pioneer and director of the lab, kept in touch with what was happening, and at the end of each day took home with him new results to study. The next day Bragg would discuss the work with Perutz. Might it be possible for me to keep in touch with Rosalind and Raymond in that kind of way? Rosalind quickly demolished my idea by saying 'But Bragg is a Nobel Prize winner.' The logic of that seemed very strong, and I could not think of an answer. Rosalind seemed very discouraging of any contact. When I wanted to compare more closely the *Sepia* sperm diffraction with the new B-type pattern of DNA that Rosalind had obtained, I began tactfully and acknowledged that the A-type pattern had some clear differences from the sperm pattern. But Rosalind dismissed me by saying that neither of the DNA patterns had any similarity to that of the sperm. To avoid any discussion with me, Rosalind was prepared to talk rubbish.

On the positive side, Stokes had been a great help in clarifying our ideas. He had a special talent for thinking about helices. When I was with Jerry Oster, looking with microscopes at zig-zag arrangements of virus particles in crystals of the tobacco mosaic virus TMV, Stokes had made a very sensible suggestion that the zig-zag appearance would be explained if TMV particles were helical. He was always very impressive and encouraging when I raised a problem with him. Sometimes I would explain the problem, and he would just say 'ah' or 'um', and then I found I had solved the problem. Stokes did not need to explain the solution to the problem: my consciousness of his understanding was enough to lead me to it.

This kind of interaction of minds acted in the opposite way in a discussion with Rosalind in December 1951. After the Fraser model failed to lead us on to further progress, I was sitting in my room, somewhat depressed. And then a very unexpected thing happened: Rosalind came into my room to discuss a new idea about helical DNA. I don't think we had discussed anything since Stokes and I had fled from her outburst. It was not a dream: I indicated a chair for her, and Rosalind sat down and explained her new idea. She spoke calmly and quietly, and I took care to do the same. She had been looking at her new B pattern (the one that Stokes and I had seen was clearly helical), and she had had a very sensible thought. The relative intensities of the layer lines seemed to indicate that, in the DNA molecule, there were two concentrations of matter separated by three-eighths of the repeat distance along the length. I vaguely thought of the helical molecule containing two clumps of matter separated by the three-eighths distance, and I could not think what they might be. Two groups of atoms? I was puzzled. Rosalind was baffled, and that was why she had come to discuss the problem. Whether she had already discussed it with Stokes I do not know, and it was foolish of me not to have made sure that he was involved. Even so, it seems clear that a mental block prevented Rosalind and me from seeing that the two concentrations of matter, separated by three-eighths of the repeat distance along the fibre, were the helical chains of two-chain DNA. Rosalind's notebook, discovered many years after her untimely death, shows that clearly: just before Jim and Francis built their Double Helix, she had begun thinking about helical two-chain DNA. And at that time I had been thinking about base-pairing. Rosalind was not thinking about that; but Francis Crick was right when he said that Rosalind was then only 'two steps away' from the Double Helix. But in 1951, a two chain-model would not have looked viable to us – the molecule clearly had a definite structure, and how would two chains maintain their relative positions? It seemed they would just flop about. Surely more chains would offer a more stable structure.

Two weeks after our colloquium at King's, I was surprised by Francis Crick, who telephoned me to say that he and Jim Watson had built a model of DNA and would I like to come to Cambridge to see it? Rushing round the labs, I collected Rosalind, Raymond, Bill Seeds and Bruce Fraser, and we were soon filling a compartment on a train to Cambridge. We knew that Francis and Jim were very bright, and we wondered what they had come up with.

We were surprised to find the model disappointing. According to our thinking it was completely inside out, with the helical regularity in its three chains being established by the phosphate groups held together along the helix axis. But magnesium ions (which we had never heard of in DNA) were needed to hold the phosphates together. On the outside of the helix, the bases seemed to flop about without being stacked on top of each other, or stabilized in any way. When Francis saw that we were not impressed, he said the model was based on a low water content that Jim had misunderstood at our colloquium. We did not take the model seriously; but if we had known that Pauling was to produce a rather similar model in a year's time, we might have been more patient and respectful. Bruce spoke about his model, but Francis and Jim were preoccupied with their own misadventure.

However, in spite of Francis and Jim's failure, which did not seem to lead anywhere, we had a strong feeling that what they had done was only a small beginning, and that they intended to press on. I had seen enough of them to expect that they could be very serious competitors if there was to be a race for the DNA structure. The idea that all of us at Cambridge and King's should work together on DNA did not occur to us: King's had opened up the field and we felt we should be free to explore the possibilities that we had created. On the other hand, we were two MRC labs managed and funded by the same agency, and it seemed silly for us to compete with each other. There certainly were some feelings of rivalry between the two labs. However, to put this situation into perspective, I should mention the important sliding filament mechanism for muscle contraction that was developed by our leading biologist Jean Hanson and the very successful biophysicist Hugh Huxley, in Bragg's lab at Cambridge. So far as I knew, there was no inter-lab rivalry between the muscle researchers. It was a very good example of co-operation.

Today, half a century on, when we can see all the important applications of DNA science, it may seem strange that inter-lab co-operation was not set up in 1951. We ought to have seen that there was a real need for collaboration. I did not foresee the need for large-scale work on the DNA problem. At the time, we did not like the idea of being in a race with Cambridge and, in December, I wrote a letter to Francis:

> *My dear Francis,*
> *I want to say I was sorry to rush off ... without seeing you again and thanking you for the pleasant time. I am afraid the average vote of opinion here, most reluctantly and with many regrets, is against your proposal to continue the work (on DNA) in Cambridge .... If you and Jim were working in a lab remote from ours [and the work could be kept separate], our attitude would be that you should go right ahead .... If your Unit thinks our suggestion selfish, or contrary to the interests as a whole of scientific advance, please let us know ....*
> *Yours very sincerely,*
> *Maurice*

Apart from my letter, our interaction with Cambridge had in many ways seemed to be developing in a co-operative way that was appropriate to the importance of the great DNA problem we were trying to solve. But, unfortunately, scientific enthusiasm was capable of developing in unexpected ways, and jarring notes tended to arise. King's was studying not only DNA but also collagen – another helical macromolecule. Collagen was a protein of great medical importance – it forms the fibrous connective tissue that is found in many parts of the body – and it was being studied in our lab on a larger scale than was DNA. Randall had a special interest in collagen because his wife had suffered from medical problems involving it for many years, and he had built up a large research group dedicated to it. After Pauling's success with the α-helix, helices were being tried out for many different biological molecules, and much excitement developed at King's as the very able Pauline Cowan (she had done her PhD in Dorothy Hodgkin's famous X-ray lab at Oxford) built helical models for collagen. Francis Crick, aided by his mathematical strength, could see very well the interest of solving the collagen problem, and thought that if he collaborated with Pauline it would be like the common practice of a theoretical physicist working with an experimentalist. But Pauline felt that Francis' interest was somewhat intrusive, and I had a word with him about it. The chemical complexities of collagen were very challenging, and, after several years, a successful model was built in a high-quality lab in India.

If Francis and Jim's helical model of DNA had more adequately demonstrated their considerable talents, it might have been possible to arrange a creative research link for DNA between King's and Cambridge. But in the end it was our MRC

Directors, Randall and Bragg, who had to decide policy, and their decision was that Francis and Jim should stop. Bragg was new to DNA, and I do not know what contact he had had with Randall over DNA policy (Bragg consistently gave me warm support) but the result was that a Moratorium was set up. I continued to have friendly social contact with Francis and Jim, but we did not discuss DNA research.

The DNA Moratorium did give rise to a generous and helpful act by Francis and Jim. They handed over to us the set of metal jigs that they had designed carefully so that the workshop mechanics could make accurate parts for constructing DNA models. This gave us a much greater exactitude in our model-building than had been possible in the Fraser model. It was nice for me to go to Cambridge and socialize with Francis and Jim; and we did need to spend some time discussing how we could link the work in Cambridge and King's. Bragg's moratorium on Cambridge research was well-intentioned, but what we needed was positive interaction. My friend John Kendrew, who was working with Max Perutz on protein structures, was beginning to widen co-operation between European labs (after much struggling, he would set up the European Molecular Biology Organization). Francis and Jim's decision to hand over their jigs was also a very good example of the way our science should have been moving. The jigs contained very valuable information about inter-atomic distances and angles between chemical bonds. All that information had been derived from a wide range of chemical structures investigated internationally in many labs. Francis and Jim were disappointed that we did not use the jigs for making DNA models: Rosalind scorned the equipment, sticking to her view that model-building was what one did after finding the structure by proper X-ray procedures. Bruce was enthusiastic about model-building, but by now he had left us for Australia, and I was in a mental log-jam because I could not see how to do better than the Fraser model. We were missing an opportunity: model-building was a way of exploring possible structures, and could have pointed us in useful directions.

Some of the difficulty came from Rosalind's view that B-DNA might be helical and A-DNA was not. Our thoughts about DNA structure were to a large extent based on Rosalind's attitude because she had four years' experience of X-ray diffraction in Paris. We disagreed about DNA being helical, but we were glad of her support for the idea that phosphate groups were on the outside of the DNA molecule. She based her thinking about the number of chains in DNA on her measurements of water content in crystalline DNA fibres. She believed that her measurements pointed to DNA having more than two chains in the molecule. Unfortunately it never occurred to me to question Rosalind about her reasoning. She submitted these ideas in a paper to *Acta Crystallographica*, the distinguished crystallography journal, and the paper was published a year or so later.

All in all, our ideas about DNA structure were fairly muddled in 1951. When I look at one of our research publications from a few years later – about DNA crystals in both A and B forms – one seems in a different world. The DNA muddles in 1951-1953 caused Stokes to lose some of his interest in DNA, and he began studying protein light-scattering problems with clear-sighted and friendly Marjorie M'Ewen. He admitted later that he had not properly recognized how very important the DNA problem was.

Our workshop had at last completed the new X-ray camera that I had designed on a bigger scale than the microcamera Rosalind was using, and which was the first stage after Raymond and I had made our important finding that DNA could really crystallize. I thought after Rosalind had discovered the A–B transition of DNA that we should move on to a bigger camera that could provide more precise and detailed images. I was very disappointed to find that Chargaff DNA (which formed fibres like those of Signer DNA) did not crystallize, and only gave B patterns like those Rosalind had at that time. I should not have let myself be carried away by enthusiasm for Chargaff's DNA. It had been prepared so as to be useful in analytical chemistry, and not for its molecular structure, and I had noticed that the fibres did not pull apart as gracefully as in the Signer DNA.

Why had I agreed not to use the Signer DNA before I had tested the Chargaff DNA properly? I had been too much impressed by Chargaff, but I did not take into account the fact that his DNA was made primarily for study of its chemical structure. In contrast, Signer specialized in making DNA that was physically intact, for studying the overall molecular weight or viscosity. My new camera could have given sharper crystalline patterns than Rosalind was obtaining with a microcamera. Many years later, it occurred to me that I should have offered my new camera to Rosalind. Sharper patterns might have helped her to see that crystalline DNA was helical. We might even have been able to share the new camera, and so begin some degree of co-operation. But I did not think of that – the barrier between us seemed so solid.

As we approached the end of 1951, the liveliness of Randall's Circus, so far as DNA structure was concerned, began dying away. I felt very depressed; but that was eased by going home for Christmas to Birmingham, where I walked in the lanes of Wylde Green with my steady, good-willed young sister Jasmine (who was training as a physiotherapist) while my mother completed preparations for Christmas dinner.

Back in the lab in January, I faced again the problem of DNA. Stokes had no brilliant thoughts, so I approached Hugh Longuet-Higgins, our new Professor of Theoretical Physics. But he was full up with other scientific problems. I did feel very low. It was during these days that John Kendrew rang me and asked if I would like to work with Francis and Jim. I said, 'what have they got to offer?', and he replied, 'They are very bright.' I thought he was right; but how could I avoid a big row over the Bragg Moratorium, and with Rosalind and Randall? I could not do it.

Then I had a brilliant thought: if I wanted Signer DNA, why not ask him for some more? I telephoned him in Switzerland. He was very friendly and invited me to his lab. I decided to go to

27 Rosalind Franklin (left) and Maurice (right), at a conference in the USA, late 1950s.

28 Maurice (late 1950s) identifying features in a model of the DNA double-helix built for lectures to general audiences. Wooden blocks form the base-pair steps of the spiral staircase and strips of sponge rubber represent the sugar-phosphate chain banisters.

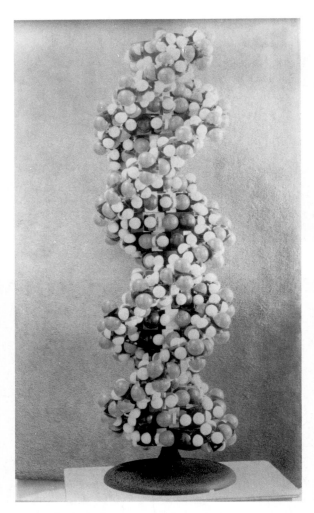

29 Space-filling model of the B form of DNA from Courtauld atomic components. A model of this type was part of the UK exhibit at the 1958 Brussels EXPO and such models and photographs of them were widely used as exhibits, in popular presentations and in textbooks, becoming a familiar icon in the second half of the twentieth century. Each atom on the sugar-phosphate chain is represented by a solid sphere representing the overall size of the atom from which a number of cuts were made to leave planar surfaces facing the directions in which the atom forms covalent bonds with other atoms.

30 Maurice (with Don Marvin) assembling a space filling model of the B form of the DNA double helix, *c*.1960.

31 Device used from early 1960s for drawing a fibre of DNA from a gel by controlled separation of two glass rods on which the gel was supported. This picture shows the final stage in the process with a fibre approximately 0.1 mm in diameter and a few mm in length held between the ends of the two glass rods.

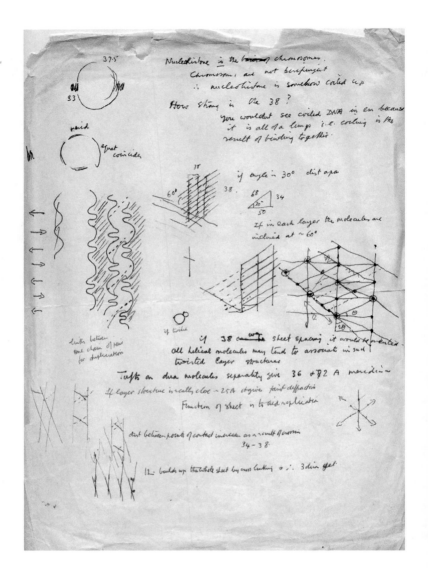

32 Notes by Maurice made in around 1960 during work on the structure of nucleohistone, the major component of chromatin. The sketch left centre represents neighbouring molecules of DNA with the wide and narrow grooves characteristic of the B form emphasized.

33   Nobel laureates, 1962. Left to right: Maurice Wilkins, John Steinbeck, John Kendrew, Max Perutz, Francis Crick, Jim Watson.

34   Christmas 1962 celebration of the award of the Nobel Prize to Francis Crick, Jim Watson, and Maurice Wilkins, showing Maurice as a Christmas angel looking out from a model of the double helix, and photographs of Maurice and Pat and their children at the Stockholm presentation celebrations.

35   Maurice and Sir John Randall at a Drury Lane party, 1960s.

36   King's College Biophysics Unit laboratory workers, Drury Lane, 1960s.

37   The Wilkins family on a cross-channel ferry on the way to Corsica, 1967.
      Left to right: Patricia, William (in pushchair), Sarah, George, Emily.

38   Maurice with Pope John Paul II, 1980s.

39 Maurice at King's, 1998.

Berne and then travel a bit further and visit Edel, who was in Munich. We could go to circuses and art galleries and up into the Alps. All that was good fun, but Signer had misunderstood me on the telephone: arriving in Berne, I found that he had no DNA, nor plans to make it; he had given it all away in London, two years ago. I had a pleasant time with Edel, but when we said goodbye we concluded our relationship. As I sat in the train *en route* to Naples, I felt very cheered at the prospect of getting some fresh *Sepia* sperm with Bruno Baltaglia, and seeing Peter Dohrn and the views of Vesuvius.

Back in London I carefully mounted some of the fresh sperm on my high resolution camera and got much clearer patterns than the previous year. The crystallinity was still less well defined than with good DNA patterns, and I wondered whether it was correct to use the term 'crystalline' when some irregularity was clearly visible. But when I met Bragg by chance I showed him the pattern and he reassured me. The pattern very clearly offered strong evidence for a helical structure for DNA. This was a very encouraging and exciting result, and I wrote to Francis, including in my letter a sketch of the pattern – the striking X formed by the dots and shadows of the X-ray diffraction.

> *My dear Francis,*
> *… I have got <u>much</u> better X-ray pictures of the* Sepia
> *sperm which show very nicely a whole series of helical*
> *layer lines. [I included my sketch here] … I have*
> *found several of your suggestions very valuable but am*
> *fairly convinced for many reasons the phosphates are*

on the outside ... [i.e. not like Francis and Jim's model]. I am really getting down to the job myself but haven't done anything on models and chemistry .... I now take my own X-ray pictures and have made new cameras. Franklin barks often but doesn't succeed in biting me .... When I saw Jim just before Christmas, he said you people could not build a model along your lines. If that is so it simplifies things a bit, anyway I am pretty certain the phosphates are on the outside. I won't start making any references to the 'business' between you people and us [over DNA] but look forward to discussing all our latest ideas and results with you again. Why don't you come and have lunch with me when you are next in town? ...

For the first time we were emerging from a very dark winter.

The sharp sperm patterns were very inspiring, and had the special interest that sperm were real live objects and not just purified DNA extracted by chemists from living material. Much later I found out that Jim Watson had written to Delbrück about my improved diffraction patterns of sperm, and had expressed his excitement with many exclamation marks. There were, however, complications in that there was protein as well as DNA in sperm heads, and in deriving the helical structure of DNA we would need to take into account the presence of the proteins. Francis had given me some advice on this. In parallel with the sharper sperm patterns, I had an encouraging thought about X-ray evidence that DNA was helical. Stokes had begun this before Rosalind had joined us. He noted that there was no diffraction along the length of the DNA apart from the clear 'pile of pennies' diffraction from the bases stacked on each other. That observation by Stokes had been the basis of all our helical thinking. The perfect continuity of the DNA helix showed itself by the absence of diffraction along the axis of the pattern. My new thought was similar. I knew that DNA molecules packed together in parallel like cylinders 20Å in diameter. I noted that in the outer part of the diffraction pattern (near the equator), there were regions where there was absence of diffraction. That fitted in with the DNA being helical and helped to cheer me up. But to be more certain, I needed better patterns.

A month or so later I received an invitation to go with a group of British biomolecular scientists to visit Brazil. The plan was to visit laboratories, hold a conference on important biomolecular advances and generally liven up Brazilian science. I was asked to represent the new kinds of microscopy that our laboratory had developed. I decided to take the new reflecting microscope I had designed for compactness and ease of use (our X-ray advances on DNA molecular structure had not yet received much attention in Brazil). As I prepared for my journey, Rosalind was preparing a bombshell attack on helical DNA. Raymond told me that she would like Stokes and me to come to her room so that she could present new X-ray results. Stokes was sent a joke invitation card that I thought fitted in well with Raymond's friendly jocularity and desire to avoid bad feeling, though many years later I discovered that the invitation had been written by Rosalind. It read:

IT IS WITH GREAT REGRET THAT
WE HAVE TO ANNOUNCE THE DEATH,
ON FRIDAY 18TH JULY, 1952,
OF D.N.A. HELIX (CRYSTALLINE).
DEATH FOLLOWED A PROTRACTED ILLNESS
WHICH AN INTENSIVE COURSE OF BESSELISED
INJECTIONS HAD FAILED TO RELIEVE.
A MEMORIAL SERVICE WILL BE HELD NEXT
MONDAY OR TUESDAY.
IT IS HOPED THAT DR. M.H.F. WILKINS WILL
SPEAK IN MEMORY OF THE LATE HELIX

R.E. FRANKLIN   R.G. GOSLING

Stokes and I went up to the pleasant airy room with two big windows that had been the Head of Department's before Randall moved down to our new basement building. Rosalind seemed in a quiet, sensible mood and told us about a recent collection of intensities from the crystalline A pattern. The directions of diffraction were at right angles to the fibre axis, or close to that. With a helical structure, the intensities would be the same for a reflection on one side of the pattern and on the opposite side. But Rosalind's careful measurements appeared to show clear differences between one side of the axis and the other. Stokes and I could see no way round the conclusion that Rosalind had reached after months of careful work. It seemed, in spite of all previous indications, that the DNA molecule was lop-sided and not helical. I felt strongly that if DNA was not helical or some other simple form, it would be very difficult to find the structure. That would be very disappointing – the helix hypothesis had given us much hope and energy.

I have no memory of Stokes or me considering the possibility that Rosalind was indulging in a deception, and that it was all a silly joke of the kind in which scientists are said to indulge sometimes (though I never met that myself or heard a first-hand account of such an experience). We had seen Rosalind giving a serious and sensible colloquium, and it seemed that her steady, quiet description of her new results was just the same as at our colloquium the previous year. Some months after Rosalind had left our lab, I felt I should look again at the data she had described to us. But Raymond did not have suitable data to show us. Several years later Watson Fuller in our lab found that the highest-resolution camera we had then was barely accurate enough to tell us about the type of intensity differences Rosalind was describing. I believe Rosalind over-estimated the suitability of her microcamera for showing deviations from helical form. Her bias against the helical idea might well have caused her to misjudge the accuracy of her measurements. Even so, I continue to believe that Rosalind believed that her 'non-helical' intensities were true.

I knew Rosalind often had very strong opinions; I respected her as a scientist, and felt we should accept her results and wait and see how non-helical ideas might develop as her work continued. Another reason why I took seriously the anti-helix talk Rosalind gave to Stokes and me was that more than six months had passed without discussion. Rosalind certainly gave the impression that she was committed to measuring the crystalline A-type pattern very carefully in order to make a proper crystallographic study of DNA structure, rather than building molecular models.

But the most disturbing question relates to an X-ray diffraction photograph that was, at this time, quite unknown to Stokes and me, and which was lying in a drawer in Rosalind's office when she made the 'death of the helix' announcement. This photograph – the now-famous 1952 pattern – was particularly clear, and everyone agreed subsequently that it provided important pro-helix evidence. I was given the pattern by Raymond on 30 January 1953, when Rosalind was preparing to leave our lab. Why would she, despite having found this evidence, give us, in July 1952, an account of why DNA was not helical? In 1962 – four years after Rosalind's death – I surveyed our 12 years of DNA structure work and referred to Rosalind's 'great ability' and her 'very valuable contributions'. I had great respect for her, but her July 1952 meeting continues to be difficult to understand. What did she think she was doing? Rosalind did not find 'open dialogue' easy. If she had shown Stokes and me the 1952 pattern, we almost certainly would have questioned her anti-helix stance.

Around this time, we all had to write a short account of our work for a report to our funders, the Medical Research Council. I expressed what I felt was a fair account of our work, and said that recent indications seemed not to point towards helices. I expressed some regret about that, saying that other more complex or less regular structures would be much harder to elucidate. The report was sent off to the MRC, and they circulated it with other labs' reports as part of their routine update to their scientists. To our colleagues, including those in Cambridge, it must have looked as though King's had given up on helices.

But I did not have much time then to engage critically with Rosalind's anti-helical arguments. I had to leave for Brazil, and I was in quite a rush to muster some clothes suitable for a month or two in a hot country – I remember Bill Astbury in Yorkshire woollies at a conference in Pasadena, in the Californian sunshine. I also had some difficulty packing my reflecting microscope, even though it was especially portable. But I did have a quiet meeting, pondering with Stokes. He said Rosalind did give numerical data and he saw no way of avoiding her conclusion. Scientists are supposed to keep cool and calm, think carefully, and try to be objective. In practice, that is often very difficult indeed.

On the way to Brazil I spent a few days at international conferences in Paris. I was very glad to meet the American scientist Harriet Ephrussi, who was one of the few DNA scientists who realized that X-rays might tell us something really important. Harriet had been working in New York as Avery led MacCartey and McCloud to show, for the first time, that genes were nothing but DNA. She told the dramatic story of Mirsky leading the great mass of scientists who believed that genes were made of protein, and criticizing Avery after a lecture he gave. Avery was a very quiet and nervous man who did not enjoy conflict, and after the lecture he disappeared for weeks. Chargaff was in Paris too, and seemed disappointed that I had not been able to do more with his DNA. Jim Watson was there, and he introduced me to his mentor Max Delbrück, who seemed rather cool when I reported Rosalind's new results which showed DNA was not helical. Jim just said 'I don't believe it.' He was very helpful in taking me to a big meeting on bacterial viruses. I was recovering from eating bad food in a restaurant, and at dinner I chose to sit next to a remote man who, I thought, would not expect me to make polite conversation. But he soon began a very exciting account of his new research which showed that when a virus infected a bacterium in order to reproduce, nothing but DNA entered the bacterium. This provided confirmation of Avery's conclusion that genes were DNA. Next day, when the conference began, I found that my dinner companion had been the geneticist Alfred D. Hershey from the Carnegie Institution of Washington, the leading speaker at the meeting, who had completed the very important experiments just before coming to Paris.

On the plane to Brazil, my head was full of the Paris talk about DNA: though Rosalind was pursuing non-helical ideas, I was more convinced than ever of the importance of DNA structure; and time would tell whether it was helical or not. It was a very long flight south, stopping at strange tropical places on the way. It was the first time I had been in the southern hemisphere since Eithne and I had left New Zealand. I got my first impression of Rio while driving in from the airport, when I was delighted by a young black man leaping gracefully through the traffic. As he jumped across our path, he gave us a great big friendly smile. I had never seen such a high-spirited pedestrian before, and after the rather gloomy big minds like Delbrück and Chargaff in Paris, that first light-hearted impression was joy to me. It fitted well with the tropical light and space; the sun, sea, the graceful skyscrapers, the monolithic Sugar Loaf Mountain, with everything dominated by the outstretched arms of the immense Corcovado Christ on the hill. On my first day, after an enormous breakfast of tropical fruits, I rested in the sun on a park bench at the side of a wide avenue, and looking around at the skyscrapers, tropical plants and traffic streaming by, I thought, 'this is the new civilization'. I had especially liked H.G. Wells' story of the crystal egg, in which an unhappy, lonely little shopkeeper appeared to see another world. But in Rio I was actually in such a world – with its strange and beautiful surroundings, and women even more dazzling than those in Naples.

Rio lived up to my first exciting impression. I was carried away by the dancing, the movements of beauty, exuberance and drama, and the joy and freedom of music. When a folk dance show in a big theatre came to its end most of the audience jumped on stage, threw off their shoes, took over the dancing, and things really got going. When our host drove us out of Rio to show us the forests and mountains, we were thrilled by our young driver tearing around every bend with tyres shrieking – 'Rudolph is a sportsman!' they said. It was great fun, in the spirit of carnival.

Having seen Brazilians leaping and dancing, and with the dramatic Sugar Loaf Mountain outside the lab window, I wondered if I might find Brazilian science as lively and dashing. Sometimes I was bored with scientists: all the whirring of their clever brains made them seem introverted and inhuman. I knew that the very intense, worm-like burrowing into the Great Mass of Nature could lead them to discover new levels of exciting exist-ence, but few scientists find it easy to communicate how that lifts up their spirits. But the science I found in Brazil was of the usual kind – most of it was low-key, the quiet serious kind of science of which scientists often proudly say that it 'knows no national boundaries'. Brazilian scientists told me that when they went to work in Europe they were caught up in the keen spirit of research, and found themselves achieving much more than they had expected. But when they returned to Brazil, their productivity faded away. Brazilian liveliness in the main had not made a con-nection with the quiet steady intensity that science needs. I did not find it easy to get research moving; supply lines for accessories and chemicals barely existed and laboratory water taps were dry by midday – 'fill up your bottles in the morning', we were told. I looked back longingly to the exciting science I had met in Naples, but I had forgotten that the Stazione there had been designed specially to meet the needs of visiting scientists, whereas Rio had very little experience of that.

However, I was glad to find in Brazilian science a special kind of dash. The famous medical scientist Carlos Chagas, who had died in 1934, was our host's father. He had discovered the disease now named after him, which is caused by a parasite that lies in wait for people in the walls and roofs of their houses. He was said to have eliminated the disease by dynamiting all the houses whose residents suffered from it. I met a similar energy when I was looking for insects called coccids whose sperm were minute threads that swam about like microscopic snakes, with DNA at one end and protein at the other. Having pushed hard to get coccids – everyone was very pleasant and encouraging, but we were achieving nothing and getting nowhere – I confronted Chagas, the powerful scientist who had invited us to Brazil, and I said if I did not get coccids I could do no research with my microscope. Immediately, Brazilian liveliness took over: straight away I was sent in a taxi to the director of the botanical gardens, and then we went over 50 miles across country to Brazil's top entomologist. He had coccids waiting for me; he showed me how to dissect them, and he presented me with his book on Brazilian insects. He could not have responded more quickly or been more helpful.

But sometimes I was out of my depth in Brazil. I was taken by a helpful member of the Rio lab, the only one not from the well-to-do class, to see how poverty-stricken black Brazilians in Rio spent Saturday nights across the tracks in the Favela shanty town. In their Macumba rituals they circled around in a kind of religious trance, and every now and then one of them would gently slip to the floor. A friendly priest-like man blew cigar-smoke in ways intended to drive away bad spirits. I felt the dancers gained a happy release after a week of hardship; but I found that evening very strange – it was yet another 'other world'.

At the end of our stay in Rio, all of us in our group of visitors had to give a lecture, and then there was a big celebration party. It was in a garden connected to a children's playground and shaded by coconut palms. Chagas was proud of his informality and, as the party warmed up, I suggested that someone should climb a palm tree and get a coconut. Possibly I was thinking of Rudolph the sportsman, but to my surprise Frey-Wissling, a German scientist who seemed rather staid, took off his shoes and socks and shot up a palm tree like a monkey. Then in the spirit of my ink-bomb pranks at school, I urged that we all, one after the other, should have a go down the children's slide in the playground. In a letter to Randall I claimed that we all went down the slide, but that was not quite true because Chagas was anxious that his prestigious gathering did not become too raucous. I had not found in Rio the fusion of science and art that I had hoped for, but the celebratory party had some of the gaiety of our lab parties back in London.

After the celebration party I was free to leave Rio. I had studied the coccid sperm, but they did not seem very hopeful for DNA X-ray work. But I had seen, in a museum, sperm bundles from giant squid pickled in ship's brandy. The bundles were much bigger than those I had got from the *Sepia* in Naples. The museums reported sea captains' claims that squid off the Pacific coast were monstrous – bigger than their ship's lifeboats. I felt I must hunt for giant squid.

For squid, I had to go to either Chile or Peru, and I chose Peru because I wanted to see its Inca civilization. Chagas arranged for me to fly over the Andes to Lima. On the way I stopped at San Paolo to visit labs and to see the outstanding theoretical physicist David Bohm, my old friend from the Berkeley Bomb project.

Like others I had known in Berkeley, he had faced the McCarthy-ite hysteria and, following Einstein's advice, he had left the USA. He was teaching and researching, but missed Berkeley. It was very good seeing him again, and we reminisced about our trip when we had climbed Pyramid Rock; but like me, Dave was very concerned about the future of nuclear weapons. As I flew on over the Andes to Peru the pilot surprised his passengers by dipping down and circling low over a live volcano so that we could look right into the smoking crater. Watching the natural energy of the Earth gently wisping up, I realized that the energy of our man-made bombs, even though it might destroy our civilization, was utterly puny compared with what lay below the Earth's crust. That was an awesome thought indeed. Looking into that crater gave me a foretaste of the extraordinary contrast of violence and beauty I was to meet in the Andes.

In Lima I made the contacts as arranged from Rio, but I could get no lead on the monster squid, and no help from ship's captains. Moving away from science I was amazed to find an enormous collection of magnificent Peruvian pottery and tapestries in the Lima Museum. Very little of that had found its way to London. I decided I must forget about squid, and explore Peruvian art and find out more about the local cultures. A tourist plane took me high up in the Andes to Cuzco, the Inca capital. Adapting to the thin air at 12,000 feet violently affected me; but after a day or two I could slowly walk out of Cuzco and up the hills to the ancient Inca buildings. Sitting there quietly looking around me I marvelled at the stupendous size of the granite blocks metres across, which had been fitted together without cement and so exactly that a penknife could barely slip between them. The shapes and relationships of the stones were outstandingly subtle and beautiful. Though the thin air weakened me, it gave me a calm sense of timelessness which added to the impressiveness of the great stones. Apart from the beauty of the stones, the sheer skill needed to cut them so exactly seemed very impressive. I felt that working stone with such sensitivity had required great respect for the material, and that seemed a wonderful relationship of man and nature, like a scientist respecting the material he or she studies.

Feeling I must go even higher, I took a crazy little tourist railcar and zigzagged up the mountains to the remains of the deserted city Machu Pichu, which had long lain undiscovered in the almost endless mountains and forest. Stepping out of the railcar I looked up at the top of a massive peak rising out of the forests, and discerned a group of buildings that reminded me of a surreal Magritte city hanging in the sky. I walked up the steep granite road to the ancient city and found the stonework even more beautiful than it was at Cuzco. And looking down, I saw the gorges and peaks below. There was so much mysterious beauty up there.

The crater of the volcano had shown beauty, associated violence and death. That closeness showed in Cuzco where the Spanish, like invaders from another planet, had smashed the Incas' world and built a cathedral of unusual beauty and richness decorated in magnificent gold. The Catholic Church had worked the Inca gold miners to their deaths, and then replaced them with men from China. When the Machu Pichu tourists had walked past poverty-stricken peasant dwellings that contrasted with the luxurious suburbs in Lima, the peasants had stood silently looking at us. I sensed despair and suppressed violence; and not long after, Maoists turned the peasants into killers. The violence continues to this day. Contrast was strong in the Andes: everywhere was beauty and death.

In the remoteness of Cuzco I remembered my recent talks with David Bohm about the possibility of nuclear war ending our civilization. Then in Cuzco, by strange coincidence, I met a German couple who expected nuclear war and had isolated themselves in the Andes hoping to escape the worldwide destruction. I told them I'd worked on the Bomb. Surrounded by the remains of one civilization, we discussed the end of all civilization. It seemed strange that the Incas, without the advantage of writing, had created a civilization of thousands of miles with beautiful cities, roads and irrigation schemes. In our modern civilization we are very proud of our writing, literature, analytical intellect and science, but, confronted by the cultures of the Andes, I found that pride beginning to fade; and I remembered that after the Bomb I had wondered about giving up science. The Andes had so much beauty; but what of the future – where was our world going now with its bombs and science?

Up in the great mountains, I had very powerful experiences. My visit was brief, but the impression I gained was deep, and lives with me long afterwards. I had seen the heights of the peaks and had looked down at a hole in the Earth's crust that led to the molten heat below. I had seen the beauty of Inca civilization and seen the surreal ruins after its brutal destruction. All this came with the shock of oxygen deprivation, and while being forced by the conviction of the German couple to confront the possible end of all civilization. As a result I had a strange feeling of timelessness and detachment. I was able to put aside everyday thoughts and stand back and see the whole world more clearly – its past, present, and future. How did it all add up?

There, in the Andes, it was easy to see that beauty and destruction went together; but was that in the very nature of things? Many questions came into my mind. We were scientists who made the Bomb. Had we shown respect for science, and for our civilization? If DNA research revealed great secrets, what would happen to the world? Would molecular biology help us to respect humanity and all living things? Disillusion with the Bomb had led me to choose molecular biology, and such fundamental biological science seemed to have real prospects, through medicine and agriculture, of benefiting humanity. But in the Andes, thinking about beauty and brutality, I began to wonder: where would it all end?

I began to see that there were no clear answers to those questions. All we could do, I realized, was to push on, exploring the world, while keeping the big questions clearly in our minds. I must go back to our lab bench again and struggle to find the DNA structure. In that struggle we were immersed in a great stream of knowledge; as we struggled, the current sometimes carried us sideways or backwards. I had left London with a great cloud hanging over our DNA work, and what Rosalind had said in the old Head of Department's room came back into my mind again as my two months in South America came to an end. If anyone had told me that out of the gloom would emerge very soon one of the most important scientific advances of the century, I would not have been surprised except by how quickly it all took place. But where would it all end?

After a long slow flight in a pre-jet propeller plane, I finally got back to my attic flat in Soho. London was dark and cold after sunny Brazil, and I was completely exhausted. Here I was, about to be immersed again in my life in London. Loaded with beautiful objects from Peru, I would have loved to share them with Edel. But I knew she would not come back – we had finally said goodbye six months ago in the Alps. I was extremely tired, and so I exploded: for a moment out of character, I smashed the beautiful things Edel had given me over the years. I did not smash the new things I had brought back from my trip – I knew my life had to go on. I suppose I was more of a quiet Hutton than a wild Wilkins.

CHAPTER 8

THE DOUBLE HELIX

When I got back to London, I was glad to find that Herbert Wilson had arrived to work with me. He had a PhD on X-ray studies. I asked him to develop further what we had done on sperm heads and to try other nucleoproteins – naturally occurring complexes of protein and DNA from which DNA can be extracted. Since Herbert would not be working on purified DNA, he could not be seen as encroaching on Rosalind's area. In any case, I had given Rosalind all our good DNA. Also, I had a special interest in studying DNA in its natural state (such as is found in sperm), because it seemed reasonable to me to think that its structure might give us new ideas about how it functioned as gene material. Herbert was puzzled by the schism between us X-ray workers, and was surprised when I forbade him to ask Rosalind for some Signer DNA when he wanted to complex it with protein. In retrospect, this was a serious mistake, but Rosalind seemed so negative that I did not want to be involved in asking her for anything.

Apart from spending some time with Herbert, I decided for a little while to 'Go back to my microscopes' until Rosalind had got further on with her non-helical DNA. I was still in touch with microscope studies of DNA in living cells. In that work, it seemed important to measure the total amount of substance (other than water) in the chromosomes and in other regions of living cells. Working with Howard Davis, I had developed a way to find the dry mass by measuring the total refraction in the various parts of cells. I decided to test this technique on a wide range of cell types – growing tissue cultures, live amoebae, dividing pollen and so on, with the help of biologists who were expert in handling the different cells. I remember a marvellous day when a group of us worked non-stop, taking it in turns to watch as pollen cells grew and the chromosomes condensed, formed pairs and separated as the cells divided. We recorded data continuously and ate a sandwich lunch as we watched the fascinating changes in the cells. The experience was both exciting and restful, like watching the changes in a baby as it grows. That was the kind of life-science I had hoped to do when I moved out of physics. It was good too to have a change from the abstractions of DNA crystal shape and symmetry, and from the lengths and directions of chemical bonds in the molecular structure. I found the sense of community in our group, and the sharing of excitement, immensely refreshing. But I realized I must fairly soon go back to that rarefied world of crystalline genes.

Then, something extraordinary happened. One day in January 1953, Raymond met me in the corridor and handed me an excellent B pattern that Rosalind and he had taken. For me to be shown raw data in such a way was quite without precedent and, even more extraordinary, Raymond made it clear that I was to keep the photograph! I had recently been relieved to hear that Rosalind was going to leave our lab for a post at Birkbeck College, and was finishing up her work. I assumed that my being shown the pattern was connected with her plans to leave, and she was handing over data so that we could follow up what she and Raymond had done. The new photograph was almost as extraordinary as its being shown to me. It was much clearer and sharper than the first clear B pattern that Rosalind had shown us in October 1951 – the one that had so excited Stokes and me. The new pattern showed the helix X-shape more clearly than ever before. Raymond gave me to understand that Rosalind was handing the pattern over to me to use as I wished.

A few days later Jim was visiting us, and I stopped him in the main passage of our lab to show him the photograph. I said that it was very frustrating that Rosalind was continuing to base her work on non-helical ideas even though she had this new pattern that was even more convincingly helical than ever. As I stood with Jim in the corridor – I had the impression he was in a hurry to leave – I felt I must tell him what I had been thinking about base-pairing in DNA. I had only recently had an idea and, because I respected him as a scientist and knew he had thought a great deal about DNA structure, I was eager to discuss the idea with him. In the event, however, I got no further than saying 'I think Chargaff's ratios are the key to DNA structure', and Jim said 'I do too' before he hurried off.

In our lab we had been well aware of Chargaff's ratios, but no one seemed to have realized that they might mean that the bases were paired in DNA. Chargaff had not mentioned that, and he gave me the impression that connecting his ratios with structure was not good science. I respected him as a very intelligent and expert scientist, and, I think, as a result, I may have had a mental block about pairing. Also, our measurements of the water content of DNA, and our thoughts about how a molecule might maintain its physical structure, seemed to indicate three chains – so that too led us away from the possibility of pairing. Jim recalled later that he and Francis had actively considered base-pairing during the summer of 1952. At a gathering in John Kendrew's college at Cambridge I remember Francis and Jim conferring over some data in a book. I asked them what they were discussing and Francis said they would tell me later. I have wondered whether they were looking at data from a researcher called Wyatt on base-pairs, which gave more exact 1:1 ratios than Chargaff's.

A month or so before I thought about pairing, Francis and Jim decided that Francis should meet me in London in order to tell me about their pairing ideas. Jim has written that when I met Francis at lunch, I talked so much about Rosalind that he forgot to mention pairing. In some ways I am glad that Francis forgot, because a few weeks later I had the satisfaction of thinking about pairing for myself. I came up with the idea of base-pairing while trying to resolve the big contradiction in our DNA work: B-DNA seemed clearly helical whereas Rosalind's patient, thorough work seemed to show that crystalline A-DNA was not. To account for this contradiction, it occurred to me that DNA might be a lop-sided helix with phosphates arranged regularly on the outside and bases lopsided inside – the big purine bases adenine and guanine on one side, and the small pyrimidines cytosine and thymine on the other. The bases would be hydrogen-bonded together in line with Chargaff's 1:1 ratios. Because I was dominated by the idea that there had to be three or more chains, my scheme had four chains with two base-pairs lying beside each other. I was not very keen on the idea, because it seemed rather artificial. But it was an important step forward to think of base-pairing at all. I noted that the distance across both pairs would be about the same, but I did not try to decide precisely where the hydrogen bonds were, or what the exact dimensions of the base pairs were. But my general idea of base-pairs linking two chains in DNA was correct. Perhaps Fraser would have had the same idea if he had not been caught in the three-chain trap.

A colloquium was planned for early in 1953 so that Rosalind could present the conclusions of her research before she left our lab. Her talk, on 28 January, was exceptionally long, and solely about her structure for A–DNA – she did not mention the B form at all. She gave much detailed argument but, in strong contrast to my experience of her excellent talk on her discovery of the B form in our hopeful days 15 months earlier, I was left with no clear impression. I could only remember bent pieces of wire, zigzags, and figure-of-eight shapes. Doubtless all that was well thought out, but to me it did not add up. In her previous talk, her anti-helical evidence had seemed convincing, and I had thought it sensible for her to follow that up. But now, Rosalind and Raymond seemed to have achieved little by struggling with non-helical structures. It did seem sad. In retrospect I can see much to admire in Rosalind's exceptional determination: good scientists probably go down the wrong track much more than non-scientists realize; but it is distressing to think of an able scientist like Rosalind struggling so hard in the wrong direction.

At question time after her talk, I asked Rosalind how the non-helical structure she had been discussing could be reconciled with the very good B pattern she had passed on to me. Her answer was quick and simple: she saw no problem: B-DNA was helical and A-DNA was not. I was taken aback by her answer, because that was the first time I had ever heard her concede that any DNA could be helical. I was even more surprised that she thought that B-DNA was helical and A-DNA was not. I do not think it had ever occurred to me that she might believe that. I was puzzled by her apparent lack of concern that DNA would need to switch easily back and forth between the helical to non-helical forms as its water content changed. As often happened when we discussed DNA, I felt we were on different wavelengths – I did not know what to say and simply sat down. No-one else said anything about B patterns, but if the striking new pattern had been shown to the audience, I think there might have been some discussion. Why did she not show it? It seemed to me hard to believe that she thought the pattern would be of no interest. But possibly that was her belief, and that was why she had handed it over to me.

Stokes and I firmly believed that, if B–DNA was helical, A–DNA would be helical too. Actually, we did not think it had to be, but we felt strongly that it was very likely. Our first reason was this: DNA was different from Astbury's hair protein which could easily be converted from its helical form into a non–helix: all one had to do was to stretch the helix until it was straight. There was only one chain of atoms in the protein molecule, and the helix untwisted by rotations that took place about the bonds between the atoms. But DNA was different because the molecule consisted of at least two chains of atoms, and it seemed very likely that the chains were twisted round each other. That meant that for a DNA helix to change into a non–helix, one chain in the DNA had to move bodily round the other, as in the tedious process of unravelling the coiled strands in a rope. That kind of unravelling did not seem to fit with Rosalind's important discovery that DNA changed rapidly and reversibly between the A and B forms when the water content changed slightly. Our second reason was as follows: both the A and B patterns showed a strong 'pile of pennies' diffraction roughly along the fibre length, and also showed similar longer periodicities coming from the overall shape of the molecule. The basic similarities of the patterns suggested that the two structures were very similar; hence, if one was helical the other would be too. That was how Stokes and I saw the problem, and we held that view consistently. But there was no certainty in it. For example, we ignored the possibility that helical chains in DNA might lie rather clumsily side by side, and not coil neatly round each other. Our view depended largely on physical intuition and faith in simplicity. I feel that all science has to be like that in some degree. Francis was later to remark, when praising Rosalind's undoubted scientific ability, that 'if she lacked anything it was intuition ... perhaps she mistrusted it.' By then, Rosalind had written that if B-DNA was helical, then A-DNA 'must' be helical, ignoring the opposite view which she had expressed previously. Her lack of faith in intuition is in line with her wanting to base conclusions solely on hard facts 'which spoke for themselves'. Science can never be as simple as that, but she seemed to want, more than most scientists, to go as far as possible in that direction.

Shortly after Rosalind's colloquium I wrote to Francis accepting an invitation to visit him and Odile in Cambridge. I began, 'Thank you for your shoal of daily letters!' In a somewhat naïve way, I did not wonder why Francis was in such a hurry to see me, but afterwards it appeared that he and Jim urgently wanted to discuss their intention to start model-building again. The idea of Francis and Jim beginning the DNA Race again was so little to my liking that I managed not to think about it, and assumed that Bragg's Moratorium was still in force. So I looked forward to a jolly, light-hearted weekend of sociability like another recent visit to the Cricks'. That memory was so cheerful that I had persuaded Geoffrey Brown to come with me to join the fun, but in my letter I explained to Francis that Geoffrey would not be coming after all. I certainly needed some cheering up: I had found Rosalind's colloquium very depressing, and had written: 'Rosie's colloquium made me a bit sicker. God knows what will become of all this business. They talked for 1¾ hours non-stop and … had a unit cell big enough to sit in but nothing in it.' I was not being facetious: it seems that Rosalind, characteristically determined, had hoped to have a non-helical model finished to put in the large Perspex box they had made to show the shape of the unit cell – the basic repeating unit. I also referred to Linus Pauling's attempt at a DNA model which Francis and Jim had been studying. I was cheered by the prospect of having some intelligent discussion about DNA; and, fed up with secrecy and lack of communication about it, I continued rather carelessly: 'I will tell you all I can remember and scribble down from Rosie.' The meeting had not been private: if Francis or Jim had wished to come to the colloquium they could have, and there had been quite a few outsiders in the audience. However, even after discussion with Stokes, I could remember no clear message about DNA structure emerging from Rosalind's talk.

When I arrived at Francis's, Jim was there and they showed me a manuscript of Linus Pauling's paper about DNA structure. Pauling had sent the paper to his son Peter, who was visiting Cambridge. I knew that Francis and Jim were not at all keen on Linus's structure, and Francis handed me the manuscript and asked me if I could see what was wrong with it. I began looking at the table of co-ordinates showing the positions of the atoms; but, not having read the paper, it was impossible to build in my mind a picture of the structure, except that it had phosphates forming the core of the helix, as had Francis and Jim's ill-fated model. I did, however, notice that there were no sodium atoms listed, and we knew that DNA does contain sodium. When I mentioned that – because I felt I should say something – Francis exclaimed 'exactly!' as though I had shown special insight. Apparently Linus, as a chemical genius, had risked trying some very weird chemical ideas, and I had spotted the flaw, like a schoolboy at an oral exam who happens to guess right. There was also no sign that the model fitted the X-ray data. Pauling did not know about our data, and that put him at a serious disadvantage.

Francis and Jim were both convinced that Pauling's bloomer would make him more determined than ever to push on with further models, and be the first to discover the DNA structure. Because of what they saw as a new and very urgent situation, Francis and Jim asked me whether I would mind if they started building models again. I found their question horrible. I did not like treating science as a race, and I especially did not like the idea of them racing against me. I was strongly attached to the idea of the scientific community; but it seemed much too complicated to try to arrange a unified DNA effort by London and Cambridge together – and Francis and Jim made no such suggestion.

Presumably Francis and Jim had spent some time considering their approach to me; but I was taken by surprise, and at first did not know what to say. I tried to consider all aspects of the situation, and I could have done with someone like John Kendrew to give me some support. But when I assessed the extent of the log-jam in our DNA work at King's, it seemed obvious that I could not ask Francis and Jim to hold off model-building any longer. And it turned out that Bragg was of the same mind: King's had had its chance – more than a year had passed and his Moratorium should go. Also, it would have been too much for Bragg if Pauling were the first to find the DNA structure as well as the α-helix that he, Perutz and Kendrew had missed. It was, however, very disappointing for me: Rosalind was about to leave and, although there was some uncertainty about Rosalind's schedule which made forward planning tricky, we did know she was leaving soon and I was looking forward to a positive, unified DNA effort in our lab. But we would instead feel a different tension – the London-Cambridge Rat Race was to begin again! What do you say if you are trudging towards the top of an unclimbed mountain and you see another group of climbers scrambling up a parallel path? When doing science, you can suggest working together – co-operation seems so much more creative than competition – but in the DNA case that did not seem possible. I do not remember thinking about the possibility that I might be The Big Shot Who Discovered the DNA Structure, but I did not enjoy making room for Francis and Jim. DNA was not private property: it was open to all to study peacefully without any one person throwing his weight about. I could see no alternative but to accept their position – I had principles and science had to march on. But I was very cast down and could not conceal it. I had come up to Cambridge looking forward to a carefree jolly time, and now there was no chance of that. I just wanted to go home, and Francis had the sense not to press me to stay. As I walked out of the house, Jim came into the street and expressed his regrets; but I was not very receptive. I believe Jim meant well, but he later wrote, with admirable honesty, that irrespective of how I had answered their question, they would have gone ahead with their model-building. It was at least good that Francis and Jim were open about their general intentions, even though they gave me no details of their plans or ideas.

With hindsight, I think we should have done more to take down the artificial barriers between London and Cambridge. I do not remember discussing with Randall how I had agreed to Francis and Jim going ahead with model-building. It was often a good thing that he, as lab Director, let senior staff like me and Jean Hanson manage our own research policies. I must, however, have put him in the general picture. We did not know how long it would be before the DNA structure might be uncovered. Since Rosalind was leaving our lab it could be simpler to arrange joint work with Cambridge, but I did not discuss that with Randall. Looking back I see that, driven by strong feeling, I reacted rather hastily to Francis and Jim's question about pushing ahead on their own. When they wished to collaborate with our lab they had used wise John Kendrew as a mediator. John was exceptionally able at sorting out such problems, and he was a good friend of mine and knew Francis and Jim well. Looking back, I am surprised I did not talk to him – it was a difficult situation, but John might have been able to show us how to deal with it.

As the many-sided body of DNA knowledge grew – from the work of Avery, Hershey, Chargaff and many others – interest in DNA had been building up. Pauling was a newcomer to DNA.

When Francis and Jim had begun again it seemed likely that they would do much better than their first hurried model. I knew that they were thinking about base pairs because Jim had agreed with me that the Chargaff ratios were the key to the structure. I felt Francis and Jim were going to push ahead hard. There was no doubt we at King's must push hard too, and I had been looking forward very much to being with DNA again. To use Coleridge's expression, I loved DNA: I wanted to savour its nature and find what that nature revealed. The gardener turns the soil and reveals the insects, worms and other life which helps the garden to grow; a geologist studies rocks and the Earth's history is revealed. What would DNA reveal? Great prospects seemed to be emerging. There was a feeling of history in the air – and a pressure of necessity. I knew that our renewed attack on DNA would not be easy, but we just had to get on, keep cool and do our best. There were changes for the better. We could achieve unity in our work; no longer was I standing aside as Rosalind worked on and on to find non-helical DNA. She was leaving soon and had handed over to me a brilliant helical B pattern, and I looked forward to getting back some of the invaluable Signer DNA that she and Raymond had been using.

Until I knew definitely when Rosalind was going, I felt we could not set up a new group and get to grips with DNA. However, very soon after my ill-fated visit to Cambridge I remembered that I had arranged to visit Harriet Ephrussi in Paris about getting some of her biologically active DNA (it could genetically transform bacteria). Harriet had always been very encouraging, and visiting her would help to fill the time while I waited to know Rosalind's date of departure. I set out with two of our very bright young men, Geoffrey Brown and Joe Chayen. Joe wanted to visit the cell biologist Jean Brachet in Brussels, and I was glad to see Brachet because I admired him not only for his studies of DNA in cells but also for his work with the Resistance in the War. We had very good talks with him about DNA in chromosomes. On the way, we were lucky to find marvellous music in Bruges Cathedral. Joe then went back to London for the Jewish Sabbath, and I went on with Geoffrey to Paris where Harriet gave us her DNA.

It was a really good little excursion and helped me to get going. We soon found Harriet's DNA gave a good crystalline X-ray pattern like that of Signer's DNA. This showed for the first time that the crystalline pattern, which gave the most detailed and exact X-ray data, was not just peculiar to DNA from a special type of cell in calf thymus – it was also given by real live genetic material. Thus, the wide significance of our work became even more clear than before. And, since Signer was no longer making his DNA, it was very good to have found an alternative source of first-class material – techniques for producing it had much improved in the three years since Signer had given away his DNA. And just a few days later, my friend Leonard Hamilton (another art enthusiast), who worked at the Sloan Kettering Cancer Institute in New York, sent us excellent quality human DNA from his lab. Leonard was to become our main supplier of DNA.

As Rosalind's departure became imminent, I began to assemble a group to continue, intensify and broaden our DNA structure work. The nature of the problem required a broad interdisciplinary approach. Also, like the Bomb Project, DNA structure was so important that a range of different approaches in parallel was needed. Randall agreed to it all. Bill Seeds was ready to give up microscope work and build molecular models of DNA. Now that we had really good DNA, Herbert Wilson put nucleo-proteins on one side and was full-time on DNA. Stokes looked forward to helping us with special mathematics. Now we could have a loosely organized group of the kind I had looked forward to when Rosalind had first arrived two years before. We could pull ourselves together, and it was very good to be working again in constructive comradeship.

I wrote to Francis on 7 March 1953, about a month after Rosalind's colloquium. I had heard nothing from him since I had walked out of his home in January, and, sad to say, I did not feel friendly enough to write 'My dear Francis'.

> *I think you will be interested to know that our dark lady leaves us next week and much of the 3-dimensional data is already in our hands. I am now reasonably clear of other commitments and have started up a general offensive on Nature's secret strongholds on all fronts; models, theoretical chemistry and interpretation of data crystalline and comparative. At last the decks are clear and we can put all hands to the pumps!*
> *It won't be long now.*
> *Regards to all.*
> *Yours ever M*
> *P.S. may be in Cambridge next week.*

Francis said later that my letter arrived on the morning they finished assembling and checking their model that is now famous as the Double Helix. He seemed to find the coincidence amusing, but I did not find it as funny as he did. I had had a faint hope that giving him news of our broad attack on DNA might deter him from pushing on too fast. Maybe that was weak logic, but in any case, I thought I should keep in touch. Looking back now I am not at all certain how serious I was when I wrote, 'It won't be long now'; but we were really going to try.

It was John Kendrew, helpful as usual, who telephoned me to invite me to Cambridge to see the new model Francis and Jim had built, and he briefly told me what it was like. Jim later wrote that neither he nor Francis had wanted the task of breaking their news to me. This was not like the relatively carefree time 18 months before when Francis called me to see their first model. Now there was tension in the air. I was in a train to Cambridge straight away. And then: there was the model in front of me, standing high on a lab bench. In some basic ways the model was familiar: I recognized features as in the Fraser model – phosphates on the outside and bases stacked in the middle and joined by hydrogen bonds. But there were only two chains in the structure, and that made it very different from the Fraser model with its three chains. As I concentrated on Francis and Jim's model, Francis kept talking and confused me by referring to a diad axis, which made no sense because the bases were all different. Then I realized he was talking about everything other than the bases. He stressed that the special new features of the model lay in the hydrogen bonds that linked the bases in pairs as in the Chargaff ratios, and also in the important fact that the sequence of atoms in one chain ran up while in the other chain it ran down (that up and down was where the twofold diad axes came in). But the really impressive feature of the structure was the extraordinary way in which the two kinds of base pairs had exactly the same overall dimensions and shape. I had recently noted that the two Chargaff pairs would be about the same size, but I had not made detailed and exact studies. That exactness led Francis and Jim directly to a mechanism for gene replication. By splitting the base pairs apart, and pairing each base with another molecule of the same partner again, this DNA could replicate itself. Whether that idea was right or not, we could only guess. But a feeling came through to me that the model, though only bits of wire on a lab bench, had a special life of its own. It seemed like an incredible new-born baby that spoke for itself, saying 'I don't care what you think – I know I am right.' (As the years went by, that baby had a lot more to say for itself.) Jim wrote later that sometimes he had feared that the DNA structure might turn out to be uninteresting. Clearly that was not the case. It seemed that non-living atoms and chemical bonds had come together to form life itself.

I was rather stunned by it all – the exactness and the replication idea, and the resolving of the paradox that DNA was so regular (even crystalline) and yet contained the complex and irregular genetic message in the sequence of base pairs. And Francis's sophisticated talk of diad axes of symmetry that had confused me was actually important, because X-rays had ruled out the Fraser model which lacked diads. New understanding of the hydrogen bonding that held the pairs of bonds together – this had come from the work of Jerry Donohue from Pauling's lab – had turned out to be vital. There was no denying that Francis and Jim were exceptionally brilliant. They had tapped into the very life of scientific knowledge and the model had appeared. Standing in front of their model, it did not occur to me to mention that I too had been thinking about Chargaff-type base pairs held together by hydrogen bonds. I had seen that the pairs were about the same size; but the exactness and symmetry of the model in front of me was well beyond where I had got to. There was only one aspect of the model that really worried me. It was a surprise that there were only two chains in the model because a large amount of water would be needed to fill the space between them. The observed water content of DNA fibres was much smaller. I said that point would have to be looked into very carefully.

Soon afterwards, when we had finished looking at the model, the discussion suddenly took a new turn. I was surprised by Francis and Jim inviting me to join them as co-author of the publication that would describe the model. John Kendrew had not said anything to me about authorship, and I do not remember thinking about that as I had sat in the train coming up to Cambridge. From the moment I had known that Francis and Jim were building models again, I had assumed that they would want to publish on their own. Now, having been completely absorbed in examining the model, I needed a rest. I had little energy and was not prepared for discussing authorship questions. For an instant I recalled the deeply satisfying times I had experienced with DNA, and I felt possessive of it. How much did Francis and Jim's model-building depend on work done at King's? I sounded bitter, and Francis said I was unfair. I did not think of thanking Francis and Jim for the generosity of their offer. One reason why I was unhappy was that a month had passed since I had last seen or heard from Francis or Jim. I had known that giving them the go-ahead might open the floodgates. But things had moved more rapidly than I had expected and it would have been nice to have had a word or two from them. But I quickly cooled and collected my thoughts, and said I could not be co-author as I had not taken part directly in building the model. I would have been embarrassed if the model had been the Watson, Crick and Wilkins model. Francis agreed, but he explained that Jim had been very concerned that I should not be left out, and he had joined Jim in their generous offer. We then returned to discussion of the science of DNA, but avoided any reference to who had made which contribution. When Jim later wrote his story of the discovery, he did not mention my angry outburst. Was that out of kindness? Talking about bad feeling can be unpleasant, but here it was probably unhelpful because it discouraged us from discussing Who Had Done What.

I think I was more deeply disturbed by the Great Discovery than I realized at the time. I was, of course, disappointed that I had not been more involved in the final great step, but on the other hand I firmly believed that what really mattered was scientific progress. I despised thoughts about fame, and perhaps that made me feel insulted by Francis and Jim's generous offer. I know that I also felt that professional recognition of what a scientist has done was important; and that connected to my own feeling that my scientific work contributed a great deal to my sense of my own identity. In any case, I could not think clearly in all the excitement.

After I had seen the Double Helix and talked with Francis and Jim, I hurried back to London and told everyone at King's what the main features of the structure were. Raymond passed the news on to Rosalind, who was now working at Birkbeck College a mile or so to the north of King's in Bloomsbury. As the days passed, I began to wish that I had behaved with more dignity when discussing co-authorship. I hoped I had not given the impression I was over-concerned about scientific priority. I tried to clarify my attitude in my letter acknowledging receipt of Francis and Jim's draft publication about their model. I began by accepting the situation reluctantly – 'I think you're a couple of old rogues' – and then went on somewhat casually with 'who the hell got it isn't what matters'. I saw such principles in science as very important: that science should be basically co-operative and grow organically with each individual scientist contributing to the whole. This is what Newton was referring to when he said he had 'stood on the shoulders of Giants'. Art, literature and music are different in that they depend more deeply on special qualities of the individual. And although I had not been directly one of the discoverers of the Double Helix, I gained satisfaction from having contributed to the discovery; and I much looked forward to the very important, careful study that would be needed to show that the Double Helix was firmly based on experimental fact.

My rejection of co-authorship led to separate papers from Cambridge and London being published together. Francis and Jim had written a short paper to be published quickly in *Nature*, but consultation and negotiation with the editor gave King's a week or two to write about our X-ray work, which would be published alongside the world-shattering announcement from Cambridge. The paper I wrote for *Nature* welcomed the general form of the model Francis and Jim had built. Many of the features had been in the Fraser model. The main problem was to check by water content that there were two chains and not three. I also noted a special feature of the model I had seen in Cambridge: the regular sequence of nucleotides along a chain was rather similar to the system of steps in a spiral staircase. Each nucleotide had roughly the shape of a step on a staircase, i.e. the bases were roughly horizontal and at right angles to the helix axis. Having noted this I went back to our lab and calculated the diffraction pattern from a spiral staircase, and I was encouraged to find that the pattern showed an overall X like that in Rosalind's first B-DNA pattern. In contrast, the crystalline A pattern of DNA did not show the overall X, but showed it was helical because there was a marked absence of diffraction along the helix axis direction. That had been the important evidence noted by Stokes in 1950. Also, in 1951, I had obtained the diffuse B pattern from DNA from different species, which indicated a helical structure. I had described that evidence for a helical structure at Perutz's July 1951 meeting, when Rosalind, very sadly, had been surprised to find me continuing DNA X-ray study. I described these helical ideas in our *Nature* paper, which was published alongside Francis and Jim's announcement of the Double Helix.

When my writing was almost complete, I was surprised by Raymond, who handed me a typescript that Rosalind and he wanted to publish alongside what I had written on the helical DNA work at King's. I was still weighed down by Rosalind's very long colloquium where she had described a very tough and unsuccessful struggle to find a non-helical DNA structure, and had not mentioned the possibility of helices, except in reply to my question-time query about the very clear helical pattern that Raymond had given me. It did not occur to me that, after that talk, Rosalind would have begun a very different, and helical, approach to DNA structure. I assumed that the typescript Raymond handed to me was nothing more than a response to the Double Helix, which had caused Rosalind to change very radically her long-standing dismissal of helices. But I should have recognized how, in answer to my question, Rosalind had said that '$\underline{B}$ is helical, $\underline{A}$ is not' – and that was an important change in her attitude to helices. Stokes and I had missed the full significance of

Rosalind's statement. Taken as a whole, it did not make sense because the transition from A to B could hardly take place as rapidly as Rosalind observed, because the two chains in DNA would have to wind round each other to form helical B. In contrast, the transition from A to B for helical DNA would be roughly like stretching or compressing a spiral spring. However, Rosalind's statement that B-DNA is helical required attention in its own right, and indicated that Rosalind had made a crucially important change in her attitude to DNA structure. As a result, she had, in January 1953, taken her 1952 pattern and told Raymond to show it to me – and I had shown it to Jim. And when the Double Helix was published in *Nature*, Rosalind published her best helical pattern: the 1952 photograph that had sat in a drawer for a year.

That photograph was to become the celebrated Double Helix pattern – possibly the most famous X-ray diffraction pattern ever photographed. In retrospect, I had been rather foolish to show it to Jim during our hurried conversation in the corridor. Part of my motive was to justify my exasperation with Rosalind for opposing helical ideas when the evidence seemed to point us clearly in that direction. I had also thought that Jim was already familiar with B patterns – for example, I had already sent Francis a sketch of the helical diffraction I had seen from the sperm heads. Jim's refusal to accept Rosalind's anti-helical evidence seemed to show that he was as firmly as ever committed to helical ideas. I did not imagine that the pattern would give Jim much new information or change his attitude to helices. However, I was wrong: Jim later wrote that seeing the pattern had spurred him on tremendously to build helical models of DNA. If I had known that, I might well not have shown him the pattern. I had forgotten that the early B patterns Jim had seen at Rosalind's colloquium more than a year before were not very clear, although they had greatly impressed Stokes and me as indicating DNA was helical. It seems that Jim, somewhat mistakenly, thought that the pattern I showed him was a new type which gave quite new evidence that DNA was helical.

The publication of separate papers about the same discovery was unusual, and questions arose about how the model had come into being. Almost everyone who believed that their work had contributed to the model got over-excited in one way or another. And, of course, I was not free of such feelings! Who was to give a special lecture on the model, who was to speak on the radio, was anything being arranged for television? Everyone who touched DNA seemed to go a little crazy. I said DNA was like the gold of Midas – touch it and you go mad. The only exception was Stokes, but he said later that he had not realized how very important DNA was. Such a very great scientific advance! There was a story about the first astronauts arriving on the Moon, who, having co-operated in their magnificent enterprise, still argued about who would be The First to step on extra-terrestrial soil. The DNA situation was a bit like that.

Much later, Rosalind's notebooks revealed clearly that, at the time she was moving from King's, she had begun to take seriously the ideas about helical DNA for the B form that she had dismissed in 1951, and was using Stokes' mathematical Bessel functions. So before the Double Helix was built, Rosalind had begun to think about a helical structure, and the *Nature* paper she and Raymond produced, for publication alongside Francis and Jim's description of their model, was honestly written and based on sound ideas we had developed at King's. While her lengthy struggle to find a non-helical structure for DNA was unsuccessful, she had stepped, in 1953, on to the right path to DNA. Jim had written that my showing Rosalind's 1952 pattern had greatly stimulated him. DNA science would have moved more rapidly forward if Rosalind had shared the pattern in May 1952 when she obtained it. At the time when the Double Helix was built, I knew nothing of Rosalind beginning helical work in early 1953. We had had no news from Rosalind after the depressing colloquium. When, many years later, her notebooks showed that she had begun to think about helical DNA, I was reminded of how, more than a year before, she had come to my room to ask me to help her think about signs that the B pattern showed that DNA contained two parts separated by three-eighths of the repeat distance. It may seem amazing that at that time neither of us saw the obvious explanation – DNA had two chains separated by three-eighths of the repeat distance. Scientists sometimes miss ideas that may later appear obvious. One of the causes of our mental block arose from reluctance to accept the idea that DNA might consist of only two chains. As our struggle to find the structure had continued for more than a year, it was not very unexpected that Rosalind was later to consider two-chain DNA. Also, I think the fact that she was trying to finish up at King's and begin new work at Birkbeck College may have helped her to consider possibilities that might otherwise have seemed unreasonable.

The discussion in Rosalind's notebook of two-chain DNA with three-eighths separation was from a month or so before the Double Helix model was built. I felt it gratifying that Rosalind had set down those thoughts independently of the new Cambridge work. She did not mention the idea of base-pairing; but I was keen about the importance of that idea, and if she and I had discussed the problem there would have been little to prevent us finding the Double Helix.

CHAPTER 9

❖

LIVING WITH THE DOUBLE HELIX

The excitement of the extraordinary discovery stressed and bewildered us. Jim was sensitive to the tension between his work with Francis and ours at King's. Soon after the Double Helix was announced he was invited to talk on the DNA structure at the Hardy Club, the leading scientific society in Cambridge, and he was concerned that I should come to hear what he had to say. Since Jim had favoured the co-authorship idea, I could understand he might wish me to hear how he acknowledged the contribution from our lab. He gave, as I expected, a good talk about the structure and what it implied for replication, and he seemed at ease; but to my surprise he said nothing at all about us at King's. There was no limelight for us. I just sat there like any other member of the large audience. I was puzzled. Then, when he finished, Jim came to me and said he was sorry that he had forgotten to mention King's. Clearly he had intended to say something about our work, but I was at a loss to know what to say to him. We just let the matter slide, neither of us being able to get to grips with the situation.

Now, I have an idea that shows how our memories may play tricks on us, and which helps to explain the Hardy Club puzzle. At that meeting I was preoccupied with what we had done on the DNA structure, and with how Jim would acknowledge us. As a result, I tended to see the talk as being about DNA model-building. I had forgotten that the Hardy Club embraced all kinds of science, and that most of the audience would at that time have known almost nothing about DNA and its significance. Clearly Jim needed to talk about the scientific context of genes and replication, because without that the importance of the Double Helix model could not be understood. As a result, most of Jim's talk was not, as I had tended to assume, about matters directly connected with our work at King's. That makes it easier to understand how he had forgotten to mention us. Similarly, all of us embroiled in the DNA affair were preoccupied with our own positions, and had somewhat distorted impressions of what had actually taken place.

It can not have been easy for Jim in his talk to decide just what to say about the work at King's, especially since Francis, Jim and I had never sat down and discussed that question. Jim's situation certainly was extraordinary, even fantastic – Harriet Ephrussi told me that he was well aware of that. He was still only 23 years old, only just with his doctorate, and already he had found his Holy Grail. With very mature scientific judgement and an especially suitable background in genetics, he could see the Double Helix as the most important discovery of the century. I do not think he was overwhelmed by that, but it was not surprising that he did not handle too well his acknowledgement of the contribution from King's.

A few weeks after Francis and Jim published their preliminary account of the Double Helix, they published a second paper in *Nature* on how the structure could suggest a mechanism for gene replication. Scientists today would consider it very sensible that they published quickly and did not leave gene replication for others to discuss for the first time. Some of Francis and Jim's friends, however, thought the second paper was rather 'going over the top'. John Kendrew was one of those critics, and at the time I was inclined to share his view. But as the excitement began to settle down, nearly all scientists realized it was sensible that the gene replication idea was published quickly, simply because it was so very important. This incident illustrates how difficult it can be, even for very good scientists, to judge the importance of new ideas.

After the publication of the discovery, and Francis's many enthusiastic talks about The Secret of Life, the response was enormous – though not at the level we might expect today. The exceptional importance of the model was clear to the press, and to a small number of scientists with special insight. Many scientists, strange though it may seem now, were too set in their ways to recognize the importance of the model – it was outside their way of thinking. I told an old friend, a very intelligent biologist, some stories about the great discovery and asked him not to repeat some of my details. He replied 'Don't worry Maurice, I am not likely to meet anyone interested in DNA.' Genetics was still a specialized area, and had barely become part of academic biology.

The Double Helix discovery was in some ways a classic victory of science. But it had many other characteristics which have not been sufficiently emphasized. The discovery was an excellent example of interdisciplinary science. A very wide range of scientific discoveries formed the foundation on which the Double Helix was built. At the biological end, there were new developments in genetics, such as those of the Phage Group. Avery's work showing that DNA was the genetic material was vital, as were biochemical studies of many kinds, organic chemistry, and physical chemistry in many forms. A special example was J.M. Gulland's work on hydrogen bonding between single DNA chains pairing up in solution. Ultraviolet light showed that the bases could be lined up, and viscosity measurements and molecular weights also pointed us in useful directions. And, of course, X-ray diffraction was crucial. I believe that the coming together of all these different branches of science was one of the factors that made the Double Helix story so important: quite new vistas arose from new combinations of approaches. When I gave lectures on DNA I drew a diagram of a pyramid with all the different scientific branches making a foundation at the bottom, and at the top was the Double Helix.

Another aspect of the Double Helix discovery that has not been properly recognized was expressed by Francis and Jim when discussing their collaboration. They made a very important and perceptive observation when they claimed that their success had depended on them being very open when the two of them discussed their differences. They argued very frankly, sometimes even taking their friendship and collaboration to its limits. That was a good way to be truly creative. In contrast, in our lab we suffered from a sad lack of openness, and would walk away from confrontation leaving matters unresolved, rather than facing up to our differences; but Francis and Jim's open discussions were uninhibited dialogue, involving very close attention to what was said. I regret that open discussion was not used to clarify the relation of the DNA work at King's and at Cambridge. We should not have hurriedly disposed of the co-authorship question: Francis and Jim would hardly have made their offer if they had not agreed that King's had contributed significantly. Wider discussion could quite possibly have led to us learning how Rosalind had used helical analysis just before the Double Helix had been completed. We might have learnt about several other matters that were not revealed until 15 years later when Jim wrote his recollections of the discovery. Thus we might have generated an atmosphere of creative co-operative science in spite of the negative Bragg Moratorium.

One reason I have mentioned Gulland's work is that he was killed in a railway accident and his name is, as a result, seldom seen. Other scientists have had a troublesome relationship with the credit they got for their contribution. Chargaff is one clear example: he discovered that the four different bases in DNA occurred in different amounts in different species, but that cytosine was always present in the same amount as guanine, and adenine in the same amount as thymine. Those 1:1 ratios were a very important part of DNA structure. But Chargaff never wrote down (or mentioned to me when we discussed it in 1951) that 1:1 ratios suggested pairing of the bases. He seemed to become very bitter when the Double Helix appeared with pairing, and near the end of his life apparently went so far as to condemn science as a whole. Jerry Donohue had given crucial information to Jim and Francis about the hydrogen bonding in the base pairs, and that help was clearly acknowledged; but Donohue was unhappy with the Double Helix. As we at King's worked steadily to make certain that the Double Helix was correct, Donohue published a series of studies of alternative structures. This was a very good idea scientifically, but it suggested that Donohue was unsettled by the Double Helix.

The question of who had thought about base-pairing also raised some tensions. I had said to Jim that the Chargaff ratios were the key to the DNA structure, and he had replied that he thought so too. I had met Francis for lunch to discuss, according to Jim, base pairing, which would explain the 1:1 ratios. But Francis did not mention pairing at lunch; according to Jim's later recollections, Francis forgot to discuss pairing. Francis apparently also forgot that in my letter to him after seeing the Double Helix model, I mentioned that I had thought about pairing. I was dismayed when Francis wrote for the twenty-first anniversary of the Double Helix that King's had 'missed the pairing of the bases and ... completely overlooked the significance of Chargaff's rule'. For the fortieth anniversary celebrations, Francis did not repeat this serious error, and his contribution had a good title: *DNA: A Cooperative Discovery*. But on the whole I think the exceptionally large number of scientists who contributed to the Double Helix made it difficult for them all to receive proper acknowledgement. As science today becomes increasingly global and interdisciplinary, the idea of any scientist standing up like someone on the top of Everest becomes increasingly inappropriate.

Strong feelings of urgency had developed in the months before the Double Helix. Francis and Jim were in a great rush to publish in case Pauling reached the DNA goal before them. In just two months, both Pauling and Francis and Jim had begun work on DNA again; Rosalind had left us, and had left behind at King's the best helical pattern; our MRC report had reached Cambridge; Bragg's Moratorium had finished; non-helical ideas had faded; and I had formed a new DNA group. We were all caught up and swept along by our own excitement and enthusiasm, and then suddenly: there was the Double Helix. Few scientists have been through such an upheaval. Most scientists spend their careers contributing to the long, slow accumulation of data and ideas, and to be involved in a dramatic victory is a very rare privilege. When the Double Helix structure was first revealed, the great excitement and publicity tended to give the impression that all one needed for exciting new ideas to emerge in science was a lot of energy and a dash of genius. As a result, some ambitious young scientists got carried away and looked around for new opportunities like the Double Helix, but did not give much attention to the painstaking task of building up new knowledge. Such scientists were seldom successful.

Let no one hurry to pass judgement on just how we DNA workers behaved in our moment of discovery. Jim, with his conscience and ethical concerns, has written about his intense involvement with genes and his sense of mission to use Pauling's method of molecular models to find the DNA structure. The very amiable Francis, who never condemned anyone except for doing poor science (or for being too slow!), enthusiastically joined in with his helical vision. And then there was me, and all three of us were caught in the whirlwind. None of us was without feelings for others, but, because of all the rush, it was difficult to find time for discussing who had done what.

It took our team at King's seven years to build up the clear body of knowledge that established the correctness of the Crick and Watson Double Helix. Francis and Jim had brought it into being less than three years after I was given DNA by Signer, Raymond and I had obtained the first clear evidence that DNA was crystalline, and Alec Stokes had pointed out signs that DNA was helical. The structure gave a new sense of direction in our work: many very important possibilities for biological and medical research could grow out of the Double Helix. We were keen to develop our X-ray studies in order to help that growth. Francis and Jim agreed that we should be responsible for extending our work and putting the Double Helix on a more detailed and accurate X-ray diffraction basis. In that way we could get closer to the truth –

science cannot give final truth, but it can move in that direction. The Double Helix was brilliant, but already alternative ideas for DNA structure were appearing. Extending our work would help science to make the best choice.

Randall, with his eye for the future, asked me if he could join in. But he was not interested in my suggestion that he should take over the sperm X-ray diffraction and other studies of DNA interacting with proteins. Randall wanted to study DNA itself, and I wanted to concentrate on that myself. Randall quietly accepted this. I had several specimens of DNA that made excellent fibres and gave diffraction as clear and sharp as Signer's DNA. By the time Rosalind left King's she and Raymond had used up all the Signer DNA, but we now had a good quality supply from Hamilton in New York.

In the *Nature* publications about the Double Helix, attention was concentrated on the B configuration of DNA. In contrast, the A configuration seemed more complicated, and not so easy to define in helical terms. Francis and Jim had made some suggestions about how the B structure might be compressed to form the A structure when the water content of DNA was reduced. Also, the B patterns were much less well defined than the crystalline A. As a result, the X-ray intensities could be more accurately measured for A than for B. In view of these difficulties we decided our first target would be to clarify the nature of the A structure. Herbert Wilson, Alec Stokes and I concentrated on the X-ray aspect, and Bill Seeds mainly built molecular models. We saw that there were 11 repeating chemical units per turn of the DNA helix, and that inclining the bases slightly enabled them to keep 3.4Å apart as in the B structure. It was only when we built a model that we were able to see this point. This illustrates how model building is not a mere illustration of thought, but enables the mind to explore and find new structures that may otherwise not appear out of imaginative processes. Looking back, I remembered the time when we realized the Fraser model was wrong because it had three chains. I did not try model building then because I could not think of what model to build. I realize now that if I had begun model building, the exploratory nature of the process might have led me to new thoughts.

Why did we think seriously of three chains, and not see that the symmetry of the DNA crystals pointed to a two-chain structure? Looking back, I now wonder whether those of us who learnt crystallography as students at Cambridge – and that included Alec Stokes, Rosalind Franklin and me – were conscious of the theory but did not know how to relate it to real structures. The crystallography teaching at Cambridge was done too much by staff who were not engaged in Bernal's pioneering research. As a result, concepts were presented in an abstract way and not linked to the process of discovering molecular structures. This may be why we failed to see that the symmetry of DNA crystals pointed to DNA having two chains. In contrast, Francis, who had learned crystallography while researching on protein structures, quickly realized that DNA crystal symmetry pointed to two chains in DNA. And Jim, as a geneticist, saw biological reasons why the material of heredity would consist of two chains.

But whatever our training, crystallography was a very demanding and laborious field. Now that we had the model, we could calculate from it the diffraction pattern we could expect to see; but that was a far from simple process, especially because computers were not yet available except in centres that specialized in mathematical research. Cambridge University had a computer, and Perutz had access to it for his X-ray work. But I was still using simple geometrical methods for the calculations – I had never liked the special X-ray card system that Rosalind and Raymond were used to. But we were able easily enough to adjust the Double Helix model so that it matched the observed diffraction pattern, and we were able to account for all the differences between the A and B patterns. The whole study was very encouraging, and we decided that next we should study the B configuration of DNA in more detail. We were greatly helped by finding a crystalline B pattern when we replaced the sodium ions in DNA with lithium ions. We could then measure B diffraction in three dimensions, and all the data would have much higher accuracy. That was a very big advance.

The three papers that had appeared in *Nature* had linked the Double Helix to the diffraction from the B-DNA. I had expected that Rosalind would then have changed to X-ray studies on virus structure when she moved to Birkbeck, so I was a little surprised when she published in *Nature* a very elegant diagram of DNA using the Patterson computational method to analyse the diffraction. Rosalind had linked the Double Helix idea with her X-ray data on crystalline A–DNA. Those data, a year earlier, had appeared to her to show that DNA could not be helical. I was therefore somewhat surprised to see them now being used to show that DNA was helical, and that the phosphate groups appeared to be separated by a distance of one half the helix pitch.

In the summer of 1953 we presented a model of our A structure, a modified Double Helix, at an exhibition in Brussels as further confirmation that the Double Helix was basically correct. After that I happened to meet Rosalind, and she surprised me by saying that I should have told her about the A-type model we had made in agreement with Francis and Jim's ideas. Rosalind was a very skilful worker, but her colleagues have since agreed that there was a mistake in her Patterson procedures in her work on A-DNA. It was right to use microcameras for exploratory work, such as her excellent B pattern, which helped to set in motion Francis and Jim's approach to the Double Helix. But, by the end of 1951, I had realized that the sharpness of crystalline A-DNA patterns was so great that bigger X-ray cameras were needed to show all the detail. Having had such a camera made in 1951, I should have suggested to Rosalind that we tried it together on Signer DNA fibres. But because of the schism in our lab that did not occur to me. The Patterson was very elegant, but our higher resolution cameras showed that Rosalind's interpretation of it was incorrect.

Our experience with trying to obtain the highest resolution from DNA X-ray patterns showed that the overlap of reflections was often considerable, and indexing a particular spot on the pattern could often be very difficult. Looking back on Rosalind and

Raymond's work in 1951-1953, we were not surprised that certain conclusions then were incorrect. Rosalind's report to me and Stokes in July 1952 that three-dimensional data showed asymmetry which ruled out helical structures was a mistake, and there was no need to suppose Rosalind's report was a spoof. The Patterson pattern published in 1953 gave a similar wrong conclusion.

The more experimental data we produced, the more laborious our calculations became. Help arrived in the form of Bob Langridge, a new PhD student, who was very keen to use computers. At first I thought it would not take us long to find the correct structure, and developing computer programmes would not be necessary. But Bob found that the pioneering computer company IBM had a large building near us in London which contained enormous computers, and could give him free time. Bob used the IBM 650 which occupied huge cabinets, but by today's standards was very modest in capacity and capability – it had a mere 2000 words of memory, all on a rotating drum. I was worried for the sake of Bob's PhD studies that many months of his time were spent before the programmes worked. Model building of the B–DNA also took up more time than I expected. Years seemed to slip by, and Francis became worried that we had not got really clear verification of the Double Helix. Spurred on by his concerns, we made a special effort and published the best results we had. However, it was not easy to get the results we wanted, and among our shortcomings was that the sugar rings in our DNA structure needed to be almost planar, which was unlikely to be correct – Perutz had pointed that out, reminding us that sugar rings are not flat. It was a mistake to allow ourselves to be pushed into premature publication: we had to do a thorough job. To do that we got an even bigger X-ray camera with a very fine collimator, lined up a group of fibres and adjusted the camera so that the X-rays fell on a new part of the specimen every week. After eight weeks we thought the X-ray film was adequately exposed, and Herbert Wilson developed the film. When he came out of the dark room I did not need to ask him if the X-ray pattern was OK – I saw his cheerful smile and knew our results were good. Despite the challenges and frustrations of the research, we were working well as a group now, sharing responsibilities, and the spirit of community was excellent. Indeed, during the years after the Double Helix, there was a very co-operative and friendly feeling among DNA workers.

During these good times, a young woman caught my eye one evening at the Institute of Contemporary Arts, a centre for modern art, dance, film and theatre just off Trafalgar Square, a short walk from King's. Seeing her walking into the crowded Institute, I immediately felt: 'There is some *spirit*!' So I introduced myself. Her name was Patricia Chidgey, and she turned out to be a lively person with wide interests in human questions, art and dancing. She was also beautiful, and much in demand as an artists' model. But when I met her she was teaching in a broad-minded Rudolph Steiner school for children with learning difficulties. That interested me very much. She was also the only woman among my special friends who impressed Eithne. Patricia and I were together for three years before we married. After my experience with Ruth, I was very concerned that I should not rush into marriage again. But we grew confident of our relationship, and in 1958 we married in a register office with some of our artist friends as witnesses, and then we went for a short honeymoon in Dorset, on the south coast of England. It was the start of a very meaningful partnership.

At King's, DNA continued to challenge us. One particular difficulty in our attempts to get agreement between the calculated diffraction from the model and the observed diffraction from real molecules was that we were unable to build a B model with the bases sufficiently close to the axis of the helix. I made a concentrated effort to overcome this difficulty just before a long holiday weekend when I planned to walk along the cliffs of Kent with Patricia. I felt I would not have peace of mind on our trip if I did not first solve the problem of the DNA model, and so I worked very intensely, making very small alterations in the directions of chemical bonds. Setting myself this deadline enabled me to overcome the difficulty, and I built a model with the base pairs where they needed to be. I then went on my long walk with Patricia, linking our enjoyment with a sense of achievement in my work.

In our DNA work, we took special care to increase the reliability of our X-ray results. To check the correctness of our computer programmes and overall procedures, we drew a diagram of the model and made holes of sizes corresponding to the X-ray scattering from each atom. We then took a diffraction photograph of the drawing using ordinary light, with the holes scattering the light just as atoms would scatter X-rays. We confirmed that the light pattern was identical to the X-ray pattern. We had enough staff now to make these detailed checks: for example, Mike Spencer published a paper comparing all the base-pairing dimensions that had become available since Donohue's data had been used in the Double Helix.

The most detailed and thorough X-ray study of DNA was begun in 1957, and led by the very able Watson Fuller, who was working for his PhD. Our first Double Helix study in 1953-1954 had been simplified and approximate because we did not have computer methods. After Bob Langridge developed computer methods with crystalline B-DNA, we hoped to define new detail in the A structure. We found that the 11-fold structure that I had noticed was arranged in the crystal in a way that was in agreement with the interatomic contacts between neighbouring molecules. Another colleague, Don Marvin, refined the B form, and, with Mike Spencer, determined the structure of a new semi-crystalline form designated C-DNA. Don began using Fourier synthesis techniques to search for water molecules in the structure. Struther Arnott extended the use of Fourier synthesis to refine the position of the base-pairs and to rule out other base-pairing schemes. Some of the positions of the water molecules associated with DNA were indicated, but most of the sodium ions and water molecules were, as one might expect, in somewhat irregular positions like those in a liquid. (The more certain locations of water around the various crystalline forms of DNA became possible three decades later, when Watson Fuller and his group at Keele University used neutron diffraction techniques at the Institute Langevin in Grenoble.)

There did, overall, seem to be basic features common to all kinds of double-helical DNA. And this basic consistency of structure was emphasized when, with Langridge's help, we found that another biological molecule related to DNA, viral RNA – they are both nucleic acids – had a very similar double-helix structure. At that stage, I began to feel that X-ray studies had clearly made the point that the Double Helix was a fundamental part of living matter. It also seemed to me that further X-ray studies in this field were not likely to reveal much of real biological interest, and I began to look around for some other field of study.

In 1960, Francis, Jim and I were given the Albert Lasker Award. These prizes were relatively new then, and came from the Lasker Foundation in San Francisco, which gave seed grants for fundamental research in basic science to encourage public funding for promising projects. The idea of the prizes was to draw attention to work that helped our understanding of serious diseases, and used novel concepts or methods. The citation referred to 'The painstaking x-ray diffraction studies of M.H.F. Wilkins [which]

provided a most important clue which was pursued in an ingenious fashion and to a logical conclusion by F.H.C. Crick and J.D. Watson ...'. It acknowledged that the details of the structure were still being elucidated, but it suggested that the Double Helix would 'nevertheless serve as a substantial contribution to a better understanding of the location of specific genetic information and of the means by which replication and mutation of genes may take place. The research of Wilkins, Crick, and Watson has provided a firm foundation for many advances in man's fight against the ravages of disease that will surely follow this enlightened discovery.'

I was specially pleased that Patricia and Sarah, our first child, were able to come with me to San Francisco to collect the Lasker Award. We enjoyed meeting Burt Tolerton, my special friend from my Atom Bomb days. We had a very enjoyable time with Burt: I remember him driving us out to see the best Californian vineyards, and we finished up going fast round a bend where Burt's skill landed us in a ditch without anyone being hurt. Burt rather took me aback during our trip, when he said that a Lasker Prize was often seen as an indication that a Nobel Prize might follow.

I gave a speech at the Award ceremony. The completion of our X-ray studies had given me time to consider wider problems of science and society, and I was drawn again to work such as I had undertaken during my student days in Cambridge 20 years earlier, before World War II. That terrible war had, unfortunately, by no means removed all possibilities of World War III. So in San

Francisco, remembering my Atom Bomb work across the Bay at Berkeley, I said that the importance of the Double Helix should be considered not only in terms of scientific knowledge but also in relation to the human benefit that may be created by applications of that knowledge. I was encouraged then by the murmur of approval that rose from the audience. I may have had thoughts about DNA and biological weapons, but an award meeting was not the place for such discussions.

Two years later, while on a visit to New York, I took a telephone call from a journalist who told me that Jim, Francis and I had been awarded the Nobel Prize. My first thought was to wonder how this journalist had known about it before I did, but I assumed that had I been at home, the news might have been delivered in a more formal manner. At first I was reluctant to participate in the Nobel ceremony, but Dick Synge, who had given me helpful advice when I was a student, had won a Nobel Prize for Chemistry in 1952 and he encouraged me to go. The Nobel citation summed up more than a decade of work: we had won for 'discoveries concerning the molecular structure of nucleic acids and its significance for information transfer in living material.' This news came in October, and the award ceremony was to take place as usual on 10 December, the anniversary of the death of Alfred Nobel, the Swedish chemist and industrialist who had endowed the prize with the profits from his many companies and patents, including one for dynamite. (Nobel thought that dynamite might bring an end to war.) Unlike the brief and informal Lasker event in California, the week-long Nobel ceremony was formal, tightly organized, and very demanding. Instructions arrived: in the intervening few weeks, we would have to think hard about the lectures we would have to deliver, as well as mustering other necessities for the trip – formal evening clothes, for example, and, in our case, a passport for our new baby, George. I made several trips to the Passport Office to try to speed that process, and although the imminent Nobel ceremony was the reason for my haste, I did feel embarrassed mentioning it in order to draw attention to my request.

After the hurried preparations, I was very tired by the time we arrived in Stockholm. We did, however, find some good ways to relax: we were very pleased to spend an enjoyable evening with the parents of Sven Blomberg, my painter friend from Birmingham, where his father had been Swedish consul. But mostly our time was taken up with Nobel formalities – being chauffeured here and there, shaking hands with important people, attending the great banquet with over a thousand guests, and generally living up to the responsibilities of being new Nobel Laureates. The more informal dinner with the Swedish Royal Family was very relaxed and enjoyable.

There were some happy coincidences in the Prizes that year. I was very pleased to meet John Steinbeck who was receiving the Nobel Prize for Literature – I much enjoyed his thoughtful novels, and he had set the scene in my mind for my time in California. The Prize for Chemistry went to our Cambridge colleagues Max Perutz and John Kendrew for their work on the structure of proteins. Haemoglobin, the important blood protein, and the related protein myoglobin were their particular successes. But the award emphasized the 25 years of work that had gone into their achievement, from the very earliest days of X-ray diffraction, and the many years when scientific understanding had been very hard won. Perutz and Kendrew were commended for their patience and perseverance, as well as their ingenuity and skill. And because their work was deemed to have great implications for the understanding of fundamental life processes, they fulfilled Alfred Nobel's criterion for the prizes in his name, which is that the work rewarded should confer 'the greatest benefit on mankind'. The great Linus Pauling was awarded the Peace Prize, to add to his 1954 Prize for Chemistry for his work on chemical bonding. Pauling's Peace award was for his 25-year campaign against nuclear weapons, and it was, as is traditional, awarded in Oslo rather than in Stockholm.

The prize to Francis, Jim and me was awarded in the category 'Physiology or Medicine', and was for work on nucleic acids generally rather than DNA in particular, embracing our years of work since the Double Helix. The official Presentation Speech, which in this category is always given by a professor from the distinguished medical university, the Royal Caroline Institute, noted the significance of nucleic acids in determining the character of living matter. It described nucleic acids as a staircase with different coloured steps, the sequence of which conveys a message, both for constructing proteins within cells, and for structuring new organisms through the biological process of inheritance. The speech concluded with the thought that while the consequences of this new knowledge were yet to be seen, it seemed very likely to lead to new understandings of disease, of the interaction of heredity and environment, and of the origin of life.

We gave our lectures the day after the award ceremony. Jim concentrated on RNA, the nucleic acid that he had been working on since DNA. He had left Cambridge shortly after the Double Helix work, and had been doing X-ray diffraction studies of RNA at the California Institute of Technology in Pasadena. He had been back to Cambridge for a couple of years in the mid-1950s to work with Francis on viruses, which consist of DNA and protein, and then he had taken a post at Harvard University, where he had concentrated on the role of RNA in the building of proteins in living cells. Jim's lecture described the roots of the nucleic acid structure work in the Phage Group and at King's, and described how RNA assembles the chemical constituents for making protein molecules.

Since the Double Helix, Francis had stayed on in Cambridge, first completing his PhD thesis and then working in several areas of biochemistry and genetics. His Nobel lecture concentrated on what the structure of nucleic acids implied for their function – the second part of our citation for the Prize. Francis had worked for many years on how the sequence of the four bases in DNA formed a genetic code that transferred biological information from one organism to its descendants. He concluded with a typically far-seeing observation that scientists' experiments would establish the complete genetic code for the synthesis of proteins within a few years – a point on which he was soon to be proved correct.

In my lecture, I concentrated on the structure of nucleic acids. I told the story of early work at King's – the remarkable Signer DNA with its threadlike fibres, and mine and Raymond Gosling's X-ray photograph that first showed we were dealing with crystalline genes. Then I described Alec Stokes' idea about helices, and Rosalind's skilful X-ray work. I noted the significance of Chargaff's pairs on the road to the Double Helix, and how the Watson–Crick model had implications for the transfer of information. But most of my talk concerned the science of confirming the Double Helix, checking that it did indeed occur in the DNA of all species, including humans, and measuring it in detail so that we might have accurate data to put the structure on a firm foundation. I also explained our work on RNA, and showed some of our X-ray results. Thinking back over such a long period of work gave me a chance to recollect the many colleagues who had contributed along the way, and I was pleased to mention Raymond and Alec, Bill Seeds and Herbert Wilson, Geoffrey Brown, Leonard Hamilton, and Harriet Ephrussi, and Bob Langridge and my current team back in London. Rosalind had recently died of cancer, and I took the opportunity to note her great ability in a career cut so short.

It was a momentous week for us all. As Patricia and I carried our children on to the plane back to London, Francis smiled at me and remarked that he was glad to see me looking so relaxed. Overwhelmed by the generosity and friendliness in Stockholm, I was glad to be heading for the peace and quiet of our family home. I was proud to be taking a Nobel Prize back to King's, and my colleagues and I enjoyed a party in Ye Olde Cheshire Cheese, a famous pub in Fleet St, just along from the College. I would soon be happy to find that a Nobel Prize would open many unexpected doors for me in the next phase of my life.

CHAPTER 10

A BROADER VIEW

After the Lasker and Nobel awards, and my confidence that the Double Helix was soundly based, I felt freer to look around and consider the wider role of science in human life, and also to enjoy life more broadly, with Patricia and our growing family. With a scientific reputation, financial security and a supportive family, I could make some choices about where to concentrate my efforts in future.

The general state of mind in the Western world was not very conducive to my continuing quiet, steady biological research. The extremely dangerous Cuban Missile Crisis had reached its highest point while I was in New York in 1962, on the trip when I heard of my Nobel award. Khrushchev then gave up his programme of delivering missiles to Cuba, within striking distance of the USA. That same year, Rachel Carson's ground-breaking book *Silent Spring* was published, and became a strong influence in helping to build up the environmental movement. During the 1960s the Hippie movement led to much broadening of the minds of young people, and sometimes there were mixed feelings about science. For example, many scientists working in genetics did their experiments with bacteria, which reproduce rapidly and so show genetic processes quickly. Bacterial genetics was a new field, and scientists had limited experience in it, and they could not at first rule out scares that dangerous mutants might escape from laboratories. In broader discussions at this time, such scares were linked with questions of the values of science and Western society. In the USA, the potential dangers of genetic research on bacteria had become a public issue, to such an extent that the Mayor of Boston had banned the research there — an area that included a number of distinguished laboratories. At King's, we were now working in our excellent new Biophysics Department which had been built in a former seed warehouse in Drury Lane, a street more famous for its theatres, just a few yards from the King's building on the Strand. In that new lab we had to face the fact that one of our colleagues wanted to use bacteria for genetic experiments. A meeting was arranged in a medical school in London to discuss this new area of science, and speakers included one of the leading American critics of the research, as well as scientists with more moderate views. The meeting concluded that there was no clear evidence of any danger from mutant bacteria escaping from a laboratory, and we decided that research at our lab in the centre of such a busy city was nevertheless safe and could go ahead.

Another sensitive issue was the role of scientists in the development of biological and chemical weapons. I had been interested in this problem since my work with the Cambridge

Scientists' Anti-War Group, when we had tested the possibility of gas-proof rooms. In the 1960s, environmental campaigners and others had drawn attention to the work being done at the Government's Porton Down laboratory where studies were made of chemical and biological weapons, and their possible danger to the British population. The lab had been set up in 1916, in response to the use of poison gases by the Germans in World War I. Research there looked at how gases such as chlorine, phosgene and mustard gas could be used in war, and at how soldiers could be protected from the dreadful injuries the gases inflicted. Britain had signed up in 1930 to the Geneva Protocol that controlled the use of chemical weapons, but was allowed to make chemical weapons in case it needed to retaliate against a chemical attack. No chemical weapons were used in World War II, but stockpiles of new and highly toxic organophosphate nerve gases were found when the Allies entered Germany. So, during the late 1940s and early 1950s, the scientists at Porton Down were looking into ways of protecting soldiers and civilians from these new weapons. When this work became a public issue, Porton Down held an Open Day, and this became an occasion for much discussion in the press. As a Nobel Laureate I was asked to write to distinguished British scientists to tell them about the event, and my young daughter Sarah helped me to push all the letters into the post-box. Many scientists came on the Open Day, and a more open-minded attitude to the work there seemed to be created. But we came away well aware that with weapons such as these, it was difficult to tell what research was for offensive use, and what was defensive, aimed at protecting people from them. I was glad to meet there a member of Porton staff who had worked with me about 10 years earlier. He was a very good scientist and a fine human being, and I was very saddened when he told me that he had suffered when the Open Day had drawn attention to the general nature of his work. His children had, in their school playground, been badly treated because we had publicized their father's work. I felt very bad about this but it illustrates the difficulty, which is still unresolved, of distinguishing defensive and offensive work on chemical and biological weapons.

Many of the contacts I had made in wartime proved very valuable in giving Patricia and me a view of life outside Britain during the post-war years. We shared an enthusiasm for France, and we spent many enjoyable family holidays in Provence where my painter friends Sven Blomberg and Raymond Mason had homes. It was only on one of these visits that I found out that when Sven had been in Birmingham, where I first met him, he had lived close to my wild schoolfriend Philip Marples' home, and had much admired Philip's high spirits. Both Sven and Raymond spent their lives as successful painters. Raymond exhibited in New York, and one of his sculptures was placed prominently in the main square in Birmingham, illustrating the pioneering spirit of the city over the centuries. Apart from our trips to Provence, for 20 years Patricia and I spent the summers with our family in a cottage in the mountains of Corsica, where we built and made good use of solar energy devices for pumping groundwater from 20 metres down in the granite, for heating water and for powering electric light. Because of the political tensions in Corsica, and with great regret, we had to leave there; and now we and various branches of the family spend many months of each year in the Massif Central in France.

Biological research still interested me. After my studies on DNA finished in 1967, I tried to find some way of increasing scientific understanding of how the human brain worked. Because of my X-ray background, research into the structure of nerve membranes seemed an obvious, though not very exciting, choice. The American physicist Allen Blaurock joined me in X-ray studies, and was very able indeed; he went on to a career in the food industry in the USA. Also, the excellent Helen Saibil came from Canada – she told me that part of her reason for coming to King's was that she had heard that I was interested in the connections between science and art. She now leads the structural biology research group at Birkbeck College.

But DNA did not stay in the background for long. In 1967 I heard from Francis Crick, who was worried about some news from Jim Watson. Jim, who was now working at Harvard University, had sent Francis the manuscript of a book he had written about the discovery of the Double Helix. The book's opening sentence read: 'I have never seen Francis in a modest mood.' This sentence was indicative of the tone of the book, for it told a racy story of scientific rivalry peopled by characters exaggerated for dramatic effect. Francis was always very brilliant, extravagant, loud and disrespectful; 'Rosy' Franklin was a mean and priggish bluestocking – many readers, including me, were bewildered by Jim's lengthy and bizarre discussion of her appearance; and I was bumbling and taciturn. The book presented the Double Helix as a kind of revelation in reward for genius, and made much of our failures, rivalries and personal lives in a way that seemed not only personally unsettling for those of us involved in the story, but also quite shocking in an era when popular science tended to present a rather noble and heroic picture of the scientific endeavour.

In retrospect, I can commend Jim for bringing science down from its pedestal in this way, and for giving readers a view of how science is really done. Almost for the first time, a scientist had written openly about his thoughts and feelings, and as a result, the world of science had been opened up more, allowing the public to see the nature of science. But at the time, we, his friends and colleagues, found it distasteful. Francis protested to Jim's publisher, Harvard University Press, and encouraged me to do the same. I did write, and I described the manuscript as badly written, juvenile and in bad taste. (Later Jim explained that he had deliberately written it in a style that reflected his youth and inexperience at the time the story took place, and I regretted that I had not seen this earlier.) The publisher was sensitive to our concerns, and they withdrew from the project. Jim soon found another publisher, and his book, *The Double Helix*, became a bestseller and a groundbreaking classic of popular science.

The atmosphere of the 1960s encouraged free discussion and democracy in the workplace, and everyone in our lab seemed to enjoy having research lectures for workshop and technical staff. Scientists became more involved in social questions, and the discussions about bacteria research and chemical and biological weapons showed that there was interest in and concern about the role of science in society. Some young natural and social scientists came together to form an organization to further discussion and campaigning on such issues. Prominent among them were the historian and philosopher of science Jerry Ravetz, social scientist Jonathan Rosenhead, and Steven and Hilary Rose. Steven Rose, a brilliant biochemist specializing in the science of the brain, was one of the youngest professors in the country. He was married to Hilary, a sociologist who was working at the London School of Economics. They had recently published their very influential book, *Science and Society*. The new organization was called the British Society for Social Responsibility in Science, or BSSRS, pronounced 'Biss-Rus'. They held their first meeting of this radical enterprise at the Royal Society – the centre of the scientific establishment in London – and it was packed with many leading scientists in the audience or on the platform. The founders of BSSRS wanted a Nobel Laureate as President, and Steven Rose asked me if I would take on the job. I was happy to do so, and I was glad to help by chairing the meetings of this exciting and important group.

The biggest and most impressive BSSRS event happened in 1970: it was a huge meeting that filled the Hall at the Quakers'

Friends' House in London for three days. The title of the conference was *The Social Impact of Modern Biology*, and the talks and discussion were published as a book edited by Watson Fuller (who had done very good work in the final years of establishing the correctness of the Double Helix). A wide range of important aspects of contemporary biology was introduced by distinguished speakers and discussed with the audience. Among the speakers at the conference were Jacques Monod, David Bohm, Jim Watson (he talked about molecular biology and cancer), Jacob Bronowski, and Steven and Hilary Rose. Looking again at the book of the meeting, I am somewhat surprised that the issue of science and war was not dealt with, except briefly in my introduction and concluding remarks. One reason for this omission may have been that biological weapons were only in an early stage of development.

The subject that raised the most interest was what were then known as 'test-tube babies'. The problems this new technique raised were discussed in a talk by the leading researcher in that field, Robert Edwards. This was useful because there had been much public opposition to his work. Edwards, a physiologist who had trained in the pioneering genetics group at Edinburgh University, had developed a technique that used hormones to control the timing of ovulation. In 1965, he had begun experiments on *in-vitro* fertilization of human eggs, and in 1967 he had teamed up with the surgeon and gynaecologist Patrick Steptoe, who was developing treatments using the controversial technique laparoscopy, the now common means for keyhole surgery. They were able to collect eggs from women, and in 1969 they had achieved the first *in-vitro* fertilization of a human egg. It would be nearly ten years before a baby was born as a result of their technique, but already questions were being asked about the ethics and value of the technique, which was seen by some as dangerous interference in natural processes. At our meeting we held an open discussion so that a range of points of view could contribute to our understanding of the potential problems and benefits. It became clear that the success of this programme was due to the scientists involved behaving in a very responsible manner, anticipating and addressing possible problems, engaging with public opinion, and doing careful work. As a whole I felt the meeting had been very useful in improving relations between scientists and the public.

I believe that, in considering the role of science in the world today, we should take a very broad view. One example of the breadth of BSSRS was its Committee on Science and Art, where one topic we considered was Buckminster-Fuller's architecture and its links with the symmetry of the virus particles that we could see with electron microscopes and X-rays. I was not the only member of BSSRS who gave talks on such subjects in Art Colleges. More important problems of the world were dealt with by BSSRS members with expertise in the philosophy, sociology and economics of science. Such work led to the setting up in our Biophysics Department at King's of an undergraduate discussion course on the Social Impact of the Biosciences. That course continues very successfully today at the Randall Centre in the King's,

Guy's, St Thomas' complex, and has led to similar courses in other institutions. Such courses, as part of scientists' education, seem to me to be valuable in helping them to deal with questions of science and society, such as those that have arisen more recently about GM crops.

By the end of the 1970s, internal divisions in BSSRS had made it less effective, and other organizations, such as those in the environmental movement, had overtaken us in debating and campaigning about the important issues. But I do feel that BSSRS helped scientists to see that there was no sharp distinction between pure and applied science, and that it paved the way for a broader, interdisciplinary approach to the problems of science and society.

In 1974, DNA came back into my life in the form of a book about Rosalind Franklin by the American writer Anne Sayre. Sayre was married to the physicist David Sayre, and the couple had moved to England in 1949 where David was to study crystallography in Oxford with the great Dorothy Hodgkin, one of Bernal's students. There they met Rosalind, and she and Anne developed a close friendship that lasted until the end of Rosalind's life. Sayre's book, *Rosalind Franklin and DNA*, cast a long shadow, and is one of the reasons why I have dwelt on my relations with Rosalind in my recollections in this book.

It appears that Jim's description of Rosalind in *The Double Helix* was important in encouraging Anne Sayre to write her book. It was of course very unfortunate that Jim's description was seriously misleading, even after Francis and I had arranged for it to be moderated. Sayre visited me while she was researching her book, and when I asked her why she was writing it she told me that her aim was to make it easier for women to do science. I replied that I thought her intention was a good one. My ancestors had worked to advance education for women, and my family was proud of my Aunt Eva who had served two months in Holloway Prison for her Suffragist activity.

When the book was published, Rosalind became emblematic of the many challenges facing women in science, and an icon of the newly prominent and vocal feminist movement; and in some people's minds I became The Enemy. Sayre said of our work at King's that all the work we had done before Rosalind had arrived was worth nothing. There was no mention of the key discovery that DNA was crystalline and so amenable to X-ray analysis; and she seriously misrepresented the number of women in our lab: Sayre reported there was only one other woman, apart from Rosalind, whereas we had an unusually good representation of able and responsible women scientists – about one third of the scientific staff were women.

In Randall's lab at King's I had enjoyed living in a community with an exceptionally high proportion of women. The fact there are generally more women students than men in our undergraduate Social Impact of the Biosciences course at King's is a matter of quiet satisfaction to me, and X-ray diffraction is an area where women have been particularly successful. It was very distressing when Rosalind had difficulties at King's, and it was a very great shock when Anne Sayre seemed to see me as a misogynist who contributed to Rosalind's unhappiness.

Some of my colleagues on the Women's Committee at BSSRS were critical of the book – they thought that Anne Sayre was not a proper feminist. The book seemed to me to be so grossly inaccurate that it did not require a response. Then another book, *The Eighth Day of Creation*, written about molecular biology by Horace Freeland Judson, implied that I had taken Rosalind's now-famous photograph out of her drawer in order to show it to Jim. I explained to Judson that if he consulted my colleagues he would not be able to confirm his story.

King's' share of the Nobel Prize for the elucidation of the structure and function of nucleic acids was awarded for a large body of work stretching from the late 1940s to the early 1960s, and over that period our group was of various sizes and an ever-changing composition; and there would be many talented and dedicated colleagues who came and went during those years whose contributions might be compared to Rosalind's. Undoubtedly Rosalind's contributions to the DNA structure were considerable, but not necessarily in a different category from those of other workers in our lab. It is true to say that she and I were never close friends, but we had been friendly in the early days in the lab, and before the tensions arose between us I had formed a high opinion of her as a colleague. Our paths crossed quite a few times after she left King's, both at conferences and in London, and after a few years we had what seemed to me to be a very satisfactory relationship. For example, after a lecture at the big MRC research institute at Mill Hill in North London, Rosalind announced 'I am motorized!', and was friendly enough to offer to drive me back to King's. I was very glad and relieved to sense that the bad feeling between us had passed.

It has distressed me to see so many stories about DNA, and about Rosalind, that those of us who lived through those times barely recognize. Opinions continue to circulate about those days, and one of the aims of this book has been to present my point of view. Rosalind never had her chance. I have a feeling that she would have very much disliked being turned into a feminist icon. Her main devotion was to doing her work in the way she wanted. There certainly were some very great tensions, including those concerning Rosalind, during the Double Helix research, but I hope this book may make those tensions more under-standable.

Having a Nobel Prize was very useful when I was working for causes I felt were important. I knew that Nobel Laureates could be specially useful in public movements, for example by being seen on public platforms. As a Laureate, I was asked in 1980 to sign a Manifesto on Third World poverty and starvation which had been written by an Argentinian Laureate. In contrast to most statements on Third World starvation, this impressive document went beyond charitable food aid and drew attention to long-standing poverty and under-development. I was glad to be one of many Laureates to sign the Manifesto, which was used by Food and Disarmament International, an organization based in Brussels and with funding from many sources. FDI assisted movements in European cities with meetings, marches and demonstrations, and was supported by a dozen or so Laureates, politicians, economists and experts on Third World development and malnutrition. Its aim was to educate people about how food shortages and underdevelopment could be caused by narrow, unjust economic and political policies. It was not only the public, but also well-educated scientists who sometimes needed to learn about Third World starvation. There has been a tendency for specialists in agriculture and food to regard their knowledge as superior to that of indigenous peoples growing food in poor countries, who sometimes have special knowledge of local pests and other factors that might be unknown to experts from other countries.

Only a small number of Laureates came to speak at FDI public meetings, but those who did were very well informed and helpful. Politicians also joined in; I greatly admired Emma Bonino, the radical Italian politician, who had led a successful campaign in Italy to legalize abortion in certain types of case, and was responsible for the referendum in which Italians rejected a civil nuclear programme for Italy. I specially admired Abdus Salam, a physics Laureate, who had worked hard to help young physicists from developing countries to advance their careers. I was able to learn about the politics and economics of Third World starvation, mainly from Philip Payne, Head of Nutrition at the London School of Hygiene and Tropical Medicine and an advisor to the Philippine government.

FDI needed not only expert knowledge but also speakers who could make a big impact at large meetings. I was not specially good at that, but I remember marching through the streets of Strasbourg at night and talking with one of the Irish women Laureates for Peace. We sat on the ground in a very big square lit by thousands of candles. When it was my turn to speak I remembered a young colleague talking to me about 'The Right to Life'. I stood up and electronics took my voice right across the enormous open space. Afterwards the organizer told me that he had not known that I could speak so well. I continued working with FDI until 1989 when it closed down because its dedicated organizer, Jean Fabre, moved to another organization.

During the 1980s, risk of nuclear war increased as US nuclear weapons arrived in Britain as part of the anti-Soviet Cold War. After World War II, a group of atomic scientists, encouraged by Einstein, had set up the Pugwash organization which was dedicated to preventing nuclear war. The idea behind Pugwash was to bring together an international group of scholars and public figures who, acting as individuals rather than as representatives of any government or institution, could consider ways of reducing the likelihood of war and of finding positive solutions to global problems. The unusual name of this organization came from its first meeting, which was held in 1957 in the village of Pugwash in Nova Scotia, the home town of its host, the American philanthropist Cyrus Eaton. The first Manifesto was signed by many well-known scientists and thinkers, including Bertrand Russell, Albert Einstein and Linus Pauling. Many of the Pugwash participants were highly regarded in their own countries, and so were able to carry the Pugwash message to policy-makers and opinion leaders. Some of the key people working for Pugwash in the early days had to remain anonymous because their political beliefs put them in danger from McCarthy's anti-communist campaign, and their names could have jeopardized Pugwash's influence in the USA. Pugwash welcomed scientists from all political persuasions. When I first came to King's after the War, I was encouraged by my Berkeley friend Eric Burhop, who was also in London, to give public lectures about the dangers of nuclear war. Eric was a brave and outspoken campaigner, and when a newspaper described him as a Stalinist, he sued the paper and was awarded a large sum of money. But in the late 1940s, there was little interest in the issue of nuclear war, and it was very dispiriting to trudge across London to speak in a draughty hall to a handful of people. In the 1980s, however, there was much more momentum in the anti-nuclear movement, and even greater need to alert the public and politicians to the danger of nuclear war. I was pleased to join the other Atom Bomb scientists and their colleagues in Pugwash, and I learnt much at their meetings. On one occasion, in Moscow, many experts from the USA and Soviet Union had gathered to discuss nuclear testing, which was largely done in the Pacific. Listening to the discussion, I realized that there had been much talk of the technical aspects of testing, but no mention at all of the Pacific Islanders whose lives had been seriously affected by the tests. I was able to remind the meeting that the people of small nations had rights too (I am impressed by the action New Zealand has taken towards the control of nuclear activity in the Pacific). I recall another Pugwash meeting that was particularly important: in Prague in 1988, news reached us of Saddam Hussein's attack on the Kurdish city of Halabja. Iraqi aircraft had shelled Halabja with chemical weapons, leaving thousands dead and injured. The pictures we saw of the Kurdish people lying dead in the streets were very shocking, and we hoped that the Russian delegates at the meeting might encourage their government to intervene in the region.

Through a Pugwash colleague, Patricia and I were invited by the Soviet Academy of Science to visit the Soviet Union. Patricia, as a member of a Russian folk dance group in London, was very interested to meet Russian experts. While we were there, I tried in vain to find my good friend from my Cambridge days, Arthur Hone, who had imagined communism leading to a just society. I had lost touch with Arthur, but I had heard that he had married an Estonian woman in the early years of the War, and had disappeared into the Soviet Union as Germans pushed Soviet troops eastwards. Then, during the War, I received a letter from Arthur, who told me he had become an interpreter in Moscow. I replied, but never heard from him again; and I was sorry not to find him on my visit to Moscow all those years later.

The visits Patricia and I made to the Soviet Union gave us the impression that memories of the horror of invasion in World

War II lived on in the minds of the Russian people, and the threat
of war may have been a motivation for reducing Cold War
tension. Of course, the Soviet public strongly disliked the idea of
nuclear war; but political economic crisis may sweep away public
opinion. In Britain at that time, public opinion was able to express
itself with the help of large organizations such as the Campaign
for Nuclear Disarmament, led by Bruce Kent, a former priest.
Where Pugwash involved scientific experts and opinion leaders,
CND took its message directly to the public. It intensified its
efforts in the early 1980s when it became known that American
cruise missiles were to arrive on British soil. These missiles flew
under their own steam and were to be placed in the UK so that
they would be within range of the Soviet Union. They were kept
at Greenham Common, a World War II airbase in the Berkshire
countryside, just west of London, that had been taken over by the
US Airforce during the 1950s, once the Soviets had developed
nuclear weapons. In 1981, a group of women organized a march
from Cardiff in Wales to Greenham Common to protest against
the missiles. They set up camp around the fence at Greenham
Common, and founded what became known as the Peace Camp.
The women kept press attention focused on the issue, and dis-
rupted the work at the base by setting up blockades and cutting
through the security fence. Patricia and I joined many CND
demonstrations there, including one at the end of 1982 that
attracted 70,000 protestors. We were surprised to see such an
enormous crowd. The beauty of the rural landscape and sky
above contrasted starkly with the glistening steel of the military

defences. The first cruise missiles arrived at Greenham Common in November 1983, and the women in the Peace Camp continued their disruptive tactics until the missiles were removed in 1991. The Camp remained a centre for anti-nuclear protest for another decade.

In marked contrast to the excitement of demonstrations, we undertook quieter work for CND in London. Patricia delivered the CND monthly newsletter to 800 local members. I gave talks on the nuclear danger, sometimes to very large audiences. One of these talks was in Trafalgar Square, in the centre of London, and was packed with supporters. We speakers stood on the base of Nelson's column, the towering landmark in the middle of the square, and when it was my turn I said that I had worked on the Bomb. A roar of disapproval contrasted with the murmur of approval years earlier at the Lasker Award ceremony.

The history of the DNA Double Helix discovery points very strongly towards the need for more open-minded attitudes in scientific research. Science needs attitudes that are opposite to those essential in military work. Today, military work depends very much on science; but the development of weapons of mass destruction makes war less and less an option in today's world. The abolition of war is more and more important. Fortunately, science is becoming increasingly global (in a positive sense) and points the way to the future of humanity as a whole. The internet and scientific organizations like the global Human Genome Project should be very helpful examples for the future. And examples of secrecy in science, as seen in DNA Double Helix research, show how important it is for humans to develop mutual understanding and the ability for open discussion. As I write, in 2003, news of terrorist attacks reverberates around the world. The destruction of the World Trade Centre on 11 September 2001 put the world on a new alert. Secrecy may be as important to terrorists as to the military. Can we learn anything from considering the DNA Double Helix history that might help us in the future? How can humans learn to be more open and less secretive? Or is that a silly question?

A dogmatic commitment to one particular viewpoint can be dangerous in many spheres of life, and this is true of science. A key problem in dealing with the mad cow disease BSE in the 1980s and 1990s in the UK was that some veterinary scientists believed the infective agent in BSE must contain nucleic acid. Their error was corrected. Science can be non-authoritarian, and that can set an example to the whole of humanity.

Open minds are crucial in the future. The concept of openness connects with breadth of mind (like Priestley, of oxygen fame, who in his Chapel read from all the Holy Books). When I use the word 'open' I must emphasize that I do not mean open in the static sense, as when one waits passively to receive messages from outside. To establish dialogue there must be interaction going in and out. It is a creative process, and one needs to be actively exploring one's own mind and the mind of the other participant. Energy, creativity, intuition and careful thought may all be needed. The same attention may be required to the concept of open dialogue itself: looking to the future, we need much further enquiry into the idea of open dialogue. The process may be tedious, exhausting and exasperating, and demand much imagination (and good luck!), but without such processes there may be no future for humanity. Perhaps with open dialogue, we may hope for a more creative and joyful community.

INDEX

A-DNA 154–6, 182, 184, 217–18
  non-helicality 199, 200, 201
  Rosalind's views 176
  structure clarification 230–3
Aberdeen University 2
Aberystwith 64
Acta Crystallographer 176
Adams, Professor (Astronomer Royal) 4
adenine:thymine ratio 226
aeroplanes 24, 25
air raids 57–8, 60, 75
Albert Lasker Award 238–9
Allen, Douglas 83
alpha helix 158–60, 174
alpha keratin 120
Amateur Telescope Making (F.A. Ellison) 28
amino acid bonding 159
Andes 191–3
Anna 111–12
aperiodic crystals 84, 115
arrest of Alan Nunn May 97
art 18, 29, 35, 74, 79, 111, 191, 192, 249
Astbury, Bill 90–1, 137, 141
astronomy 23, 28, 30–1
asymmetry 199–200
atom bomb 76–8, 81, 82, 85, 264
Auerbach, Charlotte 91, 138
authorship 66–7, 213–15, 216, 222–4, 226
Avery, Oswald 92, 114–15, 185, 186

B-DNA 154–6, 160, 161, 163, 217–19
  helicality 199, 201, 202, 203
  implications 201, 202
  Nature 230, 232
  photograph for Maurice 197
  Rosalind's views 176
  two groups of atoms 170
bacterial genetics research 247
bacteriophages 138, 186
Baldwin, Stanley 60
Baltaglia, Bruno 136, 137
Bannister, Dr 33, 45, 67, 113
Barber, Horace 146–7
Barnard, George 33
base pairs 151–2, 165, 199, 212–13, 226–7
Bath High School for Girls 4

Battle of Britain pilots 62
Battleship Potemkin 42
beauty/destruction 192, 193–4
Bedford College for Women 2
Bentley, Bill 54
Berkeley Bomb project 190–1
Berkeley, California 77–8, 80, 81, 82
Bernal, J.D. 34, 35, 36, 46, 55, 122–3
Bessel function 160, 161, 163, 220
beta keratin 120
biological weapons research 247–9
Biophysics Research Unit 99
Birkbeck College, Cambridge 164, 166, 198, 250
Birmingham 24, 26–8
  air-raids 75
  Art Gallery 29
  Bomb Lab 77
  Priestley, Joseph 1
  Town Hall public meeting 57–8
  University 49, 54, 61–5, 75
  Wylde Green 19–22, 25, 26, 72–3, 75, 87–8, 178
'The Bish' 27
Blackout 57, 62, 78
Blaurock, Allen 250
Blitzkrieg 70, 71, 72
Blomberg, Sven 51, 74, 249
blood transfusion 17–18
Blotz, Bill 75
Bluebird (Campbell) 23
Bohm, David 82, 190, 193
Bohr, Niels 77, 138, 147
Bomb Project 93
Bonino, Emma 259
Boot, Harry 53, 63, 64, 69
Brachet, Jean 209
Bragg, Lawrence 46, 64, 104–5, 169, 179
Bragg's Moratorium 175, 178, 203, 205–6
brain research 250
Brazil 181, 185–95
Bristol University 107
Brita 65, 66, 74
British Communist Party 39, 40, 59
British School Medical Service 16
British Society for Social Responsibility in
  Science 252, 254–5, 257

Brown, Geoffrey 114, 132, 203, 209
Brussels 209
BSE 265
BSSRS *see* British Society for Social
    Responsibility in Science
Bullard, Edward 46
Bunn, C.W. 126
Burch, Cyril 30, 38, 107
Burd, Mr 20
Burhop, Eric 82, 261
Butenandt, Adolf 110

C-DNA 237
California 77–8, 80–2, 85, 115, 185, 238, 243
Callan, Mick 95, 96
Cambridge Communist Party 41
Cambridge Scientists' Anti-War Group
    (CSAWG) 35–9, 54, 57, 82
Cambridge University 4, 25, 28
    Birkbeck College 164, 166, 198, 250
    Cavendish Laboratory 25, 32, 36, 46, 139, 163
    Hardy Club 222–4
    King's Moratorium on co-operation 175
    Maurice's 1951 talk 141–3
    Maurice's decision not to join forces with
        206–7
    Maurice's letter to Francis 173
    meeting with Dr Bannister 67
    Newnham College 4
    St John's College 28, 30–48
    Strangeways Laboratory 110
Campaign for Nuclear Disarmament 263–4
Campbell, Captain Malcolm 23
Carmichael 47
cars 22–3
Castle Bromwich aerodrome 25
Cavendish Laboratory, Cambridge 25, 32, 36,
    46, 139, 163
cavity magnetron 64, 66, 69–70, 71, 72, 93
Chagas, Carlos 188, 189, 190
Chargaff, Erwin 151, 152, 154, 157, 163
Chargaff's ratios 177, 198, 199, 200, 208, 226–7
Chayen, Joe 209
chemical weapons research 247–9
Chidgey, Patricia 235–6, 239, 244, 246, 249, 262,
    264
CND *see* Campaign for Nuclear Disarmament
co-authorship 213–15, 216, 222–4, 226
co-operative science 156–7, 161–2, 165, 169,
    172–3, 215–16, 226
Coal Utilization Research Laboratory 46
coccids 189, 190
Cockcroft, John 33, 46, 47
collagen 174
Communist Party 39, 40, 41, 59
computers 232, 234
conker trees 20, 26

Cooper, Bob 29
Cornford, Francis M. 41
Cornford, John 41
Corsica 249–50
Cowan, Pauline 174
Crick, Francis 109–10, 112, 120, 141, 163, 164
    approach to Maurice after Rosalind's
        departure 203, 205–6
    base pairing 199
    collaboration with Pauline Cowan 174
    DNA: A Cooperative Discovery 227
    The Double Helix 250
    Double Helix model 225–9
    first DNA model 171–2
    invitation to Maurice to be co-author 213–14
    Maurice's letters
        declining partnership 173, 179–80
        offering partnership 210–11
    Nobel Prize 240–4
    post-Rosalind plans 205–6
    second *Nature* paper 224
Crick, Odile 120, 203
cricket 101, 102
cruise missiles 263–4
crystallinity, DNA 166
crystallography *see* X-ray studies
CSAWG *see* Cambridge Scientists' Anti-War
    Group
Cuban Missile Crisis 246
Cunningham, Morris 35
Cuzco, Peru 191–3
cycling 6, 7
cyclotron lab 81, 85
cytosine:guanine ratio 151, 226
Czech refugees 73–4

D, Mrs 80, 81
Daily Worker 40
dancing 9, 125, 187, 189
Darlington, C.D. 147
Davis, Howard 108, 161, 197
De Groot 47
'death of the helix' announcement 181–4
Delbrück, Max 138, 180, 186
Denmark, seizure 70
deoxyribonucleic acid (DNA)
    see also A-DNA; B-DNA; C-DNA; Double
        Helix model
    acceptance as gene material 114
    Astbury's work 90–1
    asymmetry 182–4, 199–200, 234
    base ratios/pairing 151
    Chargaff's non-crystallising sample 177
    Crick's first model 171–2
    Ephrussi's samples 209
    Fourier synthesis 237
    helical nature 126–7

models 165–6, 175–6, 206, 213–14, 231
molecular research 106–8, 116–39
Moratorium 175
Norris, Keith 110
Pauling's paper 204–5, 206
publication of separate papers about same
  discovery 219
race to determine structure 205–6
Sepia sperm 136–7
Signer's phials 117, 118, 119, 121, 124, 140–1,
  157, 177, 196
storage conditions 123
stretching fibres 119–20, 131
stronger diffraction patterns 179–81
swelling 133, 134
two chains or three? 166–7, 169, 170–1, 176,
  199, 200, 216, 220–1, 231
water content v. crystallinity 165, 166–7
depression 45, 48–9, 67, 113
diad axes 211, 212, 213
dialectical materialism 41, 42
diffraction patterns *see* X-ray studies
dinner in the lab 94
Diploma of Public Health 16, 97
divorce 85–6, 87
DNA: A Cooperative Discovery (Francis Crick)
  227
DNA *see* deoxyribonucleic acid
Dog's Breakfast 69
Dohrn, Rheinhardt 137
Donohue, Jerry 213, 227
The Double Helix (Jim Watson) 250–1
Double Helix model 211–18, 220, 221
  Chargaff ratios 226–7
  further work at King's 229–35
  Hardy Club talk 222–4
  publication 224–5, 228
  story of its emergence 225–9
dry mass measurement 197
Dublin, Ireland 3, 4, 5, 6, 14–15

Ealing Broadway 95
ear infection 26, 79–80
The Earth (Harold Jefferies) 33
Eaton, Cyrus 260
Eddington, Arthur 31–2
Edenfield 3, 4, 5, 11
Edinburgh University 91, 138, 253
education 2–3, 4–5, 6, 11–12
Edwards, Robert 253
Ehrenberg, Werner 127
The Eighth Day of Creation (Horace Freeland
  Judson) 257
Einstein, Albert 4–5, 84, 260, 261
electron movement 46–7
electron traps 53, 66
Ephrussi, Harriet 185, 208–9, 223

Ewald, Paul 43–4
examinations 5, 30, 37, 45, 47–8

Fabre, Jean 260
Faraday, Michael 32
farts and laughter 74
FDI *see* Food and Disarmament International
Fell, Honor 107, 110, 123
feminism 256–7
fencing 113
fibres of DNA 118, 119–21, 133–4
fine-focus X-rays 127, 133, 135, 154, 157
Finland 56
Food and Disarmament International (FDI)
  259–60
Fourier synthesis 237
Franklin, Rosalind
  A-DNA/B-DNA 154, 155, 158
  anti-helical ideas 181–6
  arrival at King's College 128, 129
  B pattern photo 184, 197, 198, 218–19
  Birkbeck College move 198, 200, 208
  colloquium on research conclusions 200–4,
    219
  cool superior air over Maurice 154, 155–6
  death 244
  'death of the helix' announcement 181–5
  dismissal of Wilkins' ideas 169
  DNA structure talk 163–4
  dried DNA diffraction studies 124
  family background 133
  "Go back to your microscopes!" 142–3
  hostile reaction to 'Waves at Bessel on Sea'
    160–1
  initial meeting with Randall 129, 144
  intuition 203
  lunchtime discussions 131–2
  Maurice's impressions 130, 133
  Maurice's unquestioning acceptance 166–7
  misleading non-helical ideas 183–5
  notebooks evidence 171, 220
  Patterson computational method 232–3
  publication of best helical pattern 218
  Randall's letter of appointment 144, 145, 146,
    149–50, 156
  relationship with Maurice 257–8
  Rosalind Franklin and DNA (Ann Sayre) 255
  Signer DNA 196
  three-chain DNA 169, 170–1, 176
Fraser, Bruce 120, 131, 160, 164, 165, 168
Fraser, Mary 168
Fraser's model 168, 169, 216
Freiburg, University of 117
Fremlin, Celia 36
Fremlin, John 36, 37
Freudian psychoanalysis 112, 113
Frisch, Otto 76, 77

Fuchs, Claus 79
Fuller, Watson 183, 237
Furberg, Sven 164, 165, 166
Future, City of the 24

gas-proofed rooms 37, 39
General Electric Company 49, 52, 66, 105
General Strike 24
genes 89–92, 107, 114, 140–1, 186, 212
  see also deoxyribonucleic acid
Geneva Protocol 248
German invasion of Britain 70–1
giant squid 190, 191
Gilbert, Keith 28, 33
"Go back to your microscopes!" 142
Gollancz, Victor 59
Goodwin, Harry 20
Gordon Conference, USA 146, 151–3
Gosling, Raymond
  Randall's letter to Rosalind 145
  working with Maurice 121, 123, 124, 125,
    126, 129, 137
  working with Rosalind 161, 181, 197–8, 215,
    217, 220
Grand Tour 42–3
Great Depression 24
Greenham Common 263–4
Grenoble neutron lab 105
guanine:cytosine ratio 151, 226
Guernica (Picasso) 38
Gulland, J.M. 165, 225, 226

Haldane, J.B.S. 37, 40
Hamilton, Leonard 209
Hanson, Jean 103, 111, 173, 207
Hardy Club 222–4
Hare, Mr 27
helicality
  X pattern 216–17
  absence from Rosalind's talk on DNA
    structure 163–4
  Bruce Fraser's model 165
  collagen 174
  'death of the helix' announcement 181–4
  DNA 126–7
  protein alpha helix 159–60
  Rosalind's B pattern photo 184, 197, 198,
    218–19
  Rosalind's dismissal of Wilkins' ideas 169
  Rosalind's Patterson computational method
    232–3
  Rosalind's research conclusions 200–4
  Rosalind's sharing of ideas about double helix
    170–1
  stronger X patterns 179–81
  tobacco mosaic virus 116, 170
Henry, Philip 1

Hershey, Alfred D. 186
Hertz's copper ring 64
Hill, A.V. 96
hill-walking 10, 21–2
Hiroshima 85
Hitler, Adolf 40, 59, 67
Hodgkin, Dorothy 255
Hogben, Lancelot 53
Hone, Arthur 42, 73, 74, 262
horsechestnuts 20, 26
Human Genome Project 264–5
Hussein, Saddam 262
Hutton, Mary 3–5, 30
Huxley, Hugh 173
hydrogen bombs 83
hydrogen bonds 213
hydrogen gas 122, 123, 124, 134

IBM 234
ICI 126
in vitro fertilization 253–4
Incas 192–3, 194
incendiary bombs 37–8, 39, 75, 78
Industrial Revolution 1, 2
ink-bombs 27, 190
Institute of Contemporary Arts 235
inter-disciplinary studies 98, 99, 100, 102,
  109–10, 173–5, 225
International Brigade 41
intuition 203
Ireland 3–6, 7
Isle of Wight lab 62, 63

Japan, war with 85
Jefferies, Harold 33
John Innes plant genetics lab 95
joke invitation card 181–2
Judson, Horace Freeland 257
Jungian psychoanalysis 113

Kaiser, Ernst 73
Kelburn Parade 8
Kendrew, John 108, 137, 139, 148, 152, 178,
  224, 241–2
  Crick/Watson model 211–15
  mediation abilities 207
  Wyatt on base pairs 199
Kent, Bruce 263
keratin 120
King Edward's High School, Birmingham 25,
  26–8, 56
King's College, London 16, 18, 19
  B model 236
  Biophysics Department in Drury Lane 247
  brain research 250
  collaboration with Cambridge 173–5
  collagen 174

lab politics 142–51
laboratory colloquium (1951) 162–4, 171
lack of acknowledgement in Hardy Club talk 222–4
Randall as Head of Physics 97–111
Kirk, Professor 10
Komphner, Rudi 61, 72, 111

laboratory colloquium at King's 162–4, 171
laboratory parties 101–2
Lancashire 1, 2, 20–1, 104, 105
Lange, Edel 128, 131, 133, 153, 179, 195
Langridge, Bob 234, 237, 238
Lasker prize 238–9
Lawrence, Ernest 77, 82–3
Le Jeune Homme et la Mort 125
letters
    Maurice to Francis 179–80, 210–11
    Randall to Rosalind 144, 145, 146, 149–50, 156
Levene, Phoebus 152
Levy, Professor Hyman 55
libraries 2
light pattern checks 236–7
Lima, Peru 191, 192, 193
liveliness in Brazil 187–9
Living Machinary (A.V. Hill) 96
London 2, 4, 14, 16–19
    see also King's College, London
    Fencing Club 113
    University College 4, 37, 96, 109
Longuet-Higgins, Prof Hugh 178
luminescence 49–50, 61–6, 135
Luminescence Lab 50, 51, 52, 74
Lunar Society 1
Luria, Salvador 138, 139
Lysenko 40

Machu Pichu 192, 193
'macromolecule' concept 117
Macumba rituals 189
magnesium ions 172
Majestic, HMS 14
Makinson, Dick 44
Manchester 1, 2, 104
Manton, Mr 25, 45
Marples, Biddy 74, 78
Marples, Philip 27, 28, 56, 74, 249
Marvin, Don 237
Marx Brothers 42
Marx, Karl 41
Mason, Raymond 51, 74, 249
Massey, Harrie 79, 83, 109
Mathematics for the Million 53
Maurice, F.D. 2
Mauritania, HMS 14
Medical Inspection of Schoolchildren (Edgar H. Wilkins) 90

Medical Research Council 94, 96, 99, 100, 108
    lack of support for DNA studies 152–3
    report indicating anti-helical arguments 184–5
Memoirs for the Royal Society 104–6
men-only rule 108–9
Mendel, Helen 72–3
metal jigs 175–6
M'Ewan, Marjorie 102, 177
microscopes 115, 116, 128–9
microwave generation 62–3, 64, 69–70, 71, 72
Middendorf, Dieter 105
Mirsky, Alfred E. 92, 185
mistakes, usefulness 155
Mitcham Common 18
model-building 165–6, 175–6, 206, 213–14, 231
The Modern Boy magazine 22, 23, 24, 31
molecular biology 106–8, 116–39
Moratorium see Bragg Moratorium
Moscow Trials 40
'Mother's Workbasket' 110
Mott, Neville 50, 68
Muller, Herman 91, 138
Muritai, New Zealand 10
Museum of Modern Art, New York 79
music 8–9, 21, 43, 81
mutations 91, 106, 247

Naples conference 135–8, 179
Natural Sciences Club 33–4, 46
Nature 131, 216, 217, 220, 224, 230, 232
Nazism 38, 41, 43, 54, 72, 76
Nelson Principle 166
Neutralism 132
New York 79, 92
New Zealand, Wellington 7–12
Newnham College, Cambridge 4
Newth, Anthony 55, 56
Newth, David 55–6
Newth, H.G. 54
Newth, Nan 54, 55, 59–60, 95, 111
Newth, Thomas 56
Newton, Isaac 1
nitrogen bases see base pairs
Nobel Prize 240–5, 258–60
Norris, Keith 110, 161
Norway 70
Nottingham University 165
nuclear weapons 132, 190–1, 193, 194, 239–40, 260, 261, 263–4
'Nucleic Acid – an Extensible Molecule' 131
Nunn May family 76, 97

Official Secrets Act 97
Oliphant, Professor Marcus L.E. 32–3, 49, 50, 51
    atom bomb research 76–8

Oliphant, Professor Marcus L.E. (*contd.*)
  post-war research ideas 83
  publications 68
  radar research 61, 62, 63, 69–70
open dialogue 225–6, 264–6
Oster, Gerald 115, 116, 142, 169
Oxford 36
OXO sign 125

Pacific 80, 261–2
Paihatua, New Zealand 7
Panama Canal 13, 14
Paris 128, 131–2, 135, 165, 176, 185–6, 208–9
Parker's Piece 42
parties 101–2, 189–90
Patterson computational method 232, 233
Pauling, Linus 158–60, 163, 172, 204–5, 228, 229, 242, 261
Payne, Philip 259
Peace Camp 263–4
Peierls, Genia 79
Peierls, Rudolph 76, 79
Pencarrow lighthouse 10
Perutz, Max 110, 141, 142, 148, 169, 241–2
Phage Group 225
'the phase problem' 34
phosphate groups 172, 176, 180, 200
phosphorescence 53, 66
Picasso, Pablo 38
'pile of pennies' diffraction 181, 202
poisonous gases 248
Poland 59
Pongoroa, New Zealand 7, 8
Porton Down Laboratory 248–9
post-War research 83
Preston, Margaret 102, 130
preventive medicine 8, 12
Price, Bill 164, 165, 168
Priestley, Joseph 1
protein structures 110, 158–60, 174, 241–2
Pugwash organization 260, 261, 262

quantum mechanics 49, 65, 84, 159
Queen Elizabeth, HMS 78
Queen's College, London 2

race to determine DNA structure 173, 205–6
radar research 62–3, 64, 66–7, 68–9
railways 2
Ramsay, Margaret 44
Randall, John 49–53, 61–5
  X-ray equipment for King's 121
  A-DNA/B-DNA 158
  competitiveness 72
  conferences 135
  entrepreneurial talents 98–100
  Franklin's arrival 129

initial staff meeting with Rosalind 129, 144
King's College appointment 97–111
laboratory parties 101–2
lack of support for DNA studies 152–3
leadership style 146–50
letter to Rosalind 143–4, 145, 146, 149–50, 156
peers' jealousy 101
publications authorship 66–7, 68
radar research 63, 64, 69
request to join in research on Double Helix 230
retirement portrait 149
rivalry with Jim Sayers 71
Royal Society Memoir 104
St Andrews University Physics Department 89
US visit 92–3
'Randall's Circus' 101, 109, 178
Ravetz, Jerry 252
Redman, Roderick 30
refugees 43, 61, 72–4, 81
research authorship 66–7, 68, 213–15, 216, 222–4, 226
research funding 94, 96, 98–9
reserved scientists 61
ribonucleic acid (RNA) 238, 243
Rio, South America 186–90
RNA *see* ribonucleic acid
Rockefeller Foundation 99, 158
Rockefeller Institute, New York 92
Rosalind Franklin and DNA (Ann Sayre) 255–7
Rose, Steven and Hilary 252–3
Rosenhead, Jonathan 252
Royal Caroline Institute 242
Royal Institution 4
Royal Society Memoirs 104–6
Russell, Bertrand 261
Russia 262–3
Ruth 81, 84, 85–6, 87, 112
Rutherford, Ernest 32, 142

Saibil, Helen 250
St Andrews University, Scotland 83, 84, 88–9, 97
St John's College, Cambridge 28, 30–48
St Thomas' Medical School 103
Salam, Abdus 259
salt solutions 134–5
San Francisco 85, 95, 238–40
Sayers, Jim 71
Sayre, Ann 162, 255–7
Sayre, David 255
scholarships 25, 29, 30
school hygiene 8
Schrödinger, Erwin 83–4, 96
Science and Society (Steven Rose) 252

Scotland 83, 84, 88–9, 91, 97, 138
Scottish dancing 95
Seeds, Bill 110, 111, 119, 141, 210
'Seeing Structures' talk 34, 46
Segrave, Major 31
Segrave's *Sunbeam* 22, 23
segregation at King's College 108–9
Sepia sperm 136–7, 146, 147, 153, 179–80
septicaemia 16–18
Shapiro, 'Ship' 75
ship's engines 13
Shockley, William 47
Signer DNA phials 140–1, 157, 177, 178–9, 196
Signer, Rudolph 117, 118, 119, 124
Silent Spring (Rachel Carson) 246
Simpson, Ken 85
Skerries 5, 6, 7, 8
sliding filament mechanism 172–3
smallpox vaccination 18–19
Soc-Soc *see* Student Socialist Society
social aspects of biology 252–5
The Social Impact of Modern Biology conference 253
sodium 204–5
Solar Physics Observatory 30
Somerville College, Oxford 36
South America 181, 185–95
Southampton, England 14
Soviet Union 40, 56, 67, 262–3
Spain, Republican 37–8
Spanish Civil War 31, 36, 41, 55
Spear, Walter 127
speed machines 22–5, 31
Spencer, Mike 237
sperm DNA 121, 136–7, 179–80, 190, 191
squid 190, 191
Stalin, Joseph 40
Stanley, Wendell 115
Staudinger, Hermann 117
Stazione, Naples 136, 137
Steinbeck, John 241
Stevenson, George 2
Stockholm 153, 241
Stokes, Alec 116, 126, 133, 134, 210, 229
   Bessel function 160, 161, 163
   'death of the helix' announcement 181–4
   loss of interest in DNA 177, 178
   pro-helix 169, 170
   Randall's desire to exclude from X-ray studies 147–50
   Randall's letter to Rosalind 144, 145
Strangeways Laboratory, Cambridge 110
stretching DNA fibres 119–21, 131
Student Socialist Society 35
Students' Union 63
Sugar Loaf Mountain 187

sugar rings 234–5
survey of scientists 61
Swanwick, Anna 2–3, 4
Swanwick, Frederick 2
Switzerland 78–9
symmetry 211, 212, 213
Synge, Dick 34, 240

Taylor, Dermott 114
team spirit 156–7
telescopes 12, 28, 29, 30
'test-tube babies' 253
thermoluminescence 46, 47, 49, 52
Third World development 258–60
Thompson, Professor D'Arcy 93, 94
thymine:adenine ratio 226
tissue culture 107, 123
TMV *see* tobacco mosaic virus
toast and honey 9
tobacco mosaic virus 116, 170
Tolerton, Burt 81, 82, 239
train journeys to school 26
trapdoor spiders 10
Trinity College, Dublin 3, 4, 6
tubes of force 32
two chains evidence 166–7, 169, 170–1, 176, 199, 200, 216, 220–1, 231

ultrasonics 91, 92, 106, 109
ultraviolet microscopes 107, 116
Ulysses 5
Unitarian Church 1
universality of gene structure 140–1
University College, London 4, 37, 96, 109
uranium 76–7, 82
US 92–3, 138, 146, 151–3, 247
   Bomb project 77–8, 81–2

vegetarianism 6, 7, 9
Victoria Station, London 14
volcanos 191, 192, 194

Wales 21–2, 64
Walker, Peter 108
Warwick award 29
water in DNA 124, 133–4, 155, 165, 166–7, 202, 237–8
Watson, Jim 138, 139, 162, 164
   collaboration with King's 174–5
   DNA model 171–2
   The Double Helix 250–1
   Double Helix model 225–9
   Hardy Club talk on Double Helix 222–4
   invitation to Maurice to be co-author 213–14
   Linus's structure 205–6
   Nobel Prize 240–4
   post-Rosalind plans 205–6

Watson, Jim (contd.)
 Rosalind's B pattern photo 198, 218–19
 sperm DNA patterns 180
'Waves at Bessel on Sea' 160
Wellington, New Zealand 7–12
Welsh hills 21–2, 64
What is Life? (Erwin Schrödinger) 83–4
White, Eilleen 44
Whittacker, Eveline 7
Whittacker, Granny 15
Wilkins, Bob (uncle) 16
Wilkins, Charles 4
Wilkins, Edgar H. (father) 6–7, 8, 12, 16,
  89–90
Wilkins, Eithne (sister)
 birth 7
 childhood experiences 10–12, 13, 14, 16
 disability 20, 21
 German graduate 42
 illness 16–18, 19
 marriage to Ernst Kaiser 73
 Maurice living with 111
 music and dancing 9
 Newths' house 55
 schooling 25
 Somerville College, Oxford 36
Wilkins, Eliza 4
Wilkins, George 3–4
Wilkins, Jasmine (sister) 19, 87, 178
Wilkins, Mary (granny) 18
Wilkins, Maurice
 Assistant Directorship of MRC unit 144, 146,
  150
 attempts to restore team spirit 157
 Brazil visit 181, 185–95
 childhood experiences 8–29
 criticism by Rosalind over A-DNA/B-DNA
  154–6
 declining authorship offer 214–15
 degree exams 37, 45, 47–8
 dinner served in the lab 94
 ear infection 26, 79–80
 father's death 89–90
 first school 16
 ink-bombs 27, 190
 inviting Rosalind to dinner 150–1
 Lasker Award 238–9
 letters to Crick 173, 179–80, 210–11
 marriage to Ruth, and divorce 85–6, 87
 new X-ray camera 177
 nightmare 156
 Nobel Prize 240–5
 PhD thesis 68

 Randall's desire to exclude from X-ray studies
  147–50
 reactions to Rosalind's vehemence 162
 regret over showing B pattern to Jim Watson
  218–19
 reluctance to join Crick and Watson 206
 research assistantship to Randall 49–53
 Rosalind's negative reaction 143–4
 rows with Randall 93, 103
 St John's College, Cambridge 30–48
 scholarships 25, 29
 smallpox vaccination 18–19
 speed machines 22–5
 talk given in Cambridge 1951 141–3
 teaching experiences 91–2
 train journeys to school 26
 war time 59–86
Wilkins, Maurice (uncle) 6, 15–16
Wilkins, Sarah 239
Wilkins, William Mortimer 3, 4–5, 6
Wilson, Francesca 60, 65, 73
Wilson, Herbert 196, 210, 235
women biologists 102–3, 107, 109, 111, 256–7
Wooster, W.A. 38
Wordie, Sir James 33, 45
world cruise 12–15
World Trade Centre 265
World War II 59–86
Worshipful Company of Carpenters 30
Wright, Mr 28
Wylde Green, Birmingham 19–22, 25, 26, 72–3,
  75, 87–8, 178

X pattern 179, 216–17
X-ray studies 123, 126
 Astbury, Bill 90–1
 computer calculations 232, 234
 equipment 121, 127, 183, 233, 235
 Fuller, Watson 237
 hydrogen gas 122, 123, 124, 134
 Naples conference 137
 new good patterns 179–80
 OXO sign 125
 'pile of pennies' 181, 202
 Randall's desire to exclude Wilkins and Stokes
  147–50
 'Seeing Structures' talk 34
 Signer's DNA samples 118–19, 121, 124
 teaching 231

Zeebruge exhibition 18
zig-zag arrangements 169–70
Zosia 78